Y0-BPY-558

KISSINGER

The Uses of Power

David Landau

KISSINGER

The Uses of Power

THOMAS Y. CROWELL COMPANY
NEW YORK
Established 1834

For Bill and Jean

Library of Congress Cataloging in Publication Data

Landau, David.
  Kissinger: the uses of power.
  Bibliography: p.
  1. United States—Foreign relations—1969–
2. Kissinger, Henry Alfred.   3. United States—
Foreign relations—Vietnam.   4. Vietnam—Foreign
relations—United States.   I. Title.
E855.L36   1974   973.924′092′4 [B]   73-17190
  ISBN 0-8152-0354-3

Library of Congress Catalog Card Number 73-17190
Printed in the United States of America
ISBN 0-8152-0354-3
Apollo Edition 1974

Contents

Foreword

HENRY KISSINGER is now in title what he has long been in fact. With his appointment as Secretary of State he no longer lurks in relative obscurity as President Nixon's confidant on national security affairs; he stands forth openly as the undisputed master of American diplomacy. So great is his power and influence that he probably lacks an equal in two centuries of the American presidency; perhaps, by the time he leaves Washington, Kissinger will have taken his place alongside the great shadow-figure monarchs of Western civilization. His name may signify to future periods in history what Richelieu, Metternich, and Bismarck mean to ours. Beside the remarkable series of high government crimes and blunders which we have come to know collectively as Watergate, the ascendancy of Henry Kissinger has been the most striking fact of our recent political life.

Still, there is something incongruous about this new role for President Nixon's hitherto backstairs adviser; Secretary of State Kissinger, even more than most new titles, has an unnatural ring to it. And despite Kissinger's visible pleasure at this new accolade, he cannot at bottom feel entirely congenial with it. For by tradition, the office demands of its bearer the very things that Kissinger has most rigorously shunned and loudly deprecated throughout his government career. The Secretary of State, in theory, is not simply a diplomatic operator; he is chief of a vast network of envoys and career analysts whom he must sensibly involve in the formulation of foreign policy. As importantly, the Secretary of State is a figurehead, the public embodiment of Administration diplomacy, and as such he is accountable to Congress, press, and public. Yet for twenty years, Kissinger has repeatedly argued against giving the bureaucracy any major influence in policy; with equal fervor, he has inveighed against any role for Congress and the public, both of which he considers ill-informed and ill-tempered for the diplomatic enterprise. The solitude, secrecy and more than occasional deceptiveness in which Kissinger has acted during his term as White House adviser bears dramatic witness to these beliefs.

It is possible that Kissinger took his new position for the reason stated by the White House, that the President has decided to "institutionalize" his foreign policy, to involve the State Department and Congress in what he and Kissinger, acting largely by themselves, have up to now done. More likely, the reason was that Kissinger's own predominance had become so clear-cut that no one of any stature would serve as a puppet Secretary of State. William Rogers, a complete newcomer to foreign policy when he became Nixon's first Secretary, had clearly tired—after a surprising four-and-a-half years in the office—of playing this role; by the time of Rogers' departure, only Kissinger, no one else, could have been effective as a successor. It is probable, in other words, that Kissinger was compelled to assume an office whose powers he had usurped, but whose responsibilities he had studiedly avoided.

One year ago, I wrote in the following pages that Kissinger "has proved to be the most durable and influential figure in Washington, surpassed by the President alone." In view of subsequent events, that statement needs to be changed. Watergate, and its crippling effects on the President himself, has left Kissinger the only figure of any real stature still inside government. Whether Kissinger was directly involved in the political corruption has yet to be determined; more likely than not it will remain an open question because few people appear to have the stomach to ask it. The result, at any rate, is that Kissinger and his doctrine are riding higher than ever; and Washington's commentators, who even before Watergate had exhausted every superlative in the English language heaping praise on Kissinger, are discoursing with unmatched fervor upon the virtues of the capital city's last remaining idol. This particular reality heightens a major purpose for which this book was originally written: to remedy the lack of critical analysis about Kissinger and his policies.

Kissinger has so far been held aloof from the causes and consequences of Watergate, yet I think he must shoulder a large portion of blame. It is now understood that the purpose behind the political corruption was to insure the President's reelection. And the one element which cast most doubt on his fortunes was the conduct of the war in Vietnam. The President and Kissinger realized this, but they held to the war because, they repeatedly said, they felt that such issues of diplomacy must transcend the murky arena of domestic politics. The Watergate revelations proved quite clearly that with respect to Vietnam and other unpopular policies, many people in the White House wanted to have their cake and eat it too—that is, to pursue their policies without submitting to the risks which elected governments in democratic societies traditionally face. Prior to the election season in 1972, the Vietnam war was the most compelling and pervasive social issue in America; it had sickened and degraded our national life, and it had become the focus of opposition to the President's reelection. If the war had been abandoned, the President would have been in little danger of being ousted at the polls. But Nixon and Kissinger would not give the war up, and in so refusing they paved the way for Watergate. In retrospect, this Administration's Vietnam diplomacy, of which Kissinger had full charge, will be seen, I am sure, as much of the genesis for the most horrible political scandal of our lifetime.

David Landau

London
October 1973

Acknowledgments

THIS BOOK IS the culmination of what began in January 1971 as a handful of news stories in the Harvard *Crimson* on various aspects of Henry Kissinger's relations with his ex-colleagues on the Harvard faculty. Becoming thoroughly fascinated with this man Kissinger, I researched his impact on Washington policymaking and wrote a lengthy, three-part essay which appeared in the *Crimson* four months later. I thought then that I had done my last writing on Kissinger, but after he burst on the public scene with the announcement of his clandestine trip to Peking in July 1971, I decided that Kissinger was worthy of a book.

In addition to written sources, I have necessarily drawn on about a hundred interviews, conducted over the course of almost a year, with individuals who have had some connection with Kissinger or Nixon administration policy. The persons interviewed include high-level officials in the Johnson and Nixon administrations, policy analysts who have served — or still serve — on the Kissinger National Security Council staff, others who have consulted with the White House on policy matters, academic colleagues and friends of Kissinger at Harvard and elsewhere, a number of French authorities on Indochina, and representatives of the Provisional Revolutionary Government of South Vietnam. The great majority of these persons have requested anonymity, and I believe they are entitled to it — especially since the subject under discussion still operates from a position of considerable power and influence. And as a rule, I have kept my quotations of oral sources at a minimum, because I feel that in principle they should be protected, not exposed or defined. Let me say only that I am grateful to them for their assistance.

Kissinger himself, I am sorry to say, was not among this group. He has been aware of my project since May 1971, yet he has consistently declined my requests for an interview. Shortly before the completion of my manuscript, two of his White House assistants, acting on his instructions, talked at some length with me; to them, I also express my gratitude. As of this writing, however, I have not yet spoken with Kissinger himself.

I did obtain several hundred pages of quite useful documents which partially obviated my need to see Kissinger. They are the White House texts of background briefings which Kissinger has regularly held with the Washington press corps. The briefings are lengthy conversations on foreign policy between Kissinger and large groups of reporters; they are the most extensive and influential briefings of their kind. Nevertheless, they are not in the public domain because the ground rules of these conversations, for those who attend them, are that Kissinger cannot be identified by name, and that his words cannot be directly quoted; they can only be paraphrased. As a result, the force and impact of his pronouncements are unrecognizable in their public form. Kissinger therefore feels protected, and he talks much more freely and spontaneously than he would if he were on the record; the spontaneity of these briefings may even make a record of them as valuable in certain ways as a record of Kissinger's memoranda and policy recommendations, all of which are probably characterized by mixed motives and careful forethought.

Despite the prohibitive ground rules, the curtain has recently begun to lift on the Kissinger briefings. In December 1971, Senator Barry Goldwater abruptly placed a Kissinger India-Pakistan briefing in the *Congressional Record.* Soon afterward, the Washington *Post* and a number of other newspapers reassessed their policies of compliance with the briefing rules and decided that Kissinger was not entitled to anonymity in his policy statements. They then began identifying Kissinger as the "White House spokesman" — and stopped receiving invitations to the briefings. The briefings quoted in the following pages — all from 1969 and 1970, the period most crucial in the evolution of the Nixon-Kissinger policy — constitute absolutely fresh material; as of this writing, they have never before been aired publicly. Since I did not receive them from the White House, I have felt under no constraints and have used them freely.

Finally, I would like to mention the two men who have been my best friends — and often my most frank critics — throughout this project. The first is Stanley Hoffmann, my adviser at Harvard, whose help at every stage was kind and generous, and whose unstinting support, in an academic community that was not invariably friendly to this project, made much of my work possible. The other is Daniel Ellsberg, whom I first met in Cambridge in late 1970 and who, more than any other individual, first interested me in this project. His help since then has been — there is no other word — invaluable.

David Landau

Cambridge, Massachusetts
June 1972

A Note to the Reader

THE FOLLOWING ACCOUNT draws extensively on source material that has never before seen the light of publication, and therefore requires the documentation provided by the footnotes. For the reader's convenience, these footnotes do not encumber the pages of the text; instead, they are contained in a separate area at the back of the book. I would like to draw the reader's attention to these footnotes and to say that they form an integral part of the work.

D.L.

Part I

PROLOGUE

O N JANUARY 20, 1969, the government of the United States fell into the hands of a group of men who were undistinguished in intellect, personality, or vision. Swept into power at the end of a tormented decade, they were chosen not so much out of admiration or enthusiasm as out of fear, hatred, and desperation. No one would deign to bestow upon them the superficial accolades that had frequently adorned their predecessors, even in the worst hours of poverty and cruelty and war; in this administration, there would be no Thousand Days, no New Frontier or Great Society. It was as if everyone had instantly grasped their obvious inferiority, and hoped only that the country could somehow muddle on until a time in the future when, refreshed and reinvigorated, it would catch hold of itself and produce leadership where a simple void had existed before.

In this bleak and unpromising setting, for those who thought they knew or presumed to judge, one figure stood out. Unlike the rest, he was sharp, determined, relentlessly intellectual — one of the brightest men, some said, this country had ever produced. Open-minded and pragmatic, he was not tied to the mistakes of the past, even to those he himself had once spoken for. Brash and impenetrable, yes, but there was still a humility about him that his steelier and more arrogant predecessors had clearly lacked; he pos-

sessed a stark recognition of America's and his own limitations, and he promised again and again that neither would
be tested at its extreme. The days when America would pay
any price, would bear any burden, would meet any hardship, would fight any foe to achieve the defense of liberty
had made for a certain public spirit and élan; but, in retrospect, they had led to overcommitment, to useless loss and
destruction around the world. And in those hours of crisis,
the President of the United States had been surrounded by
men largely lacking in open-mindedness and critical perspective, men who had blindly insisted that the country continue
on the same futile course of action that they themselves had
launched. But now, it would be different; there would be a
sense of proportion. One often wondered, in fact, how he
had emerged in this crowd of banal and mediocre men, and
more important yet, how influential he would be and how
long he would last.

As Richard Nixon's special assistant for national security
affairs, Henry Kissinger has proved to be the most durable
and influential figure in Washington, surpassed by the President alone. He is completely dominant in the area of foreign policy, is snugly shielded from Congressional and public opinion, and is with the President certainly more often
than any other adviser, perhaps more frequently than the
rest of the White House coterie combined. Intellectually,
he towers over the Secretaries of State and Defense, leaving
them to cast the bureaucratic nets in their own agencies
while he advises the President on substantive policy issues.
And Kissinger has had a major hand in implementing the
very policy he has helped so much to create; many of the
crucial international negotiations have been carried out not
by the Foreign Service, but by the national security adviser

himself. He is counselor, administrator, ambassador, negotiator, resident intellectual, and briefer par excellence.

No longer the bitter, frustrated, insecure academic, Kissinger has a personality and a personal presence that are ideally suited for his job. He is thoroughly, almost exquisitely, composed, a quality that one nonetheless feels is hard-won. By nature he is ponderous and deadly serious, with merely a sardonic sense of humor; but in the company of others, he charms and quips with apparent ease. Vindictiveness comes as easily: he frequently lashes out at his sometimes abused and generally overworked staff. But with the President and with others whom he wishes to impress, he is a man of almost elaborate ceremony and tact. A German refugee with a foreign accent, yes, but his is one of the most attractive voices ever to hold forth in Washington — not at all misshapen, poorly pitched or shrill, but soft and lyrical, and at the same time deep, authoritative, deliberate, careful; whimsical yet also profound, the kind of voice that creates sympathy and confidence that the words behind it are wise and correct. And if the voice typifies anything about the man, it is his remarkable ability to argue a point and argue it well, to make his listeners seize on his views and want to make them their own. It is an ability that is indispensable to success in the inner councils of government, beyond that point where force of intellect bows out and charm of personality takes over, so that men do not feel coerced, but *persuaded*, and will go along with the arguer again and again and again.

And if we are ever to grasp this phenomenon Kissinger, if we are to visualize his ascent to power and then understand the policy he has put into effect, we must first recognize that his personality and his personal motivation — not his raw intellectual energy — are the crucial elements in his destiny. For men do not rise to power in Washington on the basis of intellectuality alone; in the scramble for political prominence, there has never been a dearth of brilliance or creative talent. Indeed, one can better argue that the political structure typically deprives the individual of the capacity to think independently and subordinates his creativity to the demands of the larger organization: such, in fact, has been Kissinger's own experience. And since the Second World War, American foreign policy has dampened many a creative impulse. Even today, in many instances, it proceeds according to the same unquestioned rationales from which it took shape so long ago: "containment" of Communism and the need for confrontation with the Communist powers; opposition to wars of national liberation, because such wars are seen only as an alternative means of the worldwide Communist advance; and, most important, the inviolability of the "Free World" alliance network which is to flourish under the aegis of America's continuing leadership. In this setting, Kissinger's intellectual energies have served not so much to challenge the underlying concepts or provide new frameworks for creative thought, but more often to manipulate a long-standing pattern of political and military relationships. His role has been not to question or criticize the existing structure, but to assimilate himself into it and to emerge as one of its leading theoreticians.

None of this is to say that Kissinger is merely an intellectual prostitute, that he is uneasy with the assumptions that have fueled American policy but has shelved his uneasiness so that he could reach a position of enormous personal strength and influence. Quite the contrary: America's postwar behavior in the international arena, her strong — if misguided — sense of mission and world destiny, are extremely well suited to Kissinger's beliefs about great power relationships. For his vision of an ideal world order is one in which America must play a central role. In Kissinger's view, international stability is possible only if individual nations conduct their business and reconcile their conflicts on strictly non-ideological grounds; and because the only global power besides the United States — the Soviet Union — is a staunch ideological monolith, Kissinger feels strongly that America, as a countervailing, non-ideological force, should continue as the leading guardian of international politics. And Kissinger's revulsion of ideology is no mere intellectual whim; it is the essence of the man himself, a man who fled from Hitler Germany as a Jewish refugee, a victim of the greatest ideological holocaust of all time.

It is no coincidence that America's most meaningful foreign policy advances under Kissinger's guidance are those which have served to moderate her own ideological approach to the international arena. The rapprochement with the People's Republic of China is a striking and imaginative break with the past, one that was as overdue as it was necessary. It will almost surely remain the outstanding achievement of Nixon administration foreign policy. And the Strategic Arms Limitation Treaty with the Soviet Union is in many ways a superb accomplishment, one which has gone far to rectify American excesses in the arms race that stretch back as far as World War II. There has been a perceptible and steady improvement in the tone of America's relationship with the Soviet Union. The President's occasional rhetorical indulgences aside, it is evident that Washington's verbal posture toward Moscow (and vice versa) has grown a great deal more moderate in the past four years; official statements no longer speak in terms of democracy versus slavery, the Free World versus the Communist Bloc. That too is a significant step forward, one that could foreshadow concrete advances in yet other areas.

But where the rationale of American policy has depended principally on the need to maintain total and constant world-wide credibility, the policy has been a shabby failure. The arms limitation talks, which were really set in motion by the previous administration, often faltered needlessly because Washington effectively linked progress in the talks to Soviet "good behavior" in other policy areas — and due to America's intransigence on issues such as Vietnam, Soviet good behavior on a global scale has not always been forthcoming. Now more than ever before, America has made herself responsible for a peaceful settlement in the Mideast, a crisis area which shows no sign of improvement. And despite the virtual absence of a policy for Africa, Latin America, and much of the remaining Third World, Washington still clings obstinately to the long-held view that it should intervene anywhere in the world, no matter what its relevance, whenever it sees the need to do so. It is this attitude that the United States must still exert worldwide prerogatives — or, in the formal phrase, undertake "global diplomacy" — that is at the heart of Nixon-Kissinger policy, its successes as well as its failures. It is simply a polished version of the Cold War's basic premise, and it is a notion to which Henry Kissinger has adhered throughout his intellectual life.

But the greatest policy failure of the United States in the past four years has been its continuation of the absurd and brutal war in Vietnam, and it is a failure that exposes the most profound weaknesses and dangers of Nixon-Kissinger policy. Not only has Washington's continued Vietnam involvement been firmly anchored in the belief that America's influence must be worldwide, that her strength and her power to enforce a given policy must never lack credibility; there is something much deeper, a problem that Kissinger has struggled with ever since he has been conscious of international relations. Perhaps more than anything else, the Vietnamese war exposes the contradiction between America's effort to maintain worldwide credibility and her need to resolve ongoing crises in specific areas of the globe. For in the concrete circumstances of international politics, America's impulse toward global predominance inevitably demands that she assume a number of burdens and commitments that would best be avoided. Such has been the case in Washington's pledge to uphold the Thieu regime in South Vietnam. True, that pledge had been inherited from earlier administrations, but beyond early 1969 it clearly became one of this administration's own making. And, ironically, it was Kissinger who, even as the President's chief foreign policy formulator, grasped the excessive foolishness of that commitment and understood that it would have to be liquidated before America's more important international business could proceed without hindrance.

Under ordinary circumstances of sovereign-power conflict, the Vietnamese war, it seems clear, would long ago have ended. The preponderance of American power was so great that Hanoi could only have been expected to surrender or to yield to Washington a favorable settlement and an "honorable" departure. But the Vietnamese war is an extraordinary one, because it has been fueled not by the mechanical ambitions of traditional nation-state aggrandizement but by popular revolution, by a movement that rejects brute coercion and fights back in spite of unusual pain and suffering because its objective is one of non-contingent principle: national self-determination. The Vietnamese war has sharply and dramatically posed for Washington the issue of revolutionary power and its role in a stable international framework.

But the revolutionary nature of the war in Vietnam does not obscure the need for a flexible American policy to find accommodation with it. In fact, Kissinger himself has recognized that the incorporation of differing ideological systems in a peaceful world order is the acid test of a sound international structure. And the existence of the revolutionary impulse in many other areas of the world only underscores the need for a truly non-ideological foreign policy. It does not stretch the imagination to suppose that a compromise settlement between the United States and the Vietnamese might once have been possible. To avoid intolerable damage to American credibility, Hanoi could quietly or implicitly have agreed to the *temporary* survival of the Thieu regime. Given the superior power position of Hanoi and the NLF in their own country, Washington could have begun and completed a withdrawal after obtaining an agreement that a "decent interval" would precede Saigon's collapse. Kissinger recognized for many years that such an arrangement was the only way to end the war in a manner that would reconcile the essential interests of both Washington and Hanoi. But the time for such a settlement has long passed.

The obstacle to a decent interval, of course, was the double-edged nature of America's credibility. Hanoi might ordinarily have rejoiced at the opportunity to come to such an agreement. But as Kissinger finally learned, the other side could not possibly have believed Washington's private assurances that it was prepared to abandon Saigon while, at the same time, America publicly preached its own superiority based on the continuing success of its aid to Saigon. In brief, Kissinger was faced with a simple choice: Should Washington relinquish its claims to global credibility by negotiating on the basis of the other side's essential demands? Or should it strive to maintain that credibility by continuing to fight what Kissinger himself recognized was a hopelessly unwinnable war? Kissinger decided that America must continue the war, only to find that four years later the war policy lay in ruins around him.

By itself, tiny Vietnam will not overthrow the world political structure if Hanoi's policies succeed. The only rationale of Washington's continued involvement there is that a "failure" in Vietnam will presage other failures elsewhere, and we are back to the Cold Warrior's paradigm. In early 1969, Kissinger and the President faced two distinct choices: modify America's goal of succeeding in every one of her undertakings, or continue the war. They could not have done both if they had done one of them well; and ironically, their current policy may cause them to be *forced* to modify their worldwide objectives if the war should be lost, with the result that the impact of Vietnam's insurgency will be all the more shattering in its implications.

In an important sense, Vietnam has exposed the shortcomings of Kissinger's world view because it is a cruel testimony to his failure to devise an accommodation between two nation-states which, for all their mistrust and animosity, *did* share a common interest in bringing the war to a close. And the futility of the war has made itself felt in areas far distant from Vietnam. It has placed one obstacle after another in the path of a safe and prudent American foreign policy. Before its completion in May 1972, the arms control agreement between the United States and the Soviet Union was doubtless repeatedly blocked by the often quiescent but ever-continuing confrontation in Vietnam; the American mining of North Vietnam's harbors last May, and the risk of causing the cancellation of the U.S.-Soviet summit two weeks later, was only the most poignant of testimonies that Washington could not make the best of its entente with Moscow at the same time that it made war on Moscow's allies in Hanoi. And it is as evident that other major American policy endeavors — détente in Europe, improved relations in China, and a peaceful settlement in the Mideast — have been gravely imperiled by America's insistence on preserving the regime of Nguyen Van Thieu.

But even more profoundly, the Southeast Asian tragedy demonstrates that Kissinger's supposedly "non-ideological" ambition for America to defend a pluralistic world order has become an aggressive and dangerous ideology after all. It has led this nation to wage a brutal and endless war against the people of Vietnam. It has caused ceaseless mass murder and wholesale destruction throughout Indochina. It augurs ill for people in other lands if Washington does not relinquish the claim that it will intervene anywhere, at any time, if it sees the need to "restore order." And its undeniable lesson is that Americans must recognize the tragedy-laden values buried beneath Kissinger's rhetoric of "stability" and "world peace" if we are not to consume other nations, and perhaps our own, in perpetual death and suffering. Vietnam does not exist in isolation. It is the core and essence of Kissinger's approach to foreign policy.

The questions surrounding Henry Kissinger's sensational rise to power and his exercise of statecraft during the past four years are numerous and compelling. But underlying all of them is Kissinger's view of what constitutes a stable international order; *that* has been the central issue of Henry Kissinger's political life, and it is in his stewardship of America's policy toward Vietnam that his view of global stability may best be grasped.

Any assessment of Henry Kissinger at this tentative moment of history must therefore lean heavily on his treatment of the Vietnam war. When President Nixon took office in 1969, Vietnam was the gravest dilemma confronting his foreign policy, and it has remained in the forefront of U.S. policy ever since that time. But Vietnam has proven to be so much more than a passing difficulty; it is still a society whose insurgent faction is tireless, whose people are extraordinarily courageous. It is a nation which the greatest military powers in the West have been unable to subdue, and it is a state whose leaders may not now negotiate except on the terms of their opponents' surrender. Most fascinatingly, and most ironically, it is a revolution whose ultimate success even Kissinger himself would not question; his only goal in Vietnam, a seemingly modest one, has been to harness the course of that revolution to the ways and prerogatives of the nation-state world order that prevails outside it. Yet even in that, he has failed; for four more years, the United States has been pitted against the revolution in Vietnam. Above all else, this essay will be an account of that failure.

Slouching Toward Washington

HEINZ KISSINGER was born in the small town of Fürth, located in the south German province of Franconia, on May 27, 1923. His father was a professor at a local high school, his mother a housewife; the setting was typical German middle class.

But the Kissingers were a Jewish family in a Germany that was on the brink of Nazism. The Kissinger children — Heinz and Walter, a younger brother — were often beaten by anti-Semitic youngsters on their way to and from their school; finally they were expelled and forced to attend an all-Jewish institution. Their father was forced to resign his professorship. And after years of social torture, the family emigrated to the United States in 1938.

Henry Kissinger never discusses his German refugee past; when asked about it, he says that it does not now exert any influence on the shape of his life. "That part of my childhood is *not* a key to anything," Kissinger insisted to one recent interviewer. "I was not consciously unhappy. I was not so acutely aware of what was going on. For children, those things are not that serious. It is fashionable now to explain everything psychoanalytically, but let me tell you, the political persecutions of my childhood are not what control my life." [1] And that is something he himself may well believe. "My friend," a long-time personal acquaintance of Kissinger has said to this writer, "about the deepest things in one's life one can say nothing. Imagine the horror of life in Nazi Germany, imagine seeing a father whom one has loved and revered, being made to give up a job, being humiliated. And all this, when one is young and defenseless, and so impressionable."

It may be true that the young Kissinger was in some way spared when the Nazis' upheaval destroyed his parents' livelihood and disfigured his own existence. But in later years, at the moment of his first mature reflection, when his intellectual life began to take shape, on what else could he have based his deepest and innermost thoughts? How could any individual in his position have ignored the most massive human dislocation of modern history, a dislocation in which he himself had been a victim? The memory of that experience, however fragmentary, would emerge in all of his later work.

There is one strain in Kissinger's writing that appears again and again, no matter what the subject under discussion. It is a gruesome, intractable fear of revolution, a deep horror of internal upheavals which cause social order and international stability to collapse around them. It is a fear that likely originated in the personal victimization he suffered during the death of the Weimar Republic, a fear he would carry with him through the rest of his life. And there is an ingrained fatalism in all of his thinking and writing, a deep apprehension of tragic possibilities and an all-pervasive recognition that failure is as likely as any other outcome. The imperfections of a stable order can be tragic, yes, but they are still more tolerable than the risks of revolutionary transformation. In the Vietnamese who are fighting for their freedom, and in the American antiwar demonstrators who may bring on the stronger and more fearsome legions of the extreme right, Kissinger sees the shades of Weimar, of political chaos and human destruction. The vision is imperfect and irrational; the Vietnamese are not Nazis, and America does not look at all like Weimar. But it is a vision that is firmly rooted in the irrational, chaotic experience of Kissinger's early life.

In America, the Kissinger family lived in New York City, in a neighborhood of Upper Manhattan among thousands of other German and Austrian refugees. Henry Kissinger was never assimilated by the culture and society that made up America; in taste and style, he would always be distinctly European. He was not among those refugees from Hitler Germany who could look back on their birthplace only with discomfort and bitterness; he was, instead, one of those refugees who regretted having to leave their country behind. He was not uncritical of the German political heritage, and he saw Nazism for what it was; his fondness for Germany would always be mixed with an abiding caution and fear. But the dominant emotion was one of warmth, an emotion that compounded the anguish of his refugee experience. His feeling for his homeland would always resemble that of a political exile; he would despise the insurgent regime which had branded him a public enemy, and he would harbor an endemic suspicion of the popular fickleness which permitted the regime to take its place — a fickleness to which, understandably, he would always feel the American people were also susceptible. And yet, at the same time, Kissinger would feel an overpowering affinity for the greater historical and cultural tradition into which he had been born. Just as it would be rare for a political exile to shed his native tongue, Kissinger — unlike most refugees of his age who erased their accents in later life — would always speak in the rich, sonorous intonation that proclaimed his Bavarian origin. And he retained his accent not because he was unable to rid himself of it, or because he was flatly untalkative, but, more probably, because he felt a deep and enduring affection for his native land. During his early years in America he sensed the eccentricity of his accent, and he was deeply self-conscious of it; yet the accent remained because, odd as he thought it might have struck others, he himself felt bound to it. And just as the political exile would never lose touch with the news of what was happening at home, Kissinger would pay close attention to the evolution of the Federal Republic; in later years, as a policy intellectual, he would feel more acutely than most of his colleagues the need to tie NATO strategy to the policy emerging from Bonn.

Beyond his identification with Germany, Kissinger would shape his thinking in a strictly European mold. He would derive his views of man's evolution and of international politics not from an American perspective, but from the historical experience of the European nation-states. When he grew interested in intellectual pursuits, his heroes would not be Thomas Jefferson or Mark Twain or Alfred Mahan; they would be Hegel, Dostoevski, Metternich, Bismarck. In one sense, his careful, seasoned approach would later provide a valuable critical alternative to those American leaders who believed that history began yesterday morning, who felt that brute military strength linked with good intentions was the key to a successful foreign policy. Kissinger's view of the world historical process would always reflect the skepticism and wariness of one who has learned that even the most appealing grand designs are likely to collapse in a heap of rubble. "Americans," he would write later in one of his most insightful moments, "live in an environment uniquely suited to a technological approach to policymaking. As a result, our society has been characterized by a conviction that any problem will yield if subjected to a sufficient dose of expertise . . . But Europeans live on a continent covered with ruins testifying to the fallibility of human foresight." [2] And yet, in areas where newer approaches were called for, many of the thoughts and policies he later applied in unfamiliar circumstances would often be quite inappropriately drawn from his observations of the Continental powers.

After four years in a New York City high school, where he had shown special talent in mathematics, Kissinger began to study accounting at night sessions of the City University of New York, earning his tuition during the daytime. But then, in 1943, he was drafted by the U.S. Army, an army which was at war with the Axis powers. Initially in a training program for especially gifted men who had been selected out by intelligence tests, he was transferred to the 84th division, which was then stationed at Camp Clairborne, Louisiana. There, as a private, Kissinger met an individual who would change the course of his life.

Fritz Kraemer was also a private, but sixteen years Kissinger's senior, an intellectual, trained in law, fiery and flamboyant yet indisputably old-world, a capricious European adventurer. He had left his homeland in Germany some years before and was now in the American army while his family continued to live in its manor house behind enemy lines. Kraemer was a highly intelligent man, winning and captivating in his brilliance, yet his was an intelligence that could not be duplicated by schooling and academic training alone; it was an intelligence filled with eccentricity and high drama, an intelligence that bemoaned the limitations of impotent scholarly thinking and pulsated with the electricity of Kraemer's own life. The impact of Kraemer's acquaintance on Kissinger would be gigantic, and its effects would be lasting.

It began when Kraemer approached the commanding general of the 84th division with an unusual request: might he, Kraemer, make use of one of the buildings on the base to address the soldiers on why they were at war with Nazi Germany? The general agreed, under the condition that he be allowed to attend the talks, and Kraemer — who now says he had never before spoken in public — snapped back, "My general, I would be honored if you would come!"

It would not be difficult to imagine this man, in his hard and stirring Teutonic voice, lashing out against Hitler Germany and exclaiming to Kissinger's unit of three thousand men — who had come straight from college campuses — that it was their duty to engage in combat as well as in intellectual exercise because, after all, one needed soldiers as well as thinkers to fight a war. The young, taciturn Kissinger was greatly impressed. He wrote Kraemer a note that said, "Dear Pvt. Kraemer: I heard you speak yesterday. This is how it should be done. Can I help you somehow? Pvt. Kissinger." [3] Shy and reticent, yet to the point. Kraemer invited him for a meeting, and their friendship had begun.

During the next two years, Kraemer bestowed a number of special favors on Kissinger. He connived to have Kissinger made personal translator to the commanding general of the 84th division by the time the division entered a ruined Germany in 1945. And at Kraemer's prodding, Kissinger for a time administered a district of occupied Germany.

But what Kraemer evoked in Kissinger himself was more

important in shaping the younger man's future: a profound interest in learning and in the intellectual process, and an almost obsessive desire to grasp the roots of man's historical experience. At a time when Kissinger's intellect was at its most formative stage, Kraemer interested the young man in Hegel, Dostoevski, and others who would play central roles in Kissinger's own development. "He told me I had a good political mind," Kissinger would later recall of Kraemer. "It was a thought that had never occurred to me." [4] Yet it was not simple bookishness which Kraemer inspired in his young friend; that, after all, was to be acquired in institutions like Harvard, where one is merely drilled in methodology. The constant company of a man like Kraemer accentuated something far more important: the *impulse* to learn, an impulse which would outlast ordinary scholarly experience. Kissinger discovered under the aegis of Kraemer that, instead of pursuing his earlier ambition of becoming a certified public accountant, he wanted to follow a career that would directly involve the giant intellectual questions with which he was just beginning to struggle.

The form his new ambition would ultimately assume was, of course, inchoate. But it sprang from another, even more important realization he had grasped from Kraemer — that as important as it was to try to understand the motivation of human existence, the central factors would defy the application of intellectual analysis because, as Kissinger well knew, man was an earthbound, contingent creature who eschewed rational standards. And to restrain the forces of irrationality, it became imperative not simply to postulate or intellectualize, but to *act*. Kraemer observed recently while speaking of Kissinger, "The medium brilliant can be overawed by their own or somebody else's brilliance. The truly brilliant will understand that brilliancy means nothing." And that, above all else, was the lesson that Kissinger derived from his acquaintance with Kraemer, the German who had wandered thousands of miles across the face of the world, finally to fight on the side of the United States against Hitler in the Second World War.

After the war, Kraemer got Kissinger a job as an instructor in an Army training school, a job that paid $10,000 a year. "That was real purchasing power in nineteen forty-six," Kraemer would remark later. "*Very* seductive." Yet Kissinger, even though he had lived a life of quite modest means, was not interested in that materialist lure; he felt he wanted an education of his own. And so this man, whom critics would accuse of blind power-hungriness in later years, won a New York State scholarship, gave up his well-paying job, and enrolled at Harvard in September 1946.

He was immediately absorbed in foreign policy; America was too large and too complicated for him to be interested in, and the world was what he knew. But first, he puzzled through the more sweeping problem of the historical process and the role of men and individual nations in it. He was concerned, especially, with the thought systems of Kant and Hegel, and with the metaphysical progression that had been postulated by Spengler.[5] The unending decay and death of successive civilizations that seemed inevitable to Spengler was a notion that the young Kissinger rejected; his experience in Germany had taught him that one must never accept inevitability, that one must do everything in one's power to wrest balance and order from chaos and destruction. Likewise, he repudiated Kantian metaphysics because it left too little room for human choice and will. In Kant, rational man performs an act because that act is moral. History is presumed to have a rational, moral end and the individual, therefore, can be presumed to act as he does because it is necessary for him to do so. The result is a teleology; there is not a clear distinction between the choice of the individual and the demands of history because the culmination of mankind's collective effort has already been predetermined. And Kissinger knew from bitter experience that men do not always act with reason and good will.

And so Kissinger fell on Hegel, a philosopher who sensed a preordained scheme in history yet would not postulate a specific historic end, who argued that only in retrospect could man fully understand the role of specific individuals and events in the total historical process because only in retrospect would mankind's ideal historical culmination become clear. Hegelian dialectic leaves room for error and tragedy; it does not demand that each specific act play a part in the construction of man's historical mission. It maintains only that in each epoch, there will arise a civilization and, more rarely, an individual, whose duty it will be to guard and transmit the historical spirit, and transmit it without ever attaining a full comprehension of all the implications it bears in the context of mankind's final destination. Hegel's belief in history as an organic process is really mystical in origin; it cannot spring from experience but only from intuition, and it may perhaps best be described as an article of faith. It is a faith to which Kissinger adheres. His belief that the United States has global responsibilities, that it is a carrier of a charge which it may perhaps sense but never entirely understand, cannot be described as nationalistic or self-centered; it is a vision exposed by Hegelian *lumière*. The word "responsibility" is not to be taken lightly; the United States and its President must not merely grasp at power and glory for their own sake, they must behave in a manner that dignifies their role as historical agents. And Kissinger's disdain for popular opinion originates in the same belief. History is made and carried forward not by the broad masses of the people, but by their leadership; the views of the public are so transitory and subject to sudden shocks and changes that they cannot stand the momentary rigors which characterize the movement of history toward its final destination. In an unusual twist of the Munich analogy, Kissinger once remarked that, "In nineteen thirty-eight, Chamberlain was the most popular man in England. Eighteen months later he was totally discredited . . ." [6] An isolated observation? Perhaps, and then perhaps not:

> [We] believe that precisely because we are not here only to liquidate one war, but because we have a larger responsibility to try to create what we hope is to be a more lasting peace, that what we do in Vietnam has to be measured in terms larger than Vietnam itself, and history teaches us that people do not forgive their leaders for producing disasters, even if what they do seems to reflect their immediate wishes. Even this, however, is a problematical statement because we are not sure that it does actually reflect their wishes.[7]

But Kissinger is not a man who blindly seeks power. For us to see him that way would be as fruitless and wrong-headed as it would be unjustified, because to approach the man so simplistically does not permit us to understand his relentless self-confidence or enable us to grasp his remarkable inner personal fortitude. An obsessively power-hungry Kissinger would be as difficult to imagine as a modest and reclusive one. It is true that he has an unusual impulse toward power and authority, but it is an impulse that springs from a strong sense of personal mission and intellectual self-duty. It is an impulse that will not stop, that will not be deterred by physical or material obstacles; it operates on a higher plane of thought and action than that of power for its own sake. And it demands an activism that is total and constant. Even of his greatest political hero, Kissinger would write: "Lacking in Metternich is the attribute which has enabled the spirit to transcend an impasse at so many crises of history; the ability to contemplate an abyss, not with the detachment of a scientist, but as a challenge to overcome — or to perish in the process." [8] These are not the words of a man interested in self-aggrandizement alone, emptied of purpose.

These instincts, even if yet unspoken, fit comfortably in the world into which Kissinger stepped in 1946. The Harvard of the late forties and early fifties was already full of the spirit that would propel its most distinguished sons to positions of enormous power in future years. Just as the United States had been wrenched out of its isolationism by the experience of World War II, so would the war and the world forces emerging from it draw classic scholarship out of its quiet, refined anonymity. Harvardians had traditionally been activists, to be sure; but now, whole disciplines were overturned and subordinated to the immediate needs of American policy. "Relevance"-oriented research institutes sprang up by the dozen at Harvard and across the country; a whole generation of philosopher-kings would be bred, mass-produced. In this exciting and uncertain atmosphere, this new burst of scholarly activity, Henry Kissinger's life underwent a drastic and enduring change.

The war had shattered the historic pattern of international relations and established bipolarity in place of a situation in which a handful of European nations had dominated the world scene. With Europe now demolished, the onus of world leadership had shifted to the superpowers in the Soviet Union and the United States. These were the frightful days of Stalin, the days of valiant Cold War confrontation, with the nations of the Free World locked in deadly combat with an ever-expanding Communist Bloc. And as a counterpoise to a hyperbolically growing Soviet world, there arose a "structuralist" tendency in American foreign policy that defined the U.S. goal as the creation of a worldwide framework that would inhibit the spread of Moscow's influence. Men in the mold of Kennan and Morgenthau, they were more subtle and sophisticated than their crusading Cold War compatriots who would themselves roll back and destroy the enemy, who saw in the very existence of the Soviet Union a deadly virus to be eliminated at any cost. They were willing to recognize Moscow's sovereignty and allow it the traditional prerogatives of sovereign powers operating in the international sphere, including the domination of certain areas bordering on it. At the same time, they saw Soviet policy as expansionist in nature and aggressive in intent; they felt the necessity to "draw the line." And they defended their policy outlook on the grounds that their larger vision was not U.S.-centered, but more essentially structural; not earthbound or transitory, but profound and rational.

And where the vision was absent in Washington, the activists from Cambridge leaped in to fill the void. Since the Civil War, Harvard had carefully nurtured its pipeline to the nation's capital. In the postwar years, the Department of State was small and unsteady; in many situations, its first reflex was to turn to Harvard's area specialists, men like

Fairbank, Reischauer, Fainsod. In this environment, no student of political science could avoid involvement in concrete policy issues, especially if his sense of mission was a keen and avid one. Kissinger's doctoral thesis was no abstract historical dissertation but a conceptual blueprint for the policy that he would have wanted the United States to enact.

The model chosen by Kissinger was the "conference system" which resolved the Napoleonic wars and launched Europe on a century of relative quietude before the outbreak of World War I. The conference system was built not by emperors or armies but by a handful of foreign ministers who monopolized the diplomatic process; theirs was a system that depended not on the perpetual use of force, but on a skillful reconciliation of interests undertaken by that small select group of ministers who were best equipped, politically and intellectually, to make compromises and avoid war. And if compromise should prove impossible, then conflicts would be settled not by a speedy resort to war and the indiscriminate application of brute military strength, but by the careful use of threats, the clever ploys and exquisite double entendres of great power diplomacy. (Of course, they did not always succeed; the history of nineteenth-century Europe is filled with small military outbreaks, though it avoided the cataclysmic burst which began at Sarajevo in 1914.) Most remarkably, these statesmen possessed an almost total degree of autonomy, not only in relation to their public and their legislative bodies, but also in relation to their own heads of state — the kind of autonomy that Kissinger often possesses vis-à-vis Richard Nixon. The European ministers, particularly Prince Metternich and Viscount Castlereagh, captured Kissinger's imagination, and their spirit would in later years impart to him a guide and an incentive for action.

The essence of the system was a common recognition by each of its members that the survival of the others must never be challenged. There might be peripheral disagreements, and wars might be fought to resolve them, but there must be universally accepted limitations on the exercise of international power. With these understandings, negotiation — defined as the prevention or limitation of physical conflict by purely verbal means — became an effective tool. Indeed, with the system functioning at its best, negotiation was the primary instrument of sovereign power relations.

And, of course, negotiation within a commonly accepted framework would allow for a measure of exaggeration and ambiguity in each of the participants' negotiating positions. Under any circumstance, negotiation was seen as a process of adjustment and compromise, a process in which disagreements could be safely manipulated and contested within the broader limitations of the accepted international system. To prevent encroachments on themselves and on the system as a whole, the participating nation-states must have armed forces at their disposal; the threat of military action, though generally unspoken, would play a central part in the negotiating process itself. And should negotiations collapse, the resort to military action by an endangered power would be permissible as long as the larger sovereign interests common to every nation-state were upheld and dutifully recognized. To avoid conflict or arrange a settlement, complex and intricate negotiating strategies would be required; implications and overtones, subtle threats and nuanced exaggerations — and outright lies — all played a central part. And the complex nature of negotiation, in turn, made it expedient to centralize the negotiating authority of every sovereign power in a single source, which happened in most cases to be the foreign minister. The autonomy of each negotiator was particularly important in complicated settlements which involved several parties to a single agreement. With all these added elements of ambiguity and flexibility, classical balance-of-power doctrine could recognize and safely assimilate the competitive impulse that was an underlying motif of great power relations. But, of course, if the basic scheme of international conduct should suddenly be abandoned by one of the competing parties, if legitimate ambitions should be exceeded and world stability endangered, if a Napoleon or a Hitler should arise on the scene, then negotiations would be useless and some form of all-out war would loom as a likely result. It was this contingency that Metternich, and Kissinger in his wake, would define as a revolutionary situation.

A revolutionary power was seen not as one with an objectionable ideology, but one that believed international relations should be conducted on ideological premises. Such a power rejected the nation-state as the only legitimate actor on the world stage, and it conducted its foreign policy in the name of a hypothetical goal. Marxist, monarchist, or capitalist, the particular ideology was of little consequence. In this setting, conservatism or counterrevolution was seen not as a competing ideology, but as an unbiased anti-ideological force enacted to prevent the floodgates of revolution and political chaos from being flung wide open. And the consequences of a revolutionary policy could be universally distressing:

> . . . When Alexander insisted on the major part of Poland, not on grounds of expediency but as a moral "right," he was not

raising the issue to a more elevated plane, but posing a dilemma which might unleash a new round of violence. For a "right" is established by acquiescence, not by a claim, and a claim not generally accepted is merely the expression of an arbitrary will. Moreover it is the essence of a moral claim that it cannot be compromised, precisely because it justifies itself by considerations beyond expediency. Thus, if the Tsar was "really" sincere in his protestations of moral duty, he was making a revolutionary contest — a contest based on the mere assertion of force — inevitable. This is the paradox which the fanatic, however well-intentioned and however sincere, introduces into international relations. His very claim to moral superiority leads to an erosion of all moral restraint.[9]

Conservatism could not be a merely reactive phenomenon; it had to be ever vigilant, constantly ready to intervene. In this respect, Kissinger felt that Metternich was the superior of Castlereagh, ultimately a prisoner of England's insular psychology, who sallied forth from his island paradise only when he felt his interests threatened. Metternich was a selfless interventionist, one who believed that it was Austria's right and duty to act anywhere and at any time, not for gain but rather to uphold Europe's social structure:

> To be a conservative, wrote Metternich, required neither return to a previous period, nor reaction, but carefully considered reform. True conservatism implied an active policy. Yet reform had to be the product of order and not of will; it had to assert the universality of law against the contingency of power . . . When the unity of Europe came to pass, it was not because of the self-evidence of its necessity, as Castlereagh had imagined, but through a cynical use of the conference machinery to define a legitimizing principle of social repression; not through Castlereagh's good faith, but through Metternich's manipulation.[10]

But above all else, Kissinger was impressed with the durability of the Metternich system. With minor interruptions, it preserved relative calm in Europe until the outbreak of World War I, even then only to be outdone by a unified and militant Germany, the creation of that talented revolutionary, Bismarck.[11]

And what emerged as Kissinger's view of modern international relations was a schema based on nineteenth-century European balance-of-power doctrine. Nation-states may pursue their foreign policies as they desire, but they must observe the limitation that they cannot infringe on the sovereignty of other nation-states and threaten the larger international structure. In this world view the threat and use of force is seen as necessary to prevent the overwhelming accumulation of strength and power by any single player, and is therefore an essential component of international politics. This common vision, these jointly held assumptions on what constitutes acceptable national ambition, make it possible for negotiation to play a crucial role in power relations. If every diplomat has the same understanding of how the international system operates, then verbal communication can be an effective means of preventing conflict or of arresting it should war break out. At the same time, the use of implied threats is central to the negotiating process itself, and the judicious application of force is a concept which nation-state diplomacy inherently recognizes.

The structure of world order has changed drastically since the nineteenth century, and Kissinger has altered his conceptual overview to accommodate the changes. Where multipolarity existed before, bipolarity between the Soviet Union and the United States is the central feature of current international relations. A century ago, the major struggles for power related strictly to European concerns and took place on the Continent; elsewhere in the world, European powers could administer vast colonial empires without infringing on their neighbors' essential interests. But now, with the liberation of the former colonies and the quest for allies, the arena of great-power confrontation encircles the globe itself. And the international responsibilities of the United States are all-embracing: "Whatever our intentions or policies, the fact that the United States disposes of the greatest single aggregate of material power in the world is inescapable. A new international order is inconceivable without a significant American contribution." [12]

America's global responsibilities are especially pronounced, in Kissinger's view, because its major rival for world influence, the Soviet Union, conducts its foreign policy on ideological grounds. Until the early sixties, Moscow's rhetoric was invariably one of world revolution; and though that tendency has abated in recent years, it has been replaced by declarations of support for wars of national liberation. Kissinger believes that the United States must demonstrate the futility of conducting policy on ideological premises; without infringing on the Soviet Union's domestic political structure, the United States must induce it to conform to the prevailing world order of nation-state diplomacy. As he said in August 1969, "We believe that the paramount problem of our time is the achievement of a stable peace in which different systems can coexist with each other." [13]

Kissinger's opposition to the idea of an ideological foreign policy is neither frivolous nor ill-considered; it springs from decades of personal experience and intense intellectual activity. It is an outgrowth of his native skepticism, his profound apprehension of tragic possibilities; it reflects a restraining awareness that unhappy endings are always possible. "We are immersed in an unending process," he wrote in 1968, "not in a quest for a final destination." [14] And if his reduction of the concept "moral consensus" to an appreciation of international stability seems unimaginative and terribly constricted, we must remember that Kissinger sees even greater danger in a foreign policy that pretends to serve ultimate yet unseen possibilities. With equal fervor, he would shun an ideological cast for American policy, and he does not see Washington's legitimate goal as the export of Western-style democracy or a capitalist economy to all corners of the globe. It is precisely this intellectual restraint which sets Kissinger apart from almost all other American policymakers of our time, men who persistently believe that the United States is a paragon of international virtue and that it has a perpetual civilizing mission in the rest of the world. If Kissinger believes in any version of an "American Century," it is one which is limited in time and in scope. His view of the U.S. role might best be described as a kind of muscular liberalism, designed to defend a pluralistic world order and prevent the emergence of forces which might threaten it. His opposition to wars of national liberation, brutal and unjustified though it has been, does not spring from any desire to suppress movements for national independence and is not without its measure of compassion for the peoples who are fighting them. It springs from an intractable fear that, if such war should appear to succeed, then other greater powers with less noble intentions will be spurred toward ideological quests. America has continued its war in Vietnam during the past four years without substantial regard for whatever political or economic benefits it may ultimately extract from the region, and Kissinger knows it. To say that Washington prolongs its policy for ideological or even self-centered reasons does not begin to get at what has gone wrong.

None of this should be taken to mean that the nation-state world order is devoid of ideology; it is not. It does presuppose a particular doctrine of international relations, and it does set limits on the acceptable extent of political behavior; it is as capable of enforcing repression as it is of encouraging growth and survival. But, in Kissinger's mind, it is not rooted in flights of imagination; it has been put into practice and has proven, by and large, to be historically durable. It does imply a political determinism of a kind; it casts the diplomat in the role of guarantor. But it rejects the self-interested determinism of the capitalist class as well as the economic determinism of the Marxist and the military ascendancy of the rightist revolutionary:

The statesman manipulates reality; his first goal is survival; he feels responsible not only for the best but also for the worst conceivable outcome. His view of human nature is wary; he is conscious of many great hopes which have failed, of many good intentions which could not be realized, of selfishness and ambition and violence. He is, therefore, inclined to erect hedges against the possibility that even the most brilliant idea might prove abortive and that the most eloquent formulation might hide ulterior motives. He will try to avoid certain experiments, not because he would object to the results if they succeeded, but because he would feel himself responsible for the consequences if they failed. He is suspicious of those who personalize foreign policy, for history teaches him the fragility of structures dependent on individuals. To the statesman, gradualism is the essence of stability; he represents an era of average performance, of gradual change and slow construction.[15]

Yet despite its internal coherence, there are serious flaws in Kissinger's application of the "Metternich parallel" in the current context of international relations. The gravest of those flaws is that, for Kissinger, the Metternich parallel is really not a parallel at all. If one disregards the twenty-year period between World Wars I and II — a period which receives practically no treatment in any of Kissinger's published work — there is nothing that stands between the last years of the Metternich system and the current postwar period. For Kissinger, the Metternich system was no mere analogy drawn from the depths of a bygone history, but a period and a world system to which he would very much have liked to return.

It is possible to maintain — and Kissinger could probably argue the point with great force — that the period between the wars has little relevance to the present age in terms of its peacekeeping accomplishments. The entire period was based on a network of faulty and poorly constructed treaty relationships, which in turn made another resort to all-out war inevitable. And it is equally true that those twenty years were characterized by a gross renunciation of vigilance, a universal lapse into thinking that "it can never happen again." In the context of diplomatic relations, the interwar period may have little to offer the present age beyond negative example. Yet because Kissinger's thinking is weighted so heavily toward a determinism of diplomacy, his analysis grossly ignores other social and political transformations which contributed to the disintegration of the Metternich system and would similarly undermine a reinstitution of it today.

In order to function effectively, the Metternich system required that the European ministers be able to operate unfettered in the management of their states' foreign policies. They had to possess full negotiating power; as a result, they were required to exercise complete mastery over their nations' bureaucratic and military machinery, and independence from the constraints of domestic opinion. In the political and technocratic milieu of the early nineteenth century, such a system could flourish with graceful ease. Government was the private preserve of a privileged few; organizational problems were smaller and relatively more manageable; and, most important, the movements for popular sovereignty and self-determination had not yet reared their threatening heads.

But by the end of the nineteenth century, all of these conditions had changed beyond recognition. The sphere of the nation-state interest had grown so drastically that international tension had spread to the remotest colonial areas of the globe. The European bureaucracies had grown monstrously, and the exercise of government had become ever more unwieldy. Military establishments had grown more sophisticated in their deadliness and, at the same time, less susceptible of diplomatic control. In some limited ways, industrialization had enabled the European elites to maintain control of a rapidly changing social structure, but it had also unleashed the quest for democracy and popular control. These changes had sown the collapse of the Metternich system well before the outbreak of World War I.

The emergence of all these forces, in turn, led to the revolutionary movements which swept the centers of European power and the colonial areas in the wake of World War I. Industrial transformation and economic polarization, in the colonies and in the homelands themselves, had produced massive human dislocation and widespread social discon-

tent; the emerging ideologies of national sovereignty and popular self-control were the ideal vehicle for the expression of
this discontent. And the historical result of this convergence
was the dramatic burst of political ideology on the international scene. The central feature of the interwar period is
not, as Kissinger would postulate, the collapse of European
diplomacy, but something far more fundamental and profound; it is the entrance of political ideology as a factor in
international relations. The Bolsheviks in Russia, the Fas-
cists in Italy, Salazar and Franco in Iberia, and the Communists and the National Socialists of Germany — these are all
very different entities, but they share as their origin the
transformation of political and economic relationships which
tore apart nineteenth-century European society. These movements did not emerge as the result of a failure of creative
diplomacy; they were the ultimate expression of forces
which could not be denied or turned back.

But Kissinger's analysis is based on a primacy of diplomacy; it seeks to ignore the underlying forces which have
revolutionized international relations and have made ideology as real a factor in world politics as the threat of war. The
events encompassed by the two World Wars have made an
indelible impact on the present period, yet it is the very
legacy of the interwar years which Kissinger seeks to eradi-
cate. His blind hatred of ideology often makes him an anach-
ronistic figure in an era where international relations proceed
in a clearly ideological context. It is understandable that
the political confusion and human horror leading to Nazism
and World War II would be repugnant to Kissinger, and
one may only sympathize with his desire to undo their ill
effects. But a humane perspective of our own era is not to
be acquired by the arbitrary erasure of the decades which

preceded it, nor should a balanced foreign policy consist of the view that the world historical forces which exploded the Metternich period can be considered merely as aberrations of the grand scheme, aberrations which can be overlooked if not swept away entirely with a skillful stroke of the diplomat's hand.

For Kissinger, foreign policy is best exercised without bureaucratic impediment. Yet the foreign policy process is today so massive that some organizational structure is vital to decision making. He believes that the larger vision of diplomacy should supersede economic or military considerations. Yet his analytical impulse has been to ignore those considerations rather than shape his diplomatic vision to them even when they are clearly relevant. Weapons technology is now a far more imposing force than it was in Metternich's day; so, for that matter, is the international economic structure. Yet Kissinger's thinking is based on the fatuous assumption that these forces will subordinate themselves to what he sees as the larger diplomatic questions.

These unstated biases, as will be shown, have often posed ruinous consequences for Kissinger's exercise of diplomacy. His tendency to view himself, and his negotiating partners in other capitals, as independent, unitary actors on the world stage have very often led him to miscalculate his opponents' responses to America's position. Most notably, his approach to the Vietnam negotiations has been that if only he could convince his counterpart from Hanoi of his individual sincerity or good will, then the entire problem of the war could be unraveled and solved in short order. He has pursued his negotiating strategy, in other words, as if the other side were incapable of a complexity of response, as if the will of the Vietnamese insurgents, and of those segments of

Vietnamese society from which the insurgents draw their support, rested in a single negotiator's hands. He also appears to believe that the United States can be "tough" on the Soviet Union without running "unacceptable risks" [16] of an upheaval in Moscow's decision-making structure, an insurgency on the part of the hard-line, militarist faction of the sort which characterized the ouster of Khrushchev following his decision to "knuckle under" at the time of the Cuban missile crisis. Not the least important, Kissinger's approach to the problem of an American negotiating strategy has been to assume that the White House can, and should, bend Congressional and public opinion to its own desires.

Indeed, the most dangerous flaw in Kissinger's line of thinking is the belief that domestic opinion should pose no obstacles to the conduct of foreign policy. For if one feels that international relations should be conducted on non-ideological grounds, he must also assume that popular sovereignty on questions of internal policy should not extend to foreign ventures, because an ideological foreign policy is by definition an extension of domestic political beliefs into the international arena. To be fair to Kissinger, it would be equally absurd to take the opposite view, that domestic political considerations should *dominate* a foreign policy; more sensibly, it should be the function of an astute policymaker to minimize the impact of domestic idiosyncrasies on international behavior. Yet Kissinger sees no middle ground on which public sentiment can have a constructive impact on foreign policymaking, because that would deprive diplomacy of its flexibility and its room to maneuver. Such a view might have been remotely defensible in the age of Metternich, when there were no vehicles for the expression of popular views even on internal political questions. But in the modern era, it would be immoral and unrealistic to ask the public to refrain from exerting influence on concrete policy issues; such an attitude ultimately implies the right of foreign policymakers to infringe on popular sovereignty in the domestic arena vis-à-vis financial and military allocations. A foreign policy conducted without regard to domestic opinion foreshadows increased regimentation and repression at home.

In the context of postwar international relations, the problem would be even more fundamental than that of undercutting domestic opinion in the United States. Since the Soviet Union was the only other sovereign power with the capacity for worldwide influence — and a power that conducted its international business in explicitly ideological terms — a policy that opposed the introduction of ideology, *any* ideology, in the global arena would become a policy characterized in concrete terms by its opposition to *Soviet* ideology. The rhetoric might be more restrained (as indeed it has been during the Nixon administration), and the policymaker would not himself conceptualize his decisions in an anti-Soviet framework, but the result would translate quickly to an anti-Soviet policy. In the struggle for global influence, the United States would ally with regimes not on the basis of their domestic structure, but on the basis of their hostility toward the Soviet Union. And in many areas of the Third World, where there would be no viable alternative between regimes headed by right-wing strongmen on the one hand and popular-front governments whose attitude toward Moscow would be sympathetic if not completely friendly, the United States would often commit its enormous power and prestige to rulers who held sway on the strength of their military power alone. Even in Europe, the cradle of civilization, Washington would bolster a number of rightist regimes in the course of maintaining NATO unity: Greece, Portugal, and Spain. The underlying rationale of bolstering rightist regimes — not the one intended for popular consumption, but the one the decision makers themselves believed — was the same as the one they would also apply to American domestic opinion: that Washington's behavior abroad should serve not the day-to-day needs of popular sovereignty, but the grander vision of nation-state diplomacy, a vision that could be grasped and then enacted only by a select few.

If Kissinger had not yet said or felt any of this by the time of his arrival at Harvard in 1946, it was all in embryo, needing only to be brought out. This doctrine then rode high among Harvard's policy intellectuals, men who were not without their influence in the outside world. Since the Civil War, Harvard had been transformed from a regional fixture to America's leading educational center. In the process, it had become unique among universities in its impact on the national arena. It would always be remarkable that Harvard attracted the most able students and scholars in the country, that it gave its favorite sons unequaled access to the vast opportunities that lay beyond its confines. If Henry Kissinger had attended college elsewhere, his life would likely have been quite different; but now, to Harvard's vast heritage, he would soon become an eager beneficiary. And one grandiose figure in the Harvard panoply would introduce him to his fortune.

He was William Yandell Elliott, small-town boy from Tennessee turned brilliant scholar, an all-American tackle at Vanderbilt who became the ruling power in Harvard's Department of Government. He had attended Balliol College, Oxford, at a time in the 1920s long after the place had been overtaken by the spirit of Benjamin Jowett, the notion that societies trained their elites — and senior scholars prepared their young disciples — for positions in government and other public service. In 1924, Elliott had written a brilliant analysis of the European political scene which described with prescience the forces that would produce the European fascist dictatorships of the following decade.[17] Sadly, he never again equaled this feat of scholarship at any time during the rest of his career, and many of his colleagues would later come to regard him as a windbag, an intellectual has-been, an excessive bore. Even by the standards of the late forties, he was a violent Cold Warrior, one who would not tolerate the slightest deviation from the path of unrelenting struggle against the Stalinist Terror. Another of Elliott's graduate students remembers that, on returning from a one-year stay in Britain, he received a lengthy harangue from the old man on the "namby pamby" quality of Clement Attlee's Labour government. Socialism had been such a failure in Britain, Elliott proclaimed, that the government could not provide enough meat for its own people. When the student presumed to inform Elliott that Britain now had the highest per capita rate of meat consumption in western Europe, Elliott threw him out of his office, and that was the end of the relationship. There are probably many other such stories etched in the minds of Elliott's colleagues and associates. Yet his personality was undoubtedly forceful and flamboyant, and he never quite lost his interesting, powerful cast of mind. One may perhaps see Elliott in the late forties as something of a King Lear figure, stalking a rainy, windy moor, constantly struggling onward in pursuit of some far-off vision and distant hope. It was this apparition, this

tattered image of a bygone age, that Kissinger latched onto
while a Harvard undergraduate, and the experience would
be lasting.

"Wild Bill" Elliott had gone to war with the rest of the
country in the early forties, and he had attained prominence
in the Office of War Mobilization. Yet now, after the war
was over, Elliott could not let go of those fascinating days in
Washington, and he continued to spend much of his time
there in spite of his scholarly duties. Doubtless there was
an intoxication of power, but Bill Elliott had long been a
dedicated internationalist, a determined advocate of American participation in world affairs, and there was a sense of
duty that underlay the self-indulgent, vainglorious obsession
with government service. It was that peculiar combination
of lust and purpose that Elliott transmitted to Kissinger.
Here was a bright young man whom Elliott felt worthy of
his tutelage; Kissinger struck him as interesting and intellectually sophisticated, yet formless enough and driftless
enough so that Elliott would want to imbue him with his
own spirit and vision, and transform him into another Elliott.
True, the relationship was rooted in academic cost-effective-
ness: Elliott made use of Kissinger's talents as a scholar's
assistant, and Kissinger established a link that was vital to
his own success. Yet it transcended the master-student relationship then so fashionable in Cambridge; one sensed reciprocal commitment, a remarkable degree of mutual élan.
At the stage of his development where the blossoming intellectual should have severed his ties with his mentor, Kissinger drew tighter. With Elliott, Kissinger founded and directed the International Seminar, under which several dozen
bright and influential foreigners spent the summer months
at Harvard; thanks to Elliott, Kissinger founded and edited

Confluence, a scholarly journal which for years served as a public forum for debate on policy issues and presaged the growth of many other similar publications in the future. And through each of these enterprises, Kissinger developed a vast nexus of personal acquaintances and contacts which proved invaluable in the progression of his own career.

After completing his dissertation, and one year as an instructor in the Department of Government, Kissinger felt the time had come for a temporary departure from Cambridge. His immediate goal — a tenured position on the Harvard faculty — was no easy matter; and the membership of his department was not uniformly friendly to him. Besides that, he was anxious to get outside and taste the real world. During the winter of 1954–55, an ideal opportunity arose, one that his unusual circle of friends made accessible. The managing editor of *Foreign Affairs,* the quarterly of the Council on Foreign Relations, quit his job, and the magazine's editor, Hamilton Fish Armstrong, was seeking a replacement. Reflexively, Armstrong turned to Harvard; he asked Arthur Schlesinger, Jr., then in the Department of History, to suggest a young scholar for the post. Schlesinger gave him Kissinger's name.[18] Armstrong invited the young man to New York for an interview; finding Kissinger's style somewhat stiff and overly labored, Armstrong decided to seek another managing editor, but found Kissinger so bright and interesting that he thought Kissinger might become the rapporteur of a study group that was then meeting at the Council on the subject of nuclear weapons.[19] Kissinger was heartily recommended for the post by Elliott; but according to Council officials, the more crucial recommendations came from Schlesinger and McGeorge Bundy, who was then Harvard's dean of faculty and another friend of Kissinger's.[20]

The Council then made the offer and Kissinger accepted; on March 8, 1955, he wrote the executive director of the Council, George Franklin, that he would take the post "not only because it seems directed in the main line of my own thought, but also because the Council seems to furnish a human environment I find attractive." [21]

The nuclear weapons study group had been meeting at the Council for several months before Kissinger's arrival, and had already conducted most of its deliberations. [22] At first, the group was unsure of whether it wanted to produce a book on the subject, but when it finally decided to do so it sought a "fresh mind" to write it. [23] Kissinger fitted that specification. He had already expressed keen interest in the military aspect of "containment," but his thoughts on the subject had not yet hardened. In fact, afraid that he would be overwhelmed by a majority opinion of the Council study group, Kissinger insisted on an entirely free hand in the composition of the book. "He didn't want to be controlled by nineteen different people in this high-powered group," George Franklin remembers. "And it was a very high-powered group." [24]

Indeed it was: State Department powers like Robert Bowie and Paul Nitze; others who would soon cut their teeth at cabinet level, McGeorge Bundy and Roswell Gilpatric; cornerstones of the private sector such as David Rockefeller. Men such as these at the Council on Foreign Relations were then in many ways the social and intellectual foundation of American policy. There were, of course, huge differences between them in shading of outlook and personality, but there was basic agreement on the central issues — the rationality of containment and of Washington's worldwide commitment, the value of NATO and foreign aid, the need for a safe international order carefully sculpted by American power. Kissinger stepped into this milieu with ease. He felt strongly, like the rest of the men in the study group, that the U.S. military must be fitted to respond to any challenge made by the Soviets in any area of the world, whether it be overt "aggression" or ambiguous encroachment, wide-ranging or limited in territorial scope. He also feared, along with the so-called "civilian strategists," that massive retaliation — the threat to wage all-out nuclear war in response to aggression of any size — was militarily constricting and lacked credibility, with America's enemies and, as critically, with her allies. Washington's experience in the Korean War had been universally rejected as a strategic model for military containment; another method of containment was in need of being devised. Might this not be accomplished by updating and improving the Pentagon's conventional capabilities, giving its forces greater firepower and increased mobility, and enabling those forces to respond to aggression anywhere in the world? This view was predominant in the study group, and it was also a view which Kissinger took in early 1955, before coming to the Council. In an article in *Foreign Affairs* that April, he argued strongly for alternatives to massive retaliation without once even mentioning nuclear weapons, much less suggesting that they might be used to fill the gaps in existing military policy.

His experience at the Council led Kissinger to change his mind. Falling under the influence of those in the study group, notably Lt. Gen. James M. Gavin, who had enormous faith in the "research and development" solutions being generated by current technology, Kissinger came to believe that small, "tactical" nuclear weapons would be the most reliable and effective means of halting the worldwide Soviet advance. He thought these weapons would overcome the Communists' manpower advantage in huge conventional war; small nuclear weapons could destroy an entire army without carrying their devastating effects beyond the battlefield, and would be especially useful against an army that had concentrated its forces closely together for massive struggles on the ground. And he felt that a reliance on tactical nuclear weapons would best exploit the fundamental superiority of the United States over the Soviet Union in the areas of industry and technology. As he argued in *Nuclear Weapons and Foreign Policy:*

> . . . limited war has become the form of conflict which enables us to derive the greatest strategic advantage from our industrial potential. It is the best means for achieving a continuous drain of our opponent's resources without exhausting both sides. The prerequisite for deriving a strategic advantage from industrial potential is a weapons system sufficiently complex to require a substantial production effort, but not so destructive as to deprive the victor of any effective margin of superiority. Thus the argument that limited war may turn into a contest of attrition is in fact an argument in favor of a strategy of limited war. A war of attrition is the one war the Soviet block could not win.[25]

So certain was he that tactical nuclear war was the wave of the future that Kissinger advocated not only their occasional use but an entire military policy based around them. He argued that the traditional branches of the armed service should be completely reorganized around strategic nuclear and tactical nuclear commands. The new policy would abolish conventional warfare. And it was bolstered by Kissinger's belief that the grander vision of great-power diplomacy could dictate the limits of military conflict, rather than the other way around.

Most important, Kissinger assumed that small nuclear wars could be prevented from escalating into a larger, all-out holocaust. His primary reason for believing in the possibility of limited war was that there would be insurmountable psychological obstacles to escalation operating on both sides. But his more immediate reason for seizing on the idea was his excessive reliance on the efficacy of great power diplomacy, on the ability of negotiators representing antagonistic and mistrustful countries to communicate their intentions in a manner that could be understood and accepted by both sides. His assumption that words would suffice to impress a weak and suspicious enemy of limited American ambitions even during the conflict itself, that "an energetic diplomacy addressed to the problem of war limitation can serve as a substitute for lack of imagination on the part of the Soviet General Staff," [26] was the real underpinning of his belief that nuclear wars could be kept limited. He even envisioned an elaborate scheme of mutual inspection that would continue throughout the atomic exchange, inspection which he felt could prevent the use of weapons above a certain level of destructive capacity, as well as insure the observance of other rules fundamental to small nuclear war.[27] In a remarkable passage, he summed up this line of thought:

> A war which began as a limited nuclear war would have the advantage that its limitations could have been established — and, what is more important — understood — well in advance of hostilities. In such a conflict, moreover, the options of the aggressor are reduced in range. Whereas in a conventional war the choice is between continuing the war with its

existing restrictions or risking an expanded *limited* war, in a
nuclear war the choice is the much more difficult one between
the existing war and all-out conflict . . .[28]

The acceptance of this idea must have required a willing
suspension, if not complete renunciation, of disbelief. Why
would the Soviets agree to limit their own possible response
to a form of warfare in which they would face certain defeat? More fundamentally, how could it ever be possible, in
a situation of total hostility, for either side to believe that
the first use of nuclear weapons by the enemy was not the
beginning of total war? And how did Kissinger ever think
that diplomacy could settle questions of such strategic importance when he himself proclaimed, in what was probably
the most pronounced internal contradiction in his thinking,
that "The emphasis of traditional diplomacy on 'good faith'
and 'willingness to come to an agreement' is a positive hand-
icap when it comes to dealing with a power dedicated to
overthrowing the international system"?[29] Considering Kissinger's view that larger questions of arms reduction and disarmament were either non-negotiable — or, in some cases,
negotiable only with major safeguards — his confidence in
the possibility of limited-war diplomacy was at best naive
and at worst quite dangerous.

At bottom, Kissinger was led to believe in limited war
through his faith in the universal applicability of Metter-
nich-style diplomacy, a diplomacy that presupposed an area
of common interest and understanding, as well as one of
conflict, between the contending parties. And that style of
negotiation, in turn, rested on the notion enunciated by
Clausewitz that war was merely an extreme expression of
the eternal political struggle which characterized interna-

tional relations. It is a strictly European notion, one that is rooted in the historical experience of the conference system begun at Westphalia and expressed most effectively in the grand meetings that resolved the Napoleonic wars. In an earlier age, the European system was less prone to disaster because the methods of violence that upheld it were not quite so total as they were in 1957. If one member of the system sought "absolute security," the other powers could collaborate in that member's defeat without destroying themselves in the process. Metternich could fail to stop the invasion of France without fear that ultimate destruction would follow his failure. What a perversely talented euphemist once called "the age of nuclear plenty" invalidates this principle. In fact, what is remarkable about Kissinger's thinking during this period is not his obsession with small nuclear weapons, but his essential lack of interest in them, his obliviousness to their consequences. Kissinger has never been interested in weapons technology, or in the use of physical force for its own sake; the epithet Strangelove emphatically does not become him. Emotionally and intellectually, he operates in the realm of old-world diplomacy; his abode is not the Situation Room at RAND, but the graceful conference halls of Vienna, with their frescoed walls and ceilings and their baroque chandeliers. Nuclear warheads were far out of place in this environment, and if they had intruded, they would likely have been misused. Kissinger himself said that "In seeking to avoid the horrors of all-out war by outlining an alternative, in developing a concept of limitation that combines firmness with moderation, diplomacy can once more establish a relationship with force even in the nuclear age." [30] Perhaps, but a system geared only to limited nuclear war was not the way to achieve that end.

More specifically, the Metternich system presupposed the ability to deter conflict by means of a policy of threat. A European diplomat could combine threat with negotiation; he could utter a warning which the recipient would acknowledge as credible and, within the framework of the system, legitimate. Among a group of equally powerful nations that shared a similar understanding about the nature of international relations, the policy of threat could prevent war. The policy was particularly effective because the threat did not have to be absolutely credible in order to work. As long as the credibility of the threat outweighed the opponent's willingness to risk its implementation, the threat could succeed. But rather than undertaking a conceptual redefinition of threat behavior to suit the requirements of the new international system — that is, to cope with a revolutionary power in the present age — Kissinger merely decided that what the United States must do was make a quantitative adjustment and insure that the threat be *absolutely* credible — in other words, to enunciate and implement it at the same time. Hence, his apparent eagerness for Washington to strike the first blow in a limited nuclear exchange. But the policy involved a grave paradox: in order to keep the war limited, the opponent must be presumed to have the same understanding of diplomacy and force as did Washington, yet it was for lack of this understanding on Moscow's part that the United States would have gone to war in the first place.

A number of important conditions would change before Kissinger would refute his own view of limited nuclear war in 1959: the United States would no longer possess clear-cut nuclear or technological superiority over the Soviet Union, and virtually the entire community of civilian strategists would come to reject the notion of an all-nuclear policy.

But the most striking element of Kissinger's self-refutation was his admission that verbal communication alone would not suffice to inform the Soviet Union of American intentions. And Kissinger then adopted the view that the broad outlines of American strategy would have to be communicated tacitly to the Russians. In the case of military conflict, the clear distinction in weapons would be nuclear versus conventional, not strategic nuclear versus tactical nuclear; as Kissinger would write, "The problem of communicating intentions to an opponent will be difficult regardless of the mode of warfare. But this makes it all the more important that the limitations which are attempted should be reasonably familiar." [31] And, as a result, Kissinger would argue in the future that the United States should not pre-empt or anticipate Soviet military action but instead respond to it, and respond in a way that would be comprehensible to the strategists who designed the Soviet move. America, he would come to feel later, should not initiate the use of force but react to it, and in doing so should raise the stakes by exceeding the opponent's thrust and confronting him with the decision to escalate further. Thus, when the Berlin Wall went up, Kissinger would suggest an invasion of the Russian sector by American troops to tear it down. And when the Soviets constructed a Moscow area antiballistic missile defense system, Kissinger would favor an American commitment to a "thin" area defense ABM, responding to the Russian population-defense rationale by posing it in a more threatening way. But though he would renounce tactical nuclear war as an everyday policy, he felt the United States should continue to maintain the capability for it, and would assail the Kennedy administration's military policies for not placing enough emphasis on it.

Kissinger's shift to a strategy of "tacit communication" was doubtless a change in the direction of restraint, but it did not grapple with the fundamental issue of possible misunderstanding on an opponent's part. If the United States could not make its desire felt by the rapid application of force, then the effect of tacit communication would be not to rectify but rather to prolong the misunderstanding. Tacit communication was in fact a strategist's euphemism for a policy of unstated threat. It made the same assumptions as did a policy of more immediate resort to military action about the nature of an opponent's comprehension and response: that the opponent shared the same appreciation of the international system as Washington's, and was willing to collaborate in the preservation of that system; that the opponent believed the United States would observe the same limits of behavior that it did; most important, that the opponent could be made to bend and compromise when confronted with the threat and use of force. In a situation that did not lend itself to easy compromise, the difference between force and tacit communication was not the difference between war and peace; it was the difference between rapid choke and slow squeeze. It did not obliterate misunderstanding; it simply gave the opponent more time to surrender. It did not ignite immediate war; it would only light a slower fuse. As Kissinger's position on the Berlin Wall would show, tacit communication could lead to all-out war just as surely as a first use of limited nuclear weapons.

We are getting ahead of our story. Kissinger's finished work, *Nuclear Weapons and Foreign Policy*, was given a gala launching by the Council on Foreign Relations, and it was an instant hit. On best-seller lists for fourteen weeks, it became the most influential public primer on nuclear policy, though it was by no means the most distinguished or searching;[32] indeed, it would presage Kissinger's unique ability to capitalize on intellectual feats of which many of his colleagues were equally capable. And Kissinger's next move upward on the political ladder would come while he was still engaged in his Council work. In 1956, the Rockefeller Brothers Fund began sponsoring a series of studies on domestic and foreign policy, and Kissinger, after obtaining the necessary leaves of absence from Council officials, became director of the panels which were set up to write the studies.

Nelson Rockefeller and Henry Kissinger had met at a conference on military policy in Quantico, Virginia, in the early fifties, and an association had continued to develop between them. It would always be hard to imagine a great deal of personal rapport in the relationship; their personalities were so disparate as to consign their association to the realm of business only. Rockefeller was always the image of a man driven — restless, enormously energetic, not a deep thinker but perpetually active to the point of being overbearing, a passionate seeker of public office who immersed himself in all the campaigning he could stand. Kissinger, by contrast, was shy and withdrawn, methodical and wary of the impulsive, obsessively intellectual, a man who frankly detested the public arena and was quietly afraid of its multitudes. But Rockefeller had always liked to gather about him a retinue of experts on every possible subject: Who's the best man? Where can I get the soundest advice? That was the Rockefeller pattern and Kissinger fit it well. The two men were dauntless interventionists, men who believed that the United States had the responsibility to show its muscle in every area of the world, and they felt strongly that America must live up to its destiny. Their first area of agreement was the

Rockefeller slogan, "A bomb shelter in every home" — the need for a vastly expanded civil defense system so that the public could be made to tolerate a tough and aggressive American policy. They shared a fear of revolution; as assistant secretary of state for Latin America during World War II, Rockefeller was largely preoccupied with eradicating Nazism and other fascist tendencies in the Western Hemisphere (a positive horror of the extreme right is a peculiar Rockefeller virtue, though one that, like Kissinger's, also incorporates the left). Above all, they were both deeply devoted to the strength and power of the United States, to its ability to survive as the major force of stability and anti-Communism in every area of the world. And it was, for both men, a devotion that transcended the smaller considerations of economic profit or military technique. To see the Rockefeller ethos purely in terms of dollars and cents would be as useless a fantasy as it would be a simple-minded one. For the Rockefellers, by the 1950s, were not so much a family who hoped to profit from the system as they were synonymous with the system; they were so deeply entrenched that they would see the enduring issues of political and social control not in terms of petty aggrandizement but rather in terms of a principle. Whatever the sacrifice — in finance or military expenditure or individual human life — the principle must be defended at any cost. Our discussion is too military, Rockefeller would say at the meetings of the panel on national security.[33] Alliances are vital to our political policy even if they do not make sense militarily, and for that reason they are not useless militarily. It was this train of thought, the need and willingness to be tough, to be an interventionist in principle, that Rockefeller found so attractive in Kissinger.

The national security panel report of the Rockefeller Brothers Fund, billed as "the answer to Sputnik," became a public document of enormous prestige and influence; Kissinger was its author. As had *Nuclear Weapons and Foreign Policy*, it argued for a strategy oriented around tactical nuclear weapons, as well as for a reorganization of the armed forces to fit America's new strategic needs. It included, of course, a lengthy plea for an expanded civil defense system, and acknowledged that these recommendations would make necessary a drastic increase in the Pentagon's budget — but then, it observed, the price of freedom has always been high. Curiously, the report masked a serious discussion of conventional war that had extended throughout the panel sessions, a discussion Kissinger himself took part in. We need physical presence in foreign countries, he argued at one point, if backward peoples are to visualize our power.[34] Nevertheless, the report itself barely even touched on the possibility of incorporating conventional tactics into an emerging American strategy.

By 1957, Kissinger was ready to return to Harvard, this time with a power base. He became associate director of Harvard's new Center for International Affairs with a virtual guarantee of tenure on the Harvard faculty, which he received five years later. His coterie of friends, contacts, and patron saints in the outside world was indeed formidable.

In his moves from Harvard to the Council on Foreign Relations to the Rockefeller Brothers Fund and, then, back to Harvard, Kissinger had proven his ability to rise in the political and social milieu of the foreign policy world. Many of his undertakings at Harvard would be geared to the same end. If Kissinger was especially well known in the Pentagon, it was because dozens of Defense Department officials and military leaders were invited to speak at Kissinger's Defense Policy Seminar for graduate students, virtually the only program of its kind in the country. And if European policy circles and journals have always had an exaggerated notion of Kissinger's role, it has been due in no small measure to the fact that hundreds of influential Europeans have spent their summers at Harvard in Kissinger's International Seminar. Yet, although Kissinger has an extremely acute perception of how to exert personal power and influence, he has never been the distinctive figure in the world of policy intellectuals: here, he has been but one among many. The great bulk of his writing contains ideas that have originated elsewhere. His first publications on limited nuclear war drew heavily from earlier work by Bernard Brodie, James Gavin, and Edward Teller.[35] His later retractions were prompted in large measure by reviews of his first book which were extremely hostile in tone and content. His ideas about negotiation and tacit communication depended almost entirely on the writings of Thomas Schelling and Herman Kahn.[36] Even his plan for "two-track" negotiations to end the Vietnam war, a plan which he publicized in January 1969, was taken directly from proposals advanced inside the government eight months earlier by analysts at the Departments of State and Defense. To say that Kissinger was an intellectual pioneer in any of these areas would be a gross overstatement.

At the same time, he has been extremely talented in adapting old ideas to new purposes and in exposing the limitations of the ideas he rejects. He brings to his work an unusually acute critical perspective, and is quite careful not to abandon his intellectual priorities for the sake of social or political gain. What creative talent he might have possessed is hampered by his conservative, innately cautious frame of mind. But his concerns are deep, and they are genuine. His views on government policy in the fifties and sixties were almost invariably unfriendly, and throughout those years intellectual independence of that sort was a quality which he jealously guarded. His current role as an official apologist is one that comes quite new to him, and, even now, he would probably shun many of the day-to-day compromises he makes if he saw them as avoidable. He has always argued against Washington's acting exclusively or even significantly in terms of internal bureaucratic motives, and he felt throughout the early sixties that the intellectual who attempted to transmit his concerns to his government by assimilating himself in the bureaucratic structure was committing the worst possible sin of betrayal. As he wrote in 1959:

> . . . in co-operating the intellectual has two loyalties: to the organization that employs him and to values which transcend the bureaucratic framework and provide his basic motivation. It is important for him to remember that one of his contributions to the administrative process is his independence, and that one of his tasks is to seek to prevent routine from becoming an end in itself . . . It is essential for him to retain the freedom to deal with the policymaker from a position of independence, and to reserve the right to assess the policymaker's demands in terms of his own standards.[37]

Kissinger believed then that intellectuals could function effectively by acting as consultants to policymakers rather than by becoming policymakers themselves; consulting was a course of influence that he tried, and failed at, in 1961. But he believed, above all, that intellectuals held an obligation to take part in policymaking, and in order to facilitate his own entrance into the policymaking world he would willfully play both sides of the White House political fence. In 1959, while a foreign policy adviser to Nelson Rockefeller, Kissinger accepted an offer to do occasional consulting for Senator John F. Kennedy's campus "brain trust," which was then beginning at Harvard and elsewhere. In 1967 and 1968, his turns of allegiance would be even greater; while still a Rockefeller adviser, Kissinger — through another friend, Secretary of Defense Robert McNamara — began building ties to Senator Robert F. Kennedy. After Governor Rockefeller's declaration of candidacy, Kissinger redoubled his efforts on behalf of his chief. Then, after Rockefeller's defeat at the Republican convention, he began to drift toward the Nixon camp, where he emerged as the President-elect's special assistant that December. Was there any rhyme or consistency in all this jockeying? Quite probably. As one friend said recently of Kissinger:

> Kissinger is a believer, always has been a believer in the notion that foreign policy has to have a lot of bipartisan support, that there is an area of central agreement which is common to both parties. Kissinger is ambitious. He certainly is a man who is not terribly interested in the role of an external critic, not a man who wants to be able to write the truth and be proved right fifty years after he's dead; that's not his temperament. He feels he can act, and I think he's a man of considerable capacity to act, so he wants to be in the action.

Kissinger got his first real chance to "be in the action," to put his thoughts and ideas into practice, in early 1961, when McGeorge Bundy, who had left Harvard to become President Kennedy's special assistant, invited Kissinger to become a White House consultant on military and security policy.

This appointment was a particularly lucky break for Kissinger; it gave him the opportunity to confer frequently with Western European leaders, particularly those of the Federal Republic, and to pass himself off in policy circles as an important White House figure. With leading decision makers, however, he had a more difficult time. He was given an office in the Executive Office Building, and he consulted on a regular basis, about once every week. During the Berlin crisis of summer 1961, he gave up his teaching duties at Harvard to be able to work full-time in Washington. But he was rarely at the center of activity; he was more often to be found skirting the edges searching eagerly for an opening. He was not given access to the more sensitive items in the cable traffic, and he was not a member of the Berlin Task Force. And to those White House officials who were not personal friends, he soon became a minor nuisance; as one aide to McGeorge Bundy now recalls of Kissinger, "After the first year I think Henry became a needler and a critic, and when you're under the kind of pressure you are in Washington you tend not to want to bring people from a distance to needle you and criticize you." But more fundamentally, he was not well suited, politically or stylistically, to the Kennedy White House. One way of characterizing this ill-suitedness might be to say that Kissinger was too German, too ponderous and heavy-handed, to be part of Camelot; another way of putting it would be that he was less arrogantly America-centered than the hard-nosed, pragmatic fix-it men who trampled recklessly on America's allies and believed that, by themselves, they could mastermind the world. Adenauer *did* have good reason to find Kissinger more to his liking than others in Washington who saw less need to pay attention to him. And even if Kissinger's global vision was as sweeping and all-encompassing as was that of Kennedy administration policy, even he did not make the absurd mistake of thinking that the United States could go it alone. On that point, Kissinger's vision left room for some doubt; his notion that "The United States is no longer in a position to operate programs globally; it has to encourage them. It can no longer impose its preferred solution; it must seek to evoke it" [38] was completely foreign to the Kennedy era. And though Kissinger consulted repeatedly with Washington policymakers throughout 1961 and early 1962 on Berlin and other related issues, those around him were so hostile to his ideas that his recommendations had little if any impact.

One lesson Kissinger drew from this period was that, as a consultant, his influence on policy could be only limited. He was rarely around when the decisions were actually made, and, more important, he rarely had access to the President. His friend, Arthur Schlesinger, Jr., would sometimes take Kissinger into Kennedy's office, but that contact was sporadic and infrequent.[39] And Kissinger's duties came to a sudden halt early in 1962 when another, erstwhile, friend — McGeorge Bundy — dislodged him from the White House out of possessive jealousy over the little access to Kennedy that Kissinger had.[40] Otherwise, he found himself completely unable to fasten onto any segment of Washington's sprawling foreign affairs bureaucracy or generate any bureaucratic interest in his ideas; one who watched Kissinger in these days would hardly have imagined that he would emerge as such a devastating bureaucratic operator as Nixon's special assistant.

And if he always found the bureaucratic treadmill so distasteful during the early sixties, it was because his divergences of opinion with Kennedy policymakers were so sweeping. Even then, he felt that America would exert its most effective influence not on its own, but through the network of alliances of which it was the hub. More particularly, he believed that Washington's military strategy did not impart confidence of commitment to the European allies. Although he had rejected his earlier notion that tactical nuclear weapons should be used in any variety of war, he strongly felt that the United States and NATO should retain the capacity to wage limited nuclear war, and he feared that the pronouncements of Secretary McNamara revealed a lack of willingness to resort to nuclear weapons in the event the Soviets attacked Western Europe. McNamara's fear of nuclear weapons, his apparent passion for a sixty-division conventional European war, was a source of constant anger and frustration to Kissinger. Not only would the West be imperiled without a nuclear option; Kissinger feared that, even in peacetime, American efforts to raise a huge conventional army for Europe would needlessly tax the physical resources of the alliance and give NATO members substantial cause to fear that the Soviets could march on Western Europe without being halted by an American nuclear response. By 1962, Kissinger had come to feel that Europe must ultimately rely on a tactical nuclear defense; any attempt to increase the level of conventional forces in Europe "could give rise to the notion that the West considers any kind of nuclear war unthinkable regardless of provocation." [41] He would write:

> The lack of a concept and capability for tactical nuclear war — conceived as control of the battlefield — is one of the greatest gaps in the present military posture of the United States as well as of NATO. It should be remedied as part of any reassessment of NATO strategy . . . If we wish to avoid

surrender or a general nuclear war, the tactical use of nuclear weapons may be our only possibility for avoiding defeat. The *worst* that could happen if nuclear weapons are used tactically is what is *certain* to happen in case a counterforce strategy is carried out.[42]

More important, he had by now come to feel that, in certain situations, tactical nuclear weapons could be used in such a way as to communicate their own extent or purpose without an accompanying verbal explanation. In some instances, then, the use of such weapons, not just the capacity to use them, could be an effective diplomatic tool. This was a distinctly minority view among Kennedy-era strategists, but Kissinger held firmly to it then, just as he does now:

The most effective method for employing nuclear weapons in a limited manner appears to be their tactical use to stop a battle and prevent a breakthrough. In the best of circumstances, the confusion attendant on *any* use of nuclear weapons will be considerable. It will be compounded by every country's lack of experience with them. The use of nuclear weapons to prevent a significant territorial advance by the attacker would have the virtue of observing well-defined geographic limitations. Of all conceivable limitations, this is the easiest to understand and to concert. If a stand-still in military operations can be forced, the major objective of the defense will be achieved.[43]

Kissinger's views on the usefulness of tactical nuclear weapons would have great bearing on his consulting activity during the summer of 1961, as the crisis over Berlin moved rapidly toward the dénouement that was to be the Wall. And Kissinger's recommendations to White House officials at the time of the Berlin crisis embodied a willingness to threaten Moscow with the use of tactical weapons over Soviet behavior in the divided city.

The crisis had opened in November 1958, when the Soviets threatened to sign a treaty giving the East German regime sovereignty over the Western access routes to Berlin unless a settlement on Berlin were reached in six months. Located more than one hundred miles inside East Germany, the four-sector city was the West's "last outpost of freedom" and a thorn in the side of the German Communists. To Moscow, the fact of an autonomous West Berlin was merely a symbol of an even more dreaded specter: a rearmed and militant West Germany. While the Soviets had kept their East German counterparts powerless and docile, preferring to govern East Germany with their own army and police, the Western powers had revived West Germany both politically and economically, and, in Soviet eyes, were allowing and encouraging Bonn to become increasingly bellicose and militaristic. Indeed, the Soviet threat on Berlin in November 1958 did not arise in a vacuum; it followed the decison of the NATO Council in December 1957 to place intermediate-range nuclear weapons on West German soil.[44] As a result Moscow had chosen to confront the NATO powers with the consequences of their decision: Allied access to the Western sectors of Berlin since the end of World War II had not been based on any formal document, but it was clear that any encroachment on access would involve a drastic departure from past practice and would infringe on long-standing Western rights.

The Soviet note of November 1958 reflected Moscow's position that the problem of Berlin would have to be settled in advance of any agreement on Germany's permanent status. The United States took a contrary view, that a settlement on Berlin should be linked to arrangements for German and Central European security. Nonetheless, Washington acceded to the Soviet threat by agreeing to a minister's conference in Geneva that May. As soon as the conference had been promised, the Soviets withdrew their May 1959 deadline for the resolution of the Berlin question; instead, having achieved their immediate goal of a meeting with the Western powers, it allowed the crux of their threat — to turn over the Berlin access routes to the East German regime — to recede temporarily into the background. As a result, the West, instead of formulating a well-defined negotiating position, approached the ministers' conference with little more than blind euphoria induced by temporary removal of the Soviet threat; it was prepared not to negotiate particulars, but more to establish and reaffirm a mood, a vacuous feeling of accomplishment, similar to the "Spirit of Camp David," the empty Khrushchev-Eisenhower summit the following September which Kissinger would so pointedly ridicule. The West had come to Geneva in May determined to discuss the broader issues as well as the specific question of Berlin; but, with typical diplomatic mastery, Gromyko induced them to confine the detailed discussion to Berlin, on which the West agreed in principle to a five-year limit on its current access rights. In addition, by receiving an East German representative, the meeting gave de facto recognition to the Ulbricht regime.

As a result of the U-2 incident and the collapse of the Paris summit meeting the following May, that is where the diplomatic positions stood at the time of President Kennedy's inauguration in January 1961. In the preceding months,

Ulbricht had undertaken selective encroachment on Bonn's access rights to the city, a situation the new President went to Vienna, unsuccessfully, to resolve. Earlier in the spring, former Secretary of State Dean Acheson had prepared for Kennedy a study of the Berlin problem which recommended a strategy of no negotiation and mobilization for a possible full-scale war. Kissinger, who was then consulting regularly for the White House, was opposed to the Acheson recommendations because they foreclosed any possibility of diplomatic exchange. The problem, he felt, was that the Allies had not put forward a coherent, carefully formulated position that could be successfully negotiated with the Soviets. He felt that if a confrontation between the United States and the Soviet Union were to come, it should come first in talks. Whereas those who argued for a hard-line policy feared that another U.S. entrance into negotiations might cause the Soviets to miscalculate Washington's intentions and assume that the U.S. was negotiating from weakness, Kissinger thought that not enough opportunity had been given to the avenues of diplomatic exchange.[45] And, of course, he advocated a firmer U.S. negotiating position than that which had been tried in 1959.

Since 1955, the Soviet position on Germany had been that there should be two German states, each disarmed and neutral. Above all else, the Soviets were fearful of German rearmament; no nation has suffered the ravages of twentieth-century German militarism more than has Russia. Sensibly, the West might have acquiesced in the division of Germany and acknowledged that the division, even if provisional, would be within the bounds of a legitimate European security arrangement. At bottom, this was the position that

Kissinger supported, and still supports today. He understood that Germany had historically been a land and a nation divided; he was not unmindful of the horror that Bismarck's artificial creation, a strong and unified Germany, had imposed on the rest of the Continent in the two World Wars. He himself had written that one of the most vital features of the Metternich system was its ability to keep Germany in fragments, to prevent the powerful eastern state of Prussia from exercising prerogatives in the many autonomous German kingdoms that separated Prussia from the Rhine. Only with the rise of Bismarck had this carefully constructed restraint collapsed. And only by keeping the western sectors of Germany firmly inside NATO, Kissinger felt, could the West restore and preserve European stability. He was quite fearful that "a militarily strong Germany without the restraint of NATO" [46] might well plunge the world into a third all-out war. "Germany," he wrote in 1960, "is the last country that should be encouraged to 'go it alone'." [47]

Unfortunately, the political realities were not so simple. If the Federal Republic were to remain inside NATO, its government would have to receive effective guarantees that NATO policy would not undermine its domestic support. And the easiest way to destroy the Federal Republic's popular base in the fifties and early sixties would have been to demonstrate that Western German membership in NATO would seriously inhibit, if not destroy, all prospects for unification. For that reason, NATO policy would have to endorse unification as an abstract goal even while not seeking it in practice. It was simply the problem of credibility posed in an unusually complicated and vexing way; and Kissinger, who has always had an unusually acute perception of how serious a problem an upset Germany can be, would want to

go further than almost any of his other colleagues in dem-
onstrating support for a goal that he himself realized was
completely chimerical:

> . . . If the West understands its interests, it *must* advocate
> German unification despite the experiences of the two World
> Wars and despite the understandable fear of a revival of Ger-
> man truculence. The West may have to acquiesce in the divi-
> sion of Germany but it cannot agree to it. The division of
> Germany may be unavoidable but the cohesion of the West
> and the future of the North Atlantic Community depends on
> our ability to demonstrate what makes it so. Any other course
> will in the end bring on what we should fear most: a militant,
> dissatisfied power in the center of the Continent . . . the issue
> in Berlin is not whether a city completely surrounded by Com-
> munist territory is "worth" a war — as is often asserted. Berlin
> has become the touchstone of the West's European policy. A
> defeat for the West — that is, a deterioration of Berlin's pos-
> sibility to live in freedom — could not help but demoralize the
> Federal Republic. It would mark the end to any hope for
> reunification. The scrupulously followed Western-oriented
> policy would be seen as a fiasco. This would become a warn-
> ing to all other states in Europe of the folly of resisting Com-
> munist pressure. Berlin would illustrate the irresistible nature
> of the Communist advance to the rest of the world . . .[48]

This sentiment typified Kissinger's view of how the United
States, as a great power, should treat a smaller ally. There
could be tactical disagreements between Washington and its
ally — and in a crisis situation, the ally usually could be the
more bellicose — but the United States must assume a public
posture of undeviating support for what its ally held to be
its fundamental political goals. In exchange for United
States support, the ally must be willing to follow Washington's lead in selecting tactics and in undertaking political

or military action. That willingness, in Kissinger's mind, constituted the acid test of a faithful and dependable ally. The current West German government, under the leadership of Willy Brandt, has taken an approach toward East Germany and toward the Soviet Union which is drastically different from that of Adenauer — and the newer approach is one with which Kissinger is in broad agreement. Yet ironically, Kissinger dislikes Brandt, not because his goals are incompatible with what Kissinger sees as the larger aims and directions of the Atlantic Alliance, but because Brandt, in his approach to the East, has acted independently of the Alliance; rather than following Washington, he has clearly been determined to take his own initiative. In 1961, Adenauer's government was repeatedly urging Washington to be tougher on the Russians in pursuit of an objective that Kissinger felt was futile; and yet, because Adenauer was willing to adjust his own behavior to Washington's, he was fulfilling what Kissinger saw as the principal duty of an ally. But Brandt, who now pursues what Kissinger himself sees as more laudable objectives, behaves according to his own — not Washington's — impulse and is treated by Kissinger and others as a difficult and bothersome ally.

At the same time, Kissinger's view of an ally's obligation was central to what he felt was a sound and practical basis for an emerging U.S.-Soviet relationship. In defending an ally, Kissinger felt, Washington must devise a negotiating position that was ambiguous enough to serve two vastly different purposes: to convince the ally (and, indirectly, all other American allies) of unswerving United States support, and at the same time to convey to Moscow an impression of America's willingness to compromise. During the crisis over Berlin, Kissinger felt Washington's objective should be to place public blame for the division of Germany on the Soviet Union in order to remove that blame from the shoulders of the Alliance and, simultaneously, to assure the Soviets that the Alliance would not actually seek unification in practice. Illuminatingly, Kissinger would see America's goal in Vietnam ten years later as inducing Hanoi to acquiesce in the continued division of Vietnam for a lengthy period following a U.S. withdrawal, not in order to preserve a non-Communist South Vietnam but to insure that when the South Vietnamese regime finally collapsed, the blame would be placed not on Washington but on Saigon.

Yet even this more moderate approach involved the same deadly paradox that had evidenced itself more obviously in the proposition of striking first with tactical nuclear weapons: how could America bring about a Soviet understanding that the West's defense of Germany was actually restrained, when all of the Alliance's public behavior — including the disposition of its military forces — repeatedly indicated otherwise? And even if the Soviet leaders, in their relatively sophisticated understanding of the U.S. position, believed that Washington was attempting to exercise restraint, then how could they — in view of their own public stance — now turn around and attempt to convince the hard-liners in their own bureaucracy and throughout the rest of the Communist world that the actions of the West on the German question did not constitute aggression of the most threatening sort? These questions would remain unanswered during Kissinger's policy activity on Berlin and throughout much of Kissinger's future government experience.

The negotiating position which Kissinger advocated for bilateral U.S.-Soviet talks on Germany was one he knew Moscow would reject: the disarmament and neutralization of East Germany under international supervision and, a number of years hence, free elections to determine the relationship of East Germany to the regime in Bonn.[49] The purpose of the position, as Kissinger himself said, was not to achieve unification but instead to "see to it that the Soviet Union is forced to accept the onus for the division of Germany." [50] At that price — Soviet acquiescence in the "onus" — the United States would not force the issue of unification in any other way. As a means of making this position acceptable to the Soviet Union, and as a persuasive method of communicating American intentions, the United States would maintain a heavy military presence in Western Europe to support the status quo. This position on Berlin and the German question was the quintessential expression of Kissinger's view of Washington's legitimate policy objectives: to satisfy an ally by prolonging an atmosphere of confrontation which would merely preserve the essential situation of both sides.

The danger, of course, was that an unpredictable event would shatter this delicate U.S.-Soviet understanding and cause the quiescent confrontation to flare up. Such an event began to unfold in June and July 1961, when huge numbers of refugees streamed across the borders of East Berlin into the Western sectors, impelled by the possible closing of the exits in the near future as well as by a drastic economic reform instituted by the Ulbricht regime. In response, the Soviet Bloc nations authorized the construction of a wall to seal off the exits from East to West. A treaty in 1949 guaranteeing the four-power status of the city would ordinarily have made the Wall impossible. But, in fact, the Wall was merely the most visible expression of a reality the city had been experiencing for some time: the erosion of four-power control. Most of official Washington accepted the Wall with complacency; there is ample evidence, in fact, that the White House breathed a sigh of relief when the Wall went up, because the politically sensitive and economically costly problem of the Eastern refugees had been ended. But Kissinger, because he viewed the problem much more symbolically, could not agree: "The partition of Berlin," he would write later, "marked the end of the belief that German unification would more or less automatically follow the strengthening of the Atlantic Alliance." [51] He then argued that this action could not go unanswered, that Washington's policy would lose credibility if there were no response. And he recommended that the President order an invasion of the Eastern sector for the purpose of tearing the Wall down.[52]

Even this action, in Kissinger's eyes, would have been symbolic in value; the West Germans would have been given confidence that America would intervene. But Kissinger's recommendation, which was also uttered simultaneously by a few other officials, would also have posed the threat of tactical nuclear weapons, albeit in a low-key way. Suppose the Soviets misunderstood? Suppose a shooting war began in East Berlin? Suppose, then, that the United States resorted to small nuclear weapons "to stop a battle and prevent a breakthrough"? The consequences could be endless . . .

. . . As they are, now, in Vietnam. The parallels between Kissinger's recommendations on the Berlin crisis, and on Vietnam a decade later, are striking; they do not give cause for reassurance. The active pursuit of an impossible goal for the simple sake of reinforcing the collective morale of America's allies; the absurd notion of credibility in each context, since neither London nor Paris would have felt reassured in the event of a nuclear obliteration of Berlin, just as they do not feel reassured now by America's actions in the defense of a Southeast Asian puppet military regime; the maintenance of tension for the purposes of diplomatic communication, a tension that can easily erupt into disaster, whether at the Wall or in Cambodia — these are the physical and emotional realities which we must recognize lie at the heart of Kissinger's present policy. And despite the fact that this policy is conceived as merely the avoidance of something that is far worse, we are tempted to ask ourselves seriously whether there is not a better way out than for man to circumvent senseless tragedy by giving in to it in the process.

The Salad Days of Henry Kissinger

HENRY KISSINGER'S ABRUPT DEPARTURE from Camelot was only the most extreme indignity visited upon him since his sudden rise to fame just a short while before. The years following the publication of *Nuclear Weapons and Foreign Policy* and the Rockefeller panel reports had riddled him with disappointment and misfortune. His initial successes in the foreign policy world were distilled in the bleak, often unfriendly setting of Harvard and Cambridge. Frustrated by stagnant surroundings, embittered by personal letdowns and unpopular with many of his colleagues, Kissinger followed ever more reliantly the paths outside of Cambridge that would lead him to Richard Nixon's Washington.

Harvard had been, and would continue to be, the focus of Kissinger's life; he had been launched on his fortune there, and his most enduring friendships and personal associations would always be centered there. And the university would serve him as a faithful way station where he could polish his sword and recoup his energies between repeated forays into the centers of national influence. Yet at those times when he was confined to Harvard alone, he was in many ways a man cut off from his most vital parts, a man whose vision was unrealized and his ambition unfulfilled.

He had arrived at Harvard in September 1946, a shy and often remote refugee student without ideas or ambitions, with only an intense desire to study and learn. Possessed of an acute native intelligence and armed with persistent, unrelenting Teutonic discipline and drive, he excelled at his studies and slowly gained confidence in his ability to do serious scholarly work. But he had also felt ill at ease in this new and strange environment, afflicted with a sense of insecurity that would color this and all his future endeavors. "Living as a Jew under the Nazis, then as a refugee in America, and then as a private in the army isn't exactly an experience that builds confidence," he would later observe of his early years.[1] And at his first taste of success, the shyness and fearful taciturnity would be complemented by a quiet arrogance and intellectual conceit. At every turn of Kissinger's fortune, each characteristic would fuel the other, the arrogance magnified by the self-consciousness and surprise of each success and the insecurity deepened by the shock and indignation at every setback. There is a story that on one occasion during his undergraduate days, Kissinger was told as the result of a clerical mistake that he had been given a failing grade. "Tell me — " the young Kissinger waxed stern and serious — "is this a joke?"

There was then a humorlessness and an abrasiveness in his approach to others that evaporated in the presence of trusted friends and yet was quite noticeable in his approach to the community at large. When, after completing his doctoral thesis, he departed for the Council on Foreign Relations, he did so not only because he was eager to escape the sterile atmosphere in Cambridge, but because if he had then attempted to scale the academic ladder, he feared he might be met with unfriendliness and animosity at every step of the way. And yet, even as his years away from Harvard would magnify his stature in the university community, they would create problems of their own when he returned to claim his rightful place.

He had left Harvard a nameless degree holder in the fall of 1955; now, two years later, he returned an international figure. Once known only as a tendentious scholar who had pursued his studies with monkish devotion, he now bore a huge coterie of patron saints in the citadels of worldly power. He had gone to the Council on Foreign Relations because he was not altogether well liked by his Harvard colleagues, because he feared they would not accord him the recognition he felt he deserved. And now, his re-entry into academia was a haughty and triumphal one, his quiet scholar's conceit now grown to the arrogance of one whose inner confidence has been affirmed by recognition and concrete success. Yet his next series of encounters in the academic and policymaking worlds would shatter much of that confidence, and would magnify the sense of native insecurity that underlay Kissinger's quest for personal distinction.

Kissinger was badly struck by the treatment of his first book, *Nuclear Weapons and Foreign Policy*, inside the intellectual community. While the book had received immediate popular acclaim due in no small measure to the huge publicity hype given it by the Council on Foreign Relations, it drew little but harshly negative comment from influential specialists in the arms field. Much of the criticism was well taken; after all, many of Kissinger's assertions were quite dangerous. But some of the commentary was also unusually vituperative, and it betrayed a sense of hostility that far transcended the bounds of scholarly etiquette. For sheer vindictiveness, it would have been difficult to surpass one reviewer, among the most respected arms specialists of the period, who abandoned all pretense of restraint and said of the book:

> Indeed, one of the many paradoxes of *Nuclear Weapons and Foreign Policy* is that it berates us for having depended too much on technology and not enough on doctrine for the solution of our problems; yet when it comes to limited war, we find Kissinger himself relying to an unbelievable extent precisely on technology to rescue him from all the dilemmas created by nuclear weapons. The result is that his discussion of limited weapons leaves the impression of special pleading rather than of systematic analysis . . . Kissinger maintains that much of the literature on military policy has been purely polemical; unfortunately, he himself has adhered to that tradition. The time for more sober, cautious studies, supported by detailed and sophisticated analysis now is at hand.[2]

This episode had a perceptible impact on Kissinger, and shaped many of his later attitudes toward his academic colleagues. Unfortunately, the attacks on *Nuclear Weapons and Foreign Policy* caused Kissinger not merely to change his thinking on limited war, but to react against them in an intensely personal way, often to assume a posture of implacable ferocity toward others, who he feared might be similarly critical toward him in the future. A less vain and personally sensitive man, one who did not feel his intellectuality tied so strongly to his inner self, would have been less vulnerable to those attacks and would have understood that they were in many ways almost routine. For the academic world has never been characterized by the pursuit of scholarly truth alone; it has always been a world oddly filled with individual jealousies and petty animosities, a world in which men, even as they pretend respect and admiration for the intellectual achievements of their colleagues, are often quite seriously pained by the success of others. In this environment, anyone who attained a measure of recognition, especially by challenging the prevailing orthodoxy as Kissinger did, would inevitably suffer a dose of harsh criticism. Indeed, since *Nuclear Weapons and Foreign Policy*, there has been a widely held attitude of subtle condescension toward Kissinger among arms specialists, a feeling that his interest lies so much in the realm of politics that his contributions to nuclear weapons literature are distinctive only for their vulgar popularization of the subject. Kissinger's attitude toward the arms community, in turn, has often been characterized by a quiet disdain for what he considers an indiscriminately technical approach to the more subtle problems of international diplomacy. And the disagreements have not been purely intellectual ones. If Kissinger's response to the initial critical salvos against him had been less extreme, his place in the academic environment might have been a more fulfilling one. But instead he oscillated ceaselessly between arrogance and self-doubt, often becoming an inward and solitary figure in his relations with others around him.

Kissinger's sense of solitude was compounded by the manner of his return to Harvard in 1957 as associate director for Harvard's new Center for International Affairs. At the same time, he had also emerged victoriously in an unseen power struggle for the directorship of Harvard's Defense Studies Program. In these two positions, Kissinger would clearly be one of the most eminent junior faculty members on campus. But, even more important, these positions virtually guaranteed that Kissinger's simultaneous appointment as an assistant professor in the Department of Government would amount to eventual academic tenure. This was no small matter to Kissinger's peers in the department, all of whom had lasted through three-year instructorships and would still have to prove themselves as assistant professors only to attain a position that Kissinger had already been given as a fait accompli. In Harvard's fiercely competitive environment, the very fact of Kissinger's emergence without the ordinary struggling upward through the bureaucratic ranks was no small cause for disaffection, a feeling that was compounded by Kissinger's own arrogance. "Have you ever known an economist who was fond of Galbraith?" queries one senior professor who still recalls his sense of slight as a junior faculty member at the fact of Kissinger's privileged status. "This did not exactly make for fraternal relations between Henry and the other junior members in the department."

Then there was Kissinger's animosity toward his superior at the Center for International Affairs. Robert R. Bowie, a high-ranking figure in the State Department of John Foster Dulles, had left government in 1957 to become the first director of the Harvard Center. In his discussions with university officials, he had been promised that an associate director would be appointed to help him run the center. At the urging of McGeorge Bundy, then dean of the Harvard faculty and a prime mover in the creation of the center, Bowie interviewed Kissinger for the job and then consented to the appointment. Within a short while, Bowie would be telling colleagues that hiring Kissinger was "the worst mistake I ever made." The two men did not agree on anything, and simply could not get along. Bowie, a formidable taskmaster, had hired an *associate* director — yet Kissinger did not take orders well. Bowie wanted the center to concentrate exclusively on research; Kissinger thought it should include a teaching facility. There was an important political clash as well. A man who retained great influence in the State Department long after his departure, Bowie was the initiator of a proposal which became the central feature of United States policy toward its European allies from 1963 to 1965; it was a scheme to which Kissinger was unusually antagonistic. The proposal was to supply NATO with a "multilateral force" of twenty-five surface ships, each to carry eight nuclear warheads and each to be manned with crew members from each of the participating countries. The purpose of the multilateral force (MLF) would be to alleviate the feeling of certain European allies, notably the Federal Republic, that they were second-class countries because they lacked an independent nuclear force. And Bowie's underlying rationale for the proposal was that Europe would eventually be politically unified, that the MLF would serve as the kernel of a European deterrent. Kissinger saw in the plan significant strategic inconsistencies, and, more important, a denial of the identity of the European nation-states; he felt that unification of the Continental powers would be a cruel hoax on history, and that the United States should not attempt to force it on its allies by encouraging an independent European striking force. (Without the "kernel" argument, of course, the strategic role of the MLF would have been ludicrous, since partial control over only two hundred warheads did not give the non-nuclear allies any real voice in the operation of the larger NATO deterrent.) Kissinger repeatedly inveighed against the MLF until its abrupt cancellation by the White House in 1965. His arguments were acute and perceptive; few NATO specialists would doubt today that Kissinger's views on the MLF were more sophisticated and far-sighted than were the official ones. Yet even those colleagues who were sympathetic to his position felt that he carried his arguments beyond the limits of political discourse into the realm of vindictiveness, because the originator of the proposal was also a personal enemy. And Kissinger's tendency to personalize intellectual disagreements would continue to evidence itself long after the MLF had died.

Kissinger felt an especially keen sense of rebuff at his failure to have any impact whatever on Kennedy-era foreign policy. And it was not as if this or that Kissinger recommendation were overlooked; his entire policy orientation was completely incongruous to the conventional wisdom of the time. After all, one did not become popular in the Kennedy White House by suggesting that the limits of America's ability to influence world developments should be considered in the formation of American foreign policy. For above all else, it was almost a point of religion with Kennedy's leading policy advisers that there was not a single problem anywhere in the world that could not be solved by the traditional pragmatic skill of American know-how. While Kissinger's thinking was firmly rooted in the European tradition of a sharing of power among the great nation-states, the popular Kennedy-era approach verged on extreme national chauvinism: America was the only true champion of freedom and it would fight anywhere and at any time to achieve its goals. The ringing oratory of President Kennedy's inaugural address — "Let every nation know, whether it wishes us well or ill, that we shall pay any price, bear any burden, meet any hardship, support any friend, oppose any foe to assure the survival and the success of liberty" — would be echoed sardonically eight years later in Kissinger's official declarations to the Washington press corps. He would always be ruthlessly pointed in his assessments of Kennedy foreign policy, of the paltry achievements measured against the sweeping claims, and, once in power, he would repeatedly contrast the idiosyncrasies of the Kennedy policy with what he considered his own more level-headed approach. It would be difficult to underestimate the sense of injury Kissinger suffered at the hands of the slick, fast-talking Kennedy White House aides who sluffed him off as a quirksome academic trying to peddle his bag of silly ideas. And as a European, Kissinger felt sadly out of place in the emphatically native American aura of Camelot, the social glamour and in-groupiness that seemed to be so much a part of Washington decision-making — and a far cry from the meager, barren social scene of Nixon's Washington that Kissinger himself, oddly enough, would dominate.

He was most deeply hurt by his brusque ejection from the White House at the hands of his former colleague and friend, McGeorge Bundy. And the issue, ironically enough, was Bundy's anger at Kissinger's attempts to circumvent him and talk directly with the President. Ironic, because Kissinger as special assistant eight years later would allow almost no one on the National Security Council staff to have any access to *his* President. Unable to exert any bureaucratic influence, Kissinger approached Bundy with a request that he be allowed to see Kennedy more regularly; Bundy, knowing full well that Kissinger was not prepared to give up his job at Harvard, confronted Kissinger with the choice of consulting full-time or not consulting at all. From all of these encounters, Kissinger suffered a feeling of powerlessness that did not go well with him, a feeling that he would not blithely forget in later years.

"One of the things he learned," a colleague would remember of Kissinger's experience in the Kennedy White House, "is that the only way to deal effectively with people at that level is to wait for them to call you and tell you they want to hear what you have to say." And so Kissinger would wait at Harvard in constant, hopeful touch with the foreign policy world but largely overlooked by leading decision makers until late 1965 — when Henry Cabot Lodge, whom Kissinger had met at the Center for International Affairs, invited him to Saigon to undertake a study of American policy in the Vietnam war. The intervening period was a difficult one for Kissinger, full of personal and intellectual agony for a man who saw little if any recognition for his work and ideas. He derived some satisfaction from teaching, and from many of his individual associations — although it had always been his unfailing habit, and an irksome one to colleagues and students alike, to postpone or cancel private engagements if Governor Rockefeller or someone of comparable status should call and ask a favor of him. But trapped in academia, Kissinger often suffered considerably, and his inner plight could scarcely be concealed even by his occasional outward grace.

When he wished to make a favorable impression, Kissinger was always able to radiate enormous tact and charm. His lilting and sympathetic voice, his superb command of language, his uncanny ability to argue, his wry, often self-effacing sense of wit, his enormous inner discipline and self-control — all combined to evoke that rare impression of intellect joined with human decency and genuine good will. And the impression was not a simple veneer; those around Kissinger during his many intellectual and political undertakings would later say that they detected in him a genuine satisfaction with many of the associations he formed, that his drive and ambition were accompanied by unfeigned personal warmth. "There's a human quality in him that I value very much," one Harvard friend would say. "There's a deep melancholy about him, and a sense that you're dealing with a guy who has known unlimited tragedy and seen some of the bleakest parts of the human landscape." If Kissinger is frequently abrasive in his approach to others, it is because he is motivated by an ingrown wariness about the limits of human charity, by an indelible suspicion about the motives and intentions of others to which his own victimization has sorrowfully earned him the right. And if his abrasiveness has been accentuated by the office he has held since 1969, even those of his underlings on the National Security Council staff who have suffered most from his harshness — and quit their jobs in frustration — are quick to compliment what they perceive as his deep and genuine sense of human purpose. These men nurture few illusions about Kissinger, and they are not easily fooled; remarkably, they are often unstinting in their praise for the man himself.

Yet the weaknesses in Kissinger's personality were often as deep-rooted and as critical as the strengths. At the heart of his behavior was that absurd combination of arrogance and insecurity, of outward insolence compounded with internal self-doubt, each feeding the other to produce in Kissinger a sense of massive unease. He was quick to feel insulted, and equally quick to wound others in turn. He felt his intellect bound inextricably to his personality, and sometimes inferred that a criticism of one was an attack on both. And just as he would insistently subordinate his private life to what he considered the more important and enduring realm of intellectual achievement, so would he personalize his intellectual disagreements with others — a trait he would carry with him to the White House in 1969. His fear of criticism often led him to avoid acknowledging or responding directly to it; to change one's mind was necessarily an act of volition or self-will, never to be occasioned by others but rather to spring from choice alone, for to do otherwise was to surrender one's autonomy, and Kissinger could not but view that as a demoralizing prospect. Even much of Kissinger's self-effacing wit was not meant, as it were, to be taken seriously; just as one resorts to humor to utter a truth that he would not dare state in a serious vein, so does one employ humor to discredit an idea that might be asserted seriously by others — and by doing so imply that the idea is so ludicrous that it can only be put as a joke. Some time after his entrance into the government, Kissinger was openly branded by Attorney General John Mitchell as an "egotistical maniac." The remark caused some public stir, and Kissinger responded by quipping to White House reporters that, "At Harvard, it took me ten years to develop a relationship of total hostility to my environment. I want you to know that here I have done it in eighteen months." [3] It is unlikely that a single reporter took the statement seriously; yet it is not entirely an inappropriate characterization of Kissinger's own experience.

His initial clashes and rivalries in Cambridge were not nearly so tied to animosity as they were to his almost total degree of personal insecurity. One close colleague remembers an occasion on which he and Kissinger attended an academic conference outside Cambridge, but accidentally saw little of each other during its course. The colleague returned home to find a long, impassioned note from Kissinger accusing him of failing to nod hello or otherwise offer greetings at certain times during the conference, and exclaiming that unless he could offer Kissinger some explanation for this conduct, their friendship would have to come to an end. The colleague responded not with an apology, but with a straightforward explanation of why Kissinger's assertions were uncalled-for and somewhat silly, and Kissinger apologized for the outburst. Such episodes reinforced the feeling that Kissinger's occasional difficulty in relating to his colleagues was not that he was personally indecent in the midst of an otherwise congenial environment, but that he was just another creature in an often inhuman jungle, a man who saw himself disliked or persecuted far more often than was the case.

In a purely academic setting, his attributes shone at their best. Kissinger was a superb teacher, one who was deeply interested in his subject matter and able to impart it in an interesting, often electric manner. His lectures vibrated with excitement, with unusual intellectual élan; he expressed his thoughts in a way that gave them a special urgency and important. There were some teaching enterprises to which Kissinger did not give his fullest, notably his seminars for graduate students, a group that Kissinger did not generally hold in high esteem. One of these seminars — on defense policy, to which he often invited leading Washington policymakers as guest speakers — was "essentially a show," as one colleague would later put it. "In a way, it was impressive just to see who he would bring." But Kissinger's International Seminar — held during the summer months for outstanding Europeans and other foreigners — was one of his favorite projects, one which yielded him a large number of friends from abroad. Even after he took office in 1969, he would continue his association with many of these friends, calling on them whenever he was in their countries and often entertaining them in Washington when they came to the United States. His fondness for the International Seminar reflected his tendency to be more at ease personally with Europeans. And his affinity for the people in the seminar enhanced his eagerness to communicate his thoughts and ideas.

But even more remarkable was his fondness for undergraduates. Most high-powered academics at Harvard have typically tended to see undergraduates as inept and driftless young bores; instead, they bestow their favors on their graduate students, the ones who teach classes and grade papers and ghostwrite academic articles for them. But Kissinger was not interested in surrounding himself with graduate students who, he felt, were less concerned with his association than with using him for their own personal advancement. Instead, he was often deeply interested in undergraduates; even though they could do nothing for him, he enjoyed the idea of imparting his knowledge to them and discussing his ideas with them and not having to feel that they wanted to manipulate him for their own ends. It was a striking fondness, born of the fact that undergraduates were intelligent, creative young people whose minds and interests were as yet unformed — not the graspy, greedy things who needed him only for the sake of their reputations and careers. Kissinger spent a good bit of his time with undergraduates (during one period at Harvard, he lunched with a group of them regularly) until his interests in the outside world cut off his teaching career.

Despite his ambitions beyond Harvard, Kissinger remained a consummate academic, devoted to his teaching and his scholarly work. Even though his outside commitments were much greater than those of any of his colleagues,

Kissinger remained as active as any — and more active than most — within the intellectual community. His undertakings at Harvard were supplemented by frequent attendance at academic conferences and gatherings of intellectuals from all over the world. Two of his most noteworthy such enterprises were in arms control discussions between influential Soviet and Western scientists, one sponsored by the Pugwash Conference and the other by the American Academy of Arts and Sciences. His ability to take part in so much activity was a testimony to his enormous — one may say tenacious — energy and personal drive. But for Kissinger, neither of his two worlds existed in contradistinction to the other; his participation in each drew on the same source, his relentless impulse toward intellectual challenge and adventure. With the same unending zeal that characterized his education of undergraduates in the relevance of Metternich to the present age, he would instruct Presidential candidates in the subtleties of contemporary American diplomacy. With the same inner conviction that embodied his debates with other colleagues at academic meetings, he would later pursue negotiation as the President's emissary with Chou or Brezhnev or Le Duc Tho. Kissinger's experience in academia did not delay or hinder his entrance into the world of power politics; it fueled his destiny and made it inevitable.

Three years after his separation from Camelot, Kissinger's political fortune made a sharp turn for the better. In late 1965, President Johnson asked Ambassador Henry Cabot Lodge to find an independent authority to investigate American involvement in Vietnam; Lodge invited Kissinger to Saigon. In the following three years, Kissinger became an active and influential behind-the-scenes figure in Vietnam diplomacy. For four months in late 1967, he nurtured a secret diplomatic channel between Washington and Hanoi, finally to negotiate as an official Presidential emissary and almost succeed in bringing about direct talks between the governments of the United States and North Vietnam. "It was a good job," one colleague would recall of Kissinger's Vietnam consultations. "His ego was under control."

At the last stretch of his teaching career, Kissinger became Nelson Rockefeller's chief foreign policy adviser during the 1968 Republican Presidential campaign. During the campaign, Kissinger had made a number of highly caustic remarks about Richard Nixon; at the Republican Convention in Miami, he reportedly went so far as to say of Nixon, "He is not fit to be President." It must have later been a shock to many people that Nixon could have appointed this man to a top foreign policy post; Kissinger had been a Rockefeller man from way back, and he had publicly scorned the President-elect. And yet, after Rockefeller's defeat, he let it be known privately that he was willing to consider an offer from the winning camp.

But why had Kissinger scorned Nixon? Not because he was less "liberal" than Rockefeller, but because in Kissinger's mind he was less attuned to the nature of America's interests and, as a mere politician, less willing to overlook popular opinion in order to pursue them. Rockefeller was of that elitist milieu which was steadfast in its convictions and willing to trample on the public will whenever it intruded on those convictions. But Kissinger feared that Nixon was so much a creature of the popular political process that he might give in to the transitory whims of public opinion rather than follow a course of action which was manifestly correct. It was only after receiving assurances that Nixon was not so simplistic in his impulses — and that Kissinger

would have a real measure of influence in a Nixon administration — that he consented to move from the drawing rooms
in Cambridge to Nixon's Washington.

As for Nixon, he had by 1968 a years-long affection for
Kissinger's work and thinking, which no doubt struck him
as appropriately hard-line. Shortly after the publication of
Nuclear Weapons and Foreign Policy in 1957, there appeared a widely circulated photograph of Vice President
Nixon with a copy of the book slung under his arm. In 1959,
Nixon wrote Kissinger a note praising an article in which
Kissinger argued against premature summitry with Soviet
leaders — a position Nixon took, probably to his own political detriment, during the 1960 televised debates. Following his first Presidential nomination, Nixon had Kissinger
summoned to work in his foreign affairs advisory group, a
request Kissinger refused. And after his 1968 nomination,
Nixon sought to retrieve Kissinger from the defeated Rockefeller camp. Most importantly, Nixon saw in Kissinger a
man of considerable intellectual independence; as a President determined to make his mark in foreign affairs, and a
strangely insecure man as well, Nixon felt that none of his
senior policy advisers should be tied to any particular interest group, that in the advice they gave they should possess
independent judgment, and should be their "own men."
Nixon was willing to overlook Kissinger's years of association with his intra-Republican rival, Nelson Rockefeller; as
one who had himself been a staunch campaigner, Nixon
could ignore Kissinger's harsh words about him, if indeed
he was even aware of them. But tempting as it may seem to
conjecture that Kissinger's transition to Nixon was part of a
pact with Rockefeller, the logic of the situation dictates
against it along with one fact that indicates Kissinger's com-

plete surprise at being offered his post. In the fall of 1968, Kissinger wrote an article on the Vietnam negotiations which *Foreign Affairs* scheduled for publication in January 1969. He would not have written a magazine article on that subject if he had felt he might soon be dealing with it as a high government official, particularly as the President's "options" man. Ever since his appointment, in fact, Kissinger has refused public comment on his views concerning matters of substance. Shortly after his acceptance of Nixon's offer, Kissinger sought to stop publication of the *Foreign Affairs* article, an attempt from which he was tactfully dissuaded by the magazine's editor, Hamilton Fish Armstrong. In light of this incident, it is hard to imagine a far-ranging plan to place Kissinger inside the government.

To Kissinger's colleagues in Cambridge — many of whom learned of the Nixon offer when Kissinger phoned them to ask their advice on whether he should accept — the appointment came as a surprise and, to a number of them, a personal jolt. A surprise, because they regarded Kissinger as far too sensible and sophisticated a foreign policy specialist for a politician of Nixon's ilk to be interested in; a jolt, because it was not entirely easy for some of those individuals to accept the fact that one of their peers, whom they considered more or less their intellectual equal, would now advance to a position of considerable power and national prominence. Their sense of shock was an ambivalent one, tempered by their happiness at having in the White House a man who might be personally responsive to their views on foreign policy — though they should have known that their potential for influence would extend only as far as their agreement with Kissinger's approach to international affairs. Still, for some time, many of Kissinger's ex-colleagues hoped to be heard by him, and until the President's decision to invade Cambodia in April 1970, Kissinger's appointment sheet was filled with the names of Harvard professors headed for Washington, just as Kissinger himself had done not so long ago, to see the great man and peddle their ideas.

Within the Nixon administration, Kissinger almost instinctively appropriated for himself the role of the President's liaison with the academic community. It was a role he played, for the most part, with *gusto*. As soon became evident, the intellectual rapport that Kissinger shared with Nixon was not enriched by the rest of the White House scene. The heavy, carnival Republicanism, the perpetual taint of electioneering and "voter appeal," the antagonism of the domestic advisers, the Haldemans and Ehrlichmans, upset that Nixon spent practically none of his time on the country's internal affairs — all of these influences operated against Kissinger's relationship with the President. So Kissinger, a man who had gone to Washington without any sort of popular or institutional base, continued to draw on the intellectuals for personal morale and support. And Nixon, it is clear, came to respect and value Kissinger's influence in the academic community, his standing in the world of thought and ideas. Kissinger, in turn, demonstrated to the President's immense satisfaction that, while he had dissolved all ties with the academic community and was beholden to Nixon alone, he was especially effective in his defense of administration policy when speaking to university representatives and groups.

The early days of the Nixon-Kissinger policy were euphoric ones for Kissinger's friends in the academic community: it appeared obvious then that Kissinger was exerting a temporizing influence on the President's decisions and policy pronouncements. Despite the administration's proposal to deploy a missile-defense ABM, Nixon's speech announcing the proposed deployment was remarkably mild in its view of the U.S.-Soviet strategic balance; rather than expound the dangerous, potentially explosive doctrine of "clear-cut" American superiority, as he had done during the Presidential campaign, Nixon said quite modestly that the United States did not wish to provoke Moscow by any reckless move that could appear to signal an intention to strike first. Neither side, he explained, should be in a position to benefit from an attack on the other, or to provoke a pre-emptive strike from the other side in return. The "arms community" breathed a sigh of relief at that speech, and assumed that Kissinger was largely responsible for the restraints implied in it. And there were other signs of Kissinger's influence as well, signs that Kissinger was having measurable success in improving on what Nixon, given what appeared to be his own instincts and personal judgment, would have otherwise done by himself. The relative openness to China, the initial announcement of troop withdrawals from Vietnam, and the President's stopover in Rumania during his round-the-world trip in July — making Nixon, oddly enough, the first American President to visit a Communist capital — were all seen in the academic community as outcomes of Kissinger's stewardship.

The reality was quite different. Nixon, though still a hard-liner, was an anti-Communist of extraordinary shrewdness and tactical flexibility. Many of his private views on foreign policy were not measurably different from Kissinger's — but of course, his public utterances were geared, as are any politician's, to the constituency from which he drew his greatest strength: the middle Republicans, the Conservatives, the ideological right wing. He pledged to enlarge America's strategic capabilities during the campaign, but knew full well that striving for military superiority, in a literal sense, over the Soviets would be a fruitless and impossible venture. And he talked tough on Vietnam, though he understood, as he put it in mid-1968, that there was "no way" for America to win the war, that the best America could do was to feign belief in the possibility of a military victory and thus strengthen her bargaining position at the Paris talks. And where the two men might have diverged in their instincts — as, for example, on the timing of opening relations with the People's Republic of China, which Nixon might have wanted to hold off until after his re-election — Kissinger could easily argue the case that a quick rapprochement between Washington and Peking would hurt the Soviet Union, a tactical chord to which Nixon was responsive. The divergence between the two men on concrete policy issues was not that great.

But Kissinger, a master of equivocation in the tradition of all talented diplomats, managed at the same time to create the illusion among intellectuals that he was a restraining and liberalizing influence on the President. And he misled ex-colleagues and others about the nature of his role by filling his private discussions with promises of imminent policy advances which, he implied, he himself had successfully urged on the President. A vast series of settlements between the United States and the Soviet Union — strategic arms limitations and East-West trade agreements, peace in the Middle East and, possibly, Vietnam — would come about in a quick progression, perhaps in nine or twelve months. Entente with the People's Republic of China would follow in rapid sequence. And most important, Kissinger left the impression with his audiences that the Vietnam war would necessarily be terminated before any other major international business took place. There was a period of mild euphoria generated by his private remarks throughout 1969 that the war would be over in six or nine months. Even today, in the aftermath of several such disappointments, many of Kissinger's associates are reluctant to acknowledge the possibility of Kissinger's concurrence on many major Vietnam policy pronouncements. Even as late as January 1971 — two weeks before the U.S.-South Vietnamese invasion of Laos — he told an assembly of credulous ex-colleagues at Harvard's Institute of Politics that by the time the United States had concluded its efforts in Vietnam, "you'll have nothing to criticize us for except that we didn't do it sooner." Kissinger's liberal audience faithfully took his remark as a promise of withdrawal; they later felt deceived and angry when the President announced after the Laotian invasion that "Vietnamization has succeeded" and that the United States would not depart from Indochina until Saigon had been given a "reasonable chance" to survive.

The invasion of Cambodia in April 1970 crystallized the many doubts held by the intellectual community about the underlying objectives of Vietnam policy and about the general drift of the administration's entire approach to foreign affairs. Early in May, a dozen of Kissinger's most eminent Harvard ex-colleagues traveled to the White House to convey personally their outrage at the President's decision. It was a painful experience for Kissinger to be chastised by a group of his former associates, many of whom had held decision-making posts in earlier administrations; and, of course, the sharp repudiation of the policy by this group of experts only exacerbated Kissinger's sensitivity to the tide of protest following the invasion. In addition to everything else, the group had made public its plans for a meeting with him before journeying to Washington, and, as a result, Kissinger read newspaper accounts of their condemnations even before his meeting with them. By any standard, then, the meeting was a deeply acrimonious one. As the organizer of the group, Thomas Schelling, said right after the meeting, "We made it clear to Henry that we weren't here lunching with him as old friends, but were talking to him solely in his capacity to communicate to the President that we regard this latest act as a disastrously bad foreign policy decision *even on its own terms.*" [4] And for many in the group, the meeting with Kissinger constituted a formal break with the White House; they would not consult for the Executive Branch until the war had ended.

To Kissinger, however, their mission was not so uncomplicated or noble. After all, he felt unenthusiastic about the Cambodia decision, and although he had not dissociated himself from it or even demurred against it, he derived great satisfaction from the fact that he was not the prime mover in it. Who did these men think they were, as Democrats who throughout the Johnson years had been less critical of the war than he was, whose prestige in some cases had been linked to it, and who were now presuming to inform him of the failure to withdraw? A few men in the group — Edwin Reischauer, Adam Yarmolinsky, and Francis Bator in particular — had actually collaborated with the war policy from official positions. Could they not now understand his predicament? Or were they seizing this opportunity to exonerate themselves by publicly repudiating him? As his irrepressible paranoia came to the fore, Kissinger began to feel that the underlying purpose of his ex-colleagues' protest visit could only be to wound him personally.

In an unusually lucid description of the encounter, based on accounts by the Harvard participants, the university's daily newspaper, the *Crimson*, described the meeting as "one of intense emotions painfully suppressed." Each member of the Harvard group addressed Kissinger at least once, each declaiming against the Cambodia decision from a different viewpoint. When their condemnations were over, Kissinger asked them if he could go off the record. To his surprise and anger, his visitors said no; they told him that this time, there would be no confidences to protect. Then, according to one of the men at the meeting, Kissinger told his visitors three things: "First, he told us that he understood what we were saying, and the gravity of our concern. Second, he said that if he could go off the record he could explain the President's action to our satisfaction. And third, he said that since we wouldn't let him go off the record, all he could do was assure us that the President had not lost sight of his original objective or gone off his timetable for withdrawal." [5]

Kissinger concluded the meeting with his familiar refrain: "When you come back a year from now, you will find your concerns are unwarranted." [6]

The Harvard group came away from the meeting with a sense of accomplishment, a sense that they had made a clear impact on Kissinger. And they believed that Kissinger would convey their sentiments to Nixon. As one of the group, Francis Bator — special assistant to President Johnson from 1965 to 1967 — put it, "He did just right with his response, actually. He could have done two other things that would have scared me more: he could have said things on-the-record that he shouldn't have said, or he could have given us a canned war briefing, which would have demeaned

whatever relation we had with him. If he'd tried to disso-
ciate himself [from] the policy, I'd have walked out. But he
behaved with great grace and dignity and courage under intense emotional pressure from his peer group." [7]

But did he really? Didn't his refusal to discuss the issue
honestly and openly "demean whatever relation" the group
had once shared with him? After all, the line which Kissinger handed them was not significantly different from his
very much "canned" presentation to other academic groups
and to the media — that they were getting out of Vietnam,
that there might be diversions along the way but everything was all right because he and the President knew better than anyone else what they were doing, that if the critics
would only sit patiently they would find six months or a year
later that their fears had been ill-founded. One year, two
years after their May 1970 encounter with Kissinger, those
in the Harvard group would find that their original concerns
had in fact not led them astray, that Nixon and Kissinger
were still very much committed to an "honorable" departure
from Vietnam. The Harvard group's good feeling after their
meeting with Kissinger reflected more their imagination
about his esteem for them than the reality of the relationship.

Indeed, Kissinger interpreted the visit as a gross insult.
He began to believe that his ex-colleagues' visit related not
so much to national policy as to their attitude about him and
about his place in the academic community. In other words,
as he saw it, they had conveyed an unstated threat that he
would not be allowed to teach at Harvard again unless he
changed the policy or quit the government. And Kissinger
thereafter began to spread the impression in Washington
circles that this had been the purpose of the visit of the ex-

colleagues, that Harvard was treating him like a pariah and would never have him back again. His allegations — all made privately — were accepted as fact and were perversely effective in discrediting his colleagues' protest; if these critics were so intolerant that they discriminated against Kissinger because of his political activity, then they must be as totalitarian as the enemy. The slander was not far removed from that of the zealous anti-Communist Richard Nixon throughout the early fifties. And since the time of the visit, one of Kissinger's greatest personal badges of honor in Republican Washington is that he has been shunned by the liberals at Harvard. Those in the Harvard group would firmly repudiate any suggestion that the purpose of their visit was to discuss Kissinger's place in the academic community, and they repeatedly asserted that they had come to see him only in his capacity as an emissary to the President; as Francis Bator would later say of the visit, "The idea that this has to do with Kissinger's relation to Harvard is grotesque on its face." [8]

Yet Kissinger, angered and upset that the group had chosen to vent their protest against him, continued to imply in private that he was the target of a vast academic conspiracy. It is possible, even likely, that during this period Kissinger received a number of hasty and random threats — or reliable reports of such threats — from individuals in the academic community. But he knew that the group had delivered no such threat; and, in continuing to imply that it had, he perpetuated a cruel fiction. At one reporters' briefing in August 1970, he referred half-jokingly to "the halls of academia from which I come and to which I may not be able to return." [9] At another briefing the following month he asserted sardonically, "I have to say from the way things are going in academia . . . I may not be able to get any job when I leave this position." [10] Later in the same briefing, he answered a question about the effectiveness of Vietnamization by saying in part that "If it doesn't succeed, not even Arizona State will take me." [11]

So, inevitably, the Washington press corps took up the clarion call. On May 8, the day the group was to meet with Kissinger, Mary McGrory wrote in the Washington *Star* — despite explicit denials to her by three of the group — that they were "descending" on the White House "with blood in their eyes" to tell Kissinger that "if he doesn't quit soon — or reverse policy — Harvard will never have him back again." And then, much more damagingly, Hugh Sidey, chief of *Time* magazine's Washington bureau, reported the visit in the magazine's May 18 issue by saying only that, "Last week a group of Kissinger's old Harvard colleagues, including Edwin Reischauer and Adam Yarmolinsky, told him *in effect* that unless the Administration's policies change, or Kissinger resigns, he will not be welcome back at Harvard." (Italics mine.) A clever turn of phrase; the group had conveyed their message not in words, but in *effect*, a distinction perhaps too subtle for the unwary reader, yet one that preserved the integrity of the report because the implication was not couched in hard, literal terms. Some in the group lodged a protest with *Time*'s editor, Hedley Donovan, but to no avail. They also asked Kissinger to correct the reports publicly, but he refused. Kissinger did "confide" to those in the group that he was *not* the source of the rumors.[12] But according to persons close to *Time* and to this writer, the source for the magazine's story was none other than Kissinger himself.

It was a superlative instance of the bittersweet ambience

that had typically marked, and would continue to characterize, Kissinger's relationship with his Harvard associates: in
public, there would be mutual respect and cordiality, but
beneath the masks would be concealed a vast network of
suspicion and innuendo. And in resolving the issue of Kissinger's place in their community, the Harvard Department
of Government would adhere to the façade that they had
always presented to the world, a façade vainly conceived
after the fashion of the United States Senate or any like-
minded gentlemen's club, that despite the underlying rivalries and animosities they must always put forward in public
a unified front, that censure of one of their colleagues, no
matter how well deserved, was in principle repugnant to
them.

There is a long-standing rule that governs leaves of absence from Harvard's faculty, that professors may not be
absent from the university for more than two successive
years without relinquishing their tenure. In late 1970, as the
war in Indochina raged onward, Henry Kissinger's Harvard
tenure was drawing to a close. If he did not quit the government by January 1971, he would lose his position in the
university. The rule had never been broken before, and
there was little reason to expect that an exception would be
made in his case: after all, as the price of remaining inside
Camelot, men of no less stature than McGeorge Bundy, Edwin Reischauer, and Arthur Schlesinger, Jr., had been forced
to relinquish their Harvard tenure after two years' absence;
others, such as John Kenneth Galbraith, Kennedy's ambassador to India, and later, Daniel Patrick Moynihan, a leading
Nixon adviser on domestic affairs, had had to cut short their
terms in government to retain their Harvard appointments.
It would of course have been possible for Kissinger to re-

linquish his tenure and then seek reappointment at some later time, as Reischauer had successfully done;[13] but that would hardly have satisfied so arrogant and at the same time so insecure a man as President Nixon's leading foreign policy adviser. Through the fall of 1970, Kissinger applied direct, private pressure on his colleagues at Harvard to make some special provision for him should he decide to retain his government position. And until they did, the intricate gossip game about the poor, destitute professor exiled by totalitarian Harvard would continue.

In December, at a closed meeting of the senior faculty members in the Department of Government, Harvard made its decision; the leaves-of-absence rule would not be explicitly broken, but it would be quietly circumvented. The Department would take no immediate action to fill Kissinger's teaching position, and would privately assure Kissinger that he would be reappointed if he gave word, at any time before the Presidential election of November 1972, that he was prepared to depart Washington at the end of Nixon's full first term. The stage had been set for the play-acting that would ensue the following month: three days before his leave of absence was to expire, Kissinger would regretfully submit his formal Harvard resignation. At the same time, the White House would release a letter from a grateful President Nixon to Kissinger saying, in part, "your decision to resign from the Faculty of Harvard University so that you can remain as a member of my administration is one that I know is very difficult for you . . ." The President's letter would add a noteworthy accolade: "Frankly, I cannot imagine what the government would be like without you." [14] This exquisite drama was soiled only by Kissinger's own indiscretion; he boasted to a *New York Times* reporter that he had received guarantees that he could return to Harvard at any time after his departure from government.[15] The day after the *Times* report, the *Crimson* disclosed the details of the arrangement;[16] questioned about the *Crimson* report, Kissinger replied coyly, "This is a matter for the Government Department and I would not know. I just resigned." [17]

The occasion on which Kissinger personally received the good news from his Harvard colleagues was a most fitting one — the retirement dinner given in Cambridge by the Department of Government for Carl Friedrich, the aged constitutional scholar who had been a fixture in the department for more than twenty years. The dinner, an artificial and often tasteless affair, was held in the baroque dining hall at Harvard's Busch-Reisinger Museum. Friedrich was not a figure unknown to Kissinger; in his younger days, Friedrich had been the great rival in the department to William Yandell Elliott, the standard-bearer of a younger Kissinger. As a result, Kissinger's scholarly relationship with Friedrich had never been more than superficially cordial. But now, at the old man's retirement dinner in late December 1971, the solidarity of the leading lights in Harvard's Department of Government would be reaffirmed for all the world to see. For one fleeting moment, amid the friendships and rivalries, the cordialities and bitter animosities that he would always know so intimately, Henry Kissinger had come back to Harvard again.

The Nixon-Kissinger Policy

"I WOULD NOT WANT to answer for his actions if he feels he has been insulted," Kissinger said of President Kennedy in the aftermath of the Berlin Wall. Lamenting the fact that his earlier recommendations had been disregarded, Kissinger voiced fears to a friend [1] at Harvard that the President might now overextend himself elsewhere in the world — and provoke a larger confrontation — as a result of his failure to take action on Berlin. The thought was timely; in November, Kennedy made a crucial decision to salvage the crumbling regime of Ngo Dinh Diem in South Vietnam, a decision whose ramifications would shape Nixon-Kissinger policy. And Kissinger's words on that early occasion reflected his view that a global foreign policy, to be effective, must be characterized not by isolated action-and-response but by conceptual unity, a balance and coordination between all the policy's disparate parts.

As special assistant to President Nixon, Kissinger has supervised a policy that is remarkably rhythmic in pattern. There is an exquisite internal harmony, a self-contained consistency in it that bears the unmistakable stamp of its creator. In order to grasp the Kissinger policy, one would do well to envision the working of a finely tuned watch. The face of the watch is obliged to change from one minute to the next; but these changes are merely gestures, no more than outward manifestations of the underlying grand design. Beneath the surface, the mechanism remains fixed, emitting identical signals through every hour of every day, churning constantly forward with the same relentless virtuosity. The eternal fluctuations of competing political and military forces are ever subject to its endless pulse. This conceptual vision has made a clear impact on the conduct of American policy. And it derives from the assumptions which Kissinger has nurtured throughout his intellectual life.

Yet as internally consistent as American foreign policy has been under Kissinger's stewardship, the policy itself has often been at odds with the realities of the world outside it. A completely harmonious policy, one that is true only to its own peculiar criteria, it has frequently been difficult to apply in a discordant, unharmonious world. The most subtle and intricate timepiece is of little ultimate value if its owner is destined to be an anachronist. And the greatest curse of Nixon-Kissinger policy — the continuation of the Vietnam war — is a direct outgrowth of the obsession to be consistent, to be credible if only to oneself, that characterizes this administration's approach to world affairs. In order to understand the Vietnam war, we must first examine the general policy from which it takes shape, and whose perpetuation it is intended to serve.

Needless to say, the Nixon-Kissinger policy has been geared primarily to the behavior of America's only rival for worldwide power and influence, the Soviet Union. Every foreign policy decision since 1969 has had the purpose of making a certain impression upon the Soviets, if not of responding directly to them. And this the Nixon administration has sought to do not by applying itself to each decision and absorbing itself in every crisis, but by attempting to generate a more durable worldwide structure in which responses to Soviet behavior can occur with greater force and certainty. Hence the network of American alliances around the globe is an essential component of America's policy toward the Soviet Union; and for that reason, every American policy decision has been geared to preserving the commitment and morale of the allies.[2]

The fundamental priority of the policy has been to convince Moscow that it is fruitless to conduct international business on ideological grounds. To do that, of course, the United States must lead by example, must demonstrate that it too is willing to behave in a non-ideological manner in the world arena. And the clearest expression so far of Kissinger's opposition to the idea of an ideologically oriented foreign policy has been Washington's rapprochement with the People's Republic of China. In one sense, the rapprochement has represented an effort to "draw" China "into a constructive relationship with the world community."[3] It arises from a perception that a global policy should not ignore an entity such as China, that "an international order cannot be secure if one of the major powers remains largely outside it and hostile toward it."[4] At the same time, Kissinger realizes that China will not come into her own as a world power for quite some time, and did not undertake the new policy on a misimpression that China would imminently emerge to challenge the U.S.-Soviet bipolar world structure. Rather, the policy — which dates back to the early days of 1969 and took its first real shape with the President's trip to Rumania in July of that year — is intended to affect American-Soviet relations in an unusually subtle way. With its christening of Peking as a legitimate player in the international sphere, the policy is calculated to temper the polemical tendencies of the Soviet Union by forcing Moscow's leaders to adopt a more conciliatory approach toward the United States. As Kissinger put it in August 1970,

> The deepest international conflict in the world today is not between us and the Soviet Union, but between the Soviet Union and Communist China . . . Therefore, one of the positive prospects in the current situation is that whatever the basic intentions of Soviet leaders, confronted with the prospect of a China growing in strength and not lessening in hostility, they may want a period of détente in the West, not because they necessarily have changed ideologically, but because they do not want to be in a position in which they have to confront major crises on both sides of their huge country over an indefinite period of time.[5]

Hence, the Nixon-Mao summit of February 1972 was essentially an anti-Soviet maneuver. Its purpose was to induce Moscow to make concessions in arms negotiations and cooperate on the handling of the crises in the Mideast and in Vietnam.

There can be little question that the Nixon-Kissinger policy has contributed to the vast improvement of America's relations with the Soviet Union and People's China. And the dual approach — reaching out to both Moscow and Peking in a single movement toward improved relations — has been a tortuously difficult one to follow, one that has demanded unusual diplomatic acumen; as obviously as it has had the effect of interesting both nations in improved relations with the United States, it could also have caused each of them to become further alienated by America's approach to the other and increasingly antagonistic in their behavior. In exploiting the Sino-Soviet split, the policy could have aggravated the two Communist giants to the same brink of war which they approached in early 1969. Since the early sixties, the Soviets have always waxed extremely nervous in the face of any American attempt to make contact or begin relations with People's China. And Peking, in turn, has come to see U.S.-Soviet conciliation as the opening of a global conspiracy against Communism in China. It must have been an extraordinary feat to convince each of these powers that America's approach to the other was undertaken not for the sake of conspiracy or petty advantage, but rather in the context of a non-ideological international structure. And it is a tribute to Kissinger's ability as a statesman, because he, more often than anyone else, has been given the great and difficult charge of conveying to Soviet and Chinese leaders a picture of the emerging American policy and Washington's view of how international relations should generally be conducted. Kissinger has many times said privately, in fact, that the most important aspects of these negotiations — especially the U.S.-Chinese exchanges — during the past four years have related not to concrete issues but instead to the larger questions of competition within a broader framework of great-power understanding — an understanding that seeks to comprehend the *total* process of how sovereign powers reconcile their interests, an understanding that not only grasps one's own predicament, but also encompasses that of the other side.

Yet the Nixon-Kissinger policy has not *created* the conditions that have allowed for the degree of great-power cooperation that is occurring today; it has *perceived* that historical conditions demand an improvement of relations. If the Soviet Union and People's China have been responsive to American approaches, they have been moved not by the competence of Kissinger's diplomacy but, more fundamentally, by their own desire to make peace with the United States and move out more comfortably on the world scene. Long before 1969, the Soviet Union had abandoned its goal of world upheaval; it had long been sheer deception for Moscow to couch its international ventures in the rhetoric of ideological principle. Moscow's interest lay not in the destruction, but rather in the perpetuation and manipulation of nation-state relationships. Before the Kissinger-Chou negotiations of 1971 and the Nixon-Mao summit the following year, the Chinese government appeared to be moving in the same direction: away from its exclusive preoccupation with internal development — a preoccupation that largely withstood America's threatening behavior in the Indochinese nations to the south — and toward establishing friendly contacts with many governments, such as Indonesia, Pakistan, and Egypt and other African nations, which did not remotely share her ideological views. Nixon and Kissinger did not bring these conditions about; they simply recognized and seized advantage of them, although it must be said in all fairness that in that comparatively modest achievement they far surpassed their predecessors, who had largely failed to do even that.

Yet despite these reconciliations, Washington is unjustified if it assumes — as it appears to do — that ideology has disappeared once and for all in Moscow's and Peking's approach to world affairs. A more sustainable view — particularly in the case of China — is that the Communist powers have opted for conciliation because it is an easier way of doing business in a technologically deadly world, and that Moscow and Peking may yet one day resume their roles as ideological centers. This is not to say that a Red Menace continues to lurk beneath the surface, or that the Soviet Union and China have been made reasonable by American "perseverance" and military strength. Indeed, the history of the Cold War seems to suggest the opposite; that the two Communist powers tend to wax fiercely ideological, not conciliatory, in the face of American intransigence. The United States may have "won" in the Cuban missile crisis, but the cost of humiliating Khrushchev was the Soviet decision to embark on a crash program to outbuild America in nuclear weaponry, a decision whose ramifications are still being felt today. Nixon and Kissinger may have gained a brief victory by forcing Moscow to swallow a U.S.-Soviet summit as American mines floated off North Vietnam's coast, but who can now say what this latest act against Hanoi — and against Moscow — will foreshadow in the long term: the erosion of the strategic arms limitation treaty, more arms spending on both sides, etc. If Nixon and Kissinger assume that Moscow and Peking have now been rendered permanently docile, and that in the face of American transgression they are incapable of anything but a meek response, then the United States may in future years become increasingly adventuristic — as is now happening in Vietnam — with the risk that the Soviet Union and China will revert to their Cold War suspicion and animosity. Beyond a certain level of American militancy, in fact, the Communist giants would likely be *forced* to such a response; they have not abandoned their literal claims of ideological supremacy, and in the event of much "toughening" on Washington's part, they would almost certainly be persuaded by their adherents, domestic and international alike, to take a firmer stand against the "capitalist" world. Nixon and Kissinger must recognize — as they have yet failed to do — that Moscow's and Peking's responses to U.S. policies do not constitute an American victory so much as they point to the rise of circumstances in the international arena that are far beyond America's singular control.

The most significant motivating force in bringing about a commonly held vision of a non-ideological world order has been the massive proliferation of nuclear arms. The very factor that once produced an unambiguous situation of U.S.-Soviet bipolarity has by now awakened the two superpowers to the possibility that if allowed to continue unblunted, that very bipolarity may unleash man's destruction. In an age of instant mass slaughter, it becomes particularly important that differences of ideology not be allowed to influence foreign policy. As the Nixon-Brezhnev declaration of May 1972 expressed it, ". . . in the nuclear age there is no alternative to conducting . . . mutual relations on the basis of peaceful coexistence." Hence, the stabilization of the arms race and the elimination of any incentive to strike first with nuclear weapons was universally recognized as the transcendent priority of U.S.-Soviet relations, and an especially urgent one at that. Indeed, this recognition extended even to the leading officials of the Johnson administration, who took the first step by proposing in 1967 that Washington and Moscow negotiate an arms agreement. By effectively eliminating the development of the antiballistic missile systems on both sides, the strategic arms limitations talks concluded in Moscow last May were a major achievement in reducing the threat of nuclear war.

At the same time, the bipolar world structure remains essentially unchanged. To be sure, the historical peculiarities of the current bipolar arrangement — the unprecedented reluctance on the part of great powers to employ all or even much of the military might at their disposal — has made for a curious phenomenon of great power impotence; and that, in turn, has encouraged the spread of political multipolarity, that is, the illusion — often a very effective one — that a superpower can be manipulated and bullied by a smaller ally. Nonetheless, the United States and the Soviet Union, because the arrangement suits their capacities and their ambitions, have undisputedly remained the leading actors on the world stage. And in that sense, it may finally evolve that the arms agreement signed in Moscow, by stabilizing and defusing the more dangerous aspects of that arrangement, may actually serve to encourage and perpetuate it, so that American and Soviet influences will continue undaunted to make themselves felt, perhaps to confront each other, in many areas of the globe. That is not to say that the SALT agreement is destined to have a negative effect; far from it. It is only to say that "looking at all the dangers, all the things that can go wrong" — Kissinger's cautionary words on the Moscow agreements[6] — it is clear that the current détente will stand or fall in the context of the two countries' interrelationship on the world scene. For their part, Nixon and Kissinger intend to continue making their influence felt on a worldwide scale. How is their approach likely to shape the future of U.S.-Soviet relations?

The single most essential requisite for a global power operating in a nation-state world order is a sturdy and dependable group of allies. Of course, a tempting criticism of Kissinger's conceptual model, the European nation-state system, is that its alliance networks caused it to break down into World War I. But Kissinger attributes this breakdown to an inflexible and otherwise poorly constructed alliance system, and a redefinition of American alliances is at the heart of Nixon-Kissinger policy. The thrust of the Nixon Doctrine,

announced at Guam in July 1969, was that, as Kissinger expressed it, "The United States alone cannot make itself responsible for every part of the world at every moment of
time against every danger and to capitalize every opportunity." [7] More fundamentally, the goal of the Doctrine was
to allow the United States to maintain worldwide credibility
at the same time that it could avoid the excessive and overbearing commitment that led the European nation-states
down the road to Sarajevo. That America has frequently
been militarily and psychologically overcommitted is a proposition that not many foreign policy critics would take exception to; the reduction of armed forces from a "two-and-a-
half-war" to a "one-and-a-half-war" posture and other parings
of material commitment spelled out during the first year of
the Nixon administration were welcomed by broad sectors
of American public opinion as well as by more seasoned observers. But while the physical presence has undergone substantial reduction, the traditional political commitment has
remained: "The Nixon Doctrine is our realistic way of remaining committed to the rest of the world. It can lay a
basis for a continuing practical relationship, not a basis for
a total withdrawal." [8]

Despite the reduction in conventional forces, the declared
obligations of American policy have, if anything, widened in
the past four years. Now more than at any other time, the
United States is pledged to guarantee a peaceful settlement
in the Mideast. The expansion of the Vietnam war that began with the invasion of Cambodia in April 1970 — and
reached an ominous peak with the mining of North Vietnam's harbors in May 1972 — has broadened the scope of
Vietnamization to include Saigon's military operations in
Cambodia and Laos, and has posed a continuous risk of di-

rect confrontation with the Soviet Union. And a remarkable statement in the 1972 State of the World Message warning against "The use or threat of force by the Soviet Union in Eastern Europe" [9] seems to declare that·the Soviet bloc nations will henceforth be considered within the legitimate sphere of America's worldwide concerns.

Thus, the most striking aspect of the Nixon Doctrine is the dichotomy between America's military presence, which the Doctrine proposes to reduce, and the political pledge, which is to remain intact. The effect of this disparity has been to place a premium on U.S. credibility, and to make U.S. policy more reliant on the use of threats. To be sure, the threat of the Nixon Doctrine is double-edged; besides warning America's opponents that Washington may intervene, the reduction in physical aid forces America's client regimes more and more to assume the burden of their own fate. And in many ways, the Doctrine is a quite pragmatic recognition of the fact that America's patronizing her more mature allies is incompatible with the notion of genuine and sustained partnership — a recognition exemplified by the reversion of Okinawa to Japan. Nonetheless, the expanded political commitment of the Nixon Doctrine has placed increased emphasis on the confrontationist tendencies in Washington's policy.

Ironic as it may seem, the all-embracing obligations spelled out in the Doctrine demand that the role of the United States in every confrontation be particularly "tough" or convincing. For Washington may make sweeping global pretensions only if it can demonstrate that, when called upon to act, it will invariably act with force and resolve. To put it another way, the more widespread the area in which America commits itself, the more important the notion of credibility becomes. Under ordinary circumstances, a policy does not either "have" or "lack" credibility; it possesses a certain *degree* of credibility, and the measure of a policy's success is whether that degree outweighs an opponent's willingness to risk a showdown; no threat has to be *absolutely* credible in order to succeed. But under the circumstances of America's worldwide commitment — a commitment that, by its very scope, would seem to defy belief — each action in each area must be geared to the whole if the commitment is to remain intact; Washington's credibility must be total and constant.

In particular, the overall reduction of American ground forces around the world places greater reliance on the threat to use nuclear weapons if the sweeping political claims of the Nixon Doctrine are to be taken seriously; the 1970 State of the World Message is quite explicit in this regard.[10] American NATO policy is still grounded in the assumption that the United States must not be denied the added flexibility of tactical nuclear threats in the event of Soviet misbehavior over Berlin or, apparently, Eastern Europe. And against lesser nuclear powers such as the People's Republic of China, the resort to nuclear weapons could come with a lesser provocation. Clearly, Nixon and Kissinger would like to avoid nuclear war, but the excessive political commitments of the Nixon Doctrine are edging them closer in that direction.

The risks of overcommitment and confrontation are often underlain by Kissinger's peculiar expectation of how America's allies must pursue their own foreign policies. His criterion for judging correct allied behavior is not domestic ideology or even tactical sensibility on international matters, but simply allied willingness to shape all foreign behavior according to American judgments. It is an extremely simplistic approach, one that blurs his vision about what is possible in concrete foreign policy situations and one that strains America's allied relationships as well. It is an approach that leads him at various times to see Nguyen Van Thieu as a convenient ally not because he is reasonable but merely because he is compliant, and to regard Willy Brandt as a difficult ally not because his policies are unsound or even incompatible with America's long-range goals but because his timing and his tactical judgments are reached independently of Washington and the other NATO powers. In fact, the White House's entire approach to the present West German government is an object lesson in how paternalistic a fashion Nixon and Kissinger expect to be able to treat their allies.

The President and Kissinger have never been particularly fond of Willy Brandt — a fact exemplified by Nixon's premature victory congratulations to then-Chancellor Kurt Georg Kiesinger after the first inconclusive returns of the September 1969 elections in which Brandt finally captured the Chancellorship. Their predispositions were soon fueled by Brandt's decision to pursue détente with the Soviet Union and East Germany outside the framework of American and NATO negotiations with the Soviet Union. In Nixon's and Kissinger's eyes, the fundamental thrust of *Ostpolitik* — acknowledging the division of Germany and easing tension in Central Europe — was a sound one; yet they feared that Brandt's initiative might disrupt NATO unity by encouraging other Western European governments to behave independently of Washington in their relations with Moscow. That, they felt, would decrease America's power to bargain with the Soviet Union, not only because concrete issues of mutual U.S.-Soviet interest would already have been negotiated but also because Washington's ability to influence and mold the behavior of its allies would have been rendered questionable. The 1972 State of the World Message contained an indirect condemnation of Brandt's policies:

> Some of our allies were pursuing détente in bilateral contacts with the East, but it was clear that most bilateral questions were part of a wider web of European security issues. The Soviet Union could not be given the opportunity to offer selective détente, smoothing relations with some Western nations but not others.
>
> Thus, Western cohesion must be the bedrock of our pursuit of détente. We and our allies have a responsibility to consult together in sufficient depth to ensure that our efforts are complementary and that our priorities and broad purposes are essentially the same.[11]

There can be little doubt that German détente is integrally related to the larger picture of U.S.-Soviet negotiations. Most importantly, the recent access agreement on Berlin — without which *Ostpolitik* would have been meaningless — was negotiated not by Bonn, but by the three allied powers legally in charge of the city's western sectors, the United States, Britain, and France. It is further true that German security was a focal issue in the SALT negotiations — especially on the question of intermediate-range nuclear weapons in Europe, a question that the negotiations did not resolve — and that it would also figure centrally in any discussion of European conventional force reductions. There are even matters that do not seem to relate directly to U.S.-Soviet arms negotiations — most notably, the psychological importance of the status of Germany, to which the Russians have historically been peculiarly sensitive — which would heavily influence East-West discussions; indeed, it seems likely that the Soviets' recent decision to receive the President in Moscow and consecrate the SALT agreement despite the presence of American mines in North Vietnamese harbors was based on the fact that, a short while before, the Federal Republic's closely contested treaties with Moscow and with Poland easily passed in Parliament despite what appeared earlier to be an even split among the West German deputies — a split that was likely resolved when Washington influenced its friends in the Christian Democratic opposition to let the treaties pass. In any discussion the Soviets hold with the United States, one East Germany is worth two dozen North Vietnams.

The question, as Brandt himself acknowledges, is not whether United States policy will continue to play an important part in Germany's approach to her own foreign affairs — the protection of the U.S. deterrent and even that of conventional American forces is too important to allow otherwise — or whether Bonn will fail to *consult* meticulously with Washington on any basic foreign policy decision. It is whether American influence can effectively or legitimately extend to those historical-cultural or psychological issues which the Germans themselves must address. The dividing line beyond which Washington should not venture is sometimes unclear, but *Ostpolitik*, as a phenomenon that speaks to a peculiarly German problem, seems to fall beyond it. Yet the dividing line — in German and in other allies' affairs — is not one that Kissinger scrupulously observes. In the case of Germany, it is not even an issue that Kissinger fully acknowledges; he insists frequently that "We respect Willy Brandt" [12] when the opposite is more frequently the truth. America's ability to bring about the Moscow summit by means of gracing the German parliament's ratification of the Eastern treaties, if it so happened, was an adept tactical maneuver. But that does not remove the distinct possibility that *Ostpolitik* was made more painful by America's insistence on holding out for bargaining power — as probably occurred in the excessively lengthy negotiations on Berlin — nor does it resolve the issue of where such an approach toward one's allies, in Europe and elsewhere, is likely to lead.

Indeed, the current administration's obsession with manipulating allies is even more pronounced in the Third World, where America's possessiveness is less politically excusable — and more psychologically dangerous. Washington's impulse to control allies and, through them, to control events, is ill-suited to the many situations which, unlike some of those in Europe, are neither traditionally nor justifiably susceptible of American stewardship. As a result, the regimes that America chooses to work with — and seeks to uphold—are quite frequently at odds with the collective traditions and the political will of the peoples over whom those regimes exercise their rule. And that tendency is underlain by the guiding principle of Nixon-Kissinger policy, a principle which maintains that each American decision, every allied motion throughout the world, must be orchestrated into a unified, harmonious gesture toward the Soviet Union.

The most characteristic device in Nixon-Kissinger policy is the concept of "linkage." The rationale of linkage is that all the world's trouble spots exist on a single continuum which connects the Soviet Union and the United States. In this context, the resolution of individual issues depends not so much on the merits of the specific case as on the overall balance of power between the two sides. And the underlying assumption of linkage is that the settlement of a crisis in one area of the world can be predetermined by the strength and degree of resolution which one or both of the contending parties have shown in other areas.

Doubtless there are many international developments that are appropriate subjects of linkage. As a general rule, it would be dangerous for American decision makers to pursue each policy venture in complete disregard of the policy's general thrust and direction; indeed, any competent policy must have some such identifiable direction. And in closely connected frameworks, opposing U.S. and Soviet positions may appropriately be traded off against each other to produce a mutually beneficial settlement encompassing more than a single crisis area. It seems necessary, for example, for U.S. negotiators to make an emphatic connection between the status of intermediate-range nuclear weapons facing each other across Eastern Europe and European security agreements. More remotely, it would be justifiable under certain circumstances to draw connections between Soviet behavior in Europe and in the Mideast; to take an example offered by one of Kissinger's present assistants, the United States and the Soviet Union cannot engage in Europe-related negotiations if the two sides are also at loggerheads in a Mideast war. Yet at a certain remove, linkage becomes unjustified; it is silly to think that Soviet assistance to the Arab nations in the Mideast is in any way comparable to, or closer to a solution by virtue of, America's prosecution of a full-scale Indochina war. And it is even less reasonable to suppose that America's steadfastness in Southeast Asia measurably affects Washington's credibility in the European theater, with the Soviet Union, or even with the West European allies; from Europe's vantage point, the war is an exercise not in credibility, but in irrational and absurd theatricality. Above all else, it is mistaken to predicate the reduction of nuclear tensions on Moscow's willingness to assist Washington in the Mideast and Vietnam, because the specter of strategic nuclear warfare should transcend the other categories of international relations. Easing the threat of instant and mutual mass slaughter should not be equated with the resolution of other crises that can and must be settled without resort to intercontinental missiles.

Kissinger's tendency has been to link Europe, the Mideast, and Vietnam without much regard to political or conceptual subtleties. Seeing no viability in modified linkage, he has chosen total linkage over no linkage at all. Rather than opting for what James C. Thomson, Jr., has described as a "ripple" approach, supposing, in other words, that like ripples in a pond, events in the world arena are only as strongly interconnected as their geographic or conceptual distances are brief, Kissinger prefers to see equally firm "links" between all U.S.-Soviet intersections in every area of the globe. As Kissinger once defined linkage in an unusually bold way:

> We are trying to get a [Mideast] settlement in such a way that the moderate regimes are strengthened, and not the radical regimes. We are trying to expel the Soviet military presence, not so much the advisors, but the combat pilots and the combat personnel, before they become so firmly established . . .
> It is, of course, nonsense to say that we did what we did in Cambodia to impress the Russians in the Middle East. It was not as simple as that. But we certainly have to keep in mind that the Russians will judge us by the general purposefulness of our performance everywhere. What they are doing in the Middle East, whatever their intentions, poses the gravest threats in the long term for Western Europe and Japan and, therefore, for us.[13]

There is a disturbing tendency in Nixon-Kissinger linkage theory to postulate an overall decline in U.S.-Soviet tensions before the consecration of specific agreements. The 1972 State of the World Message noted petulantly that "The Soviets sought détente in Europe without a relaxation of hostility toward the United States." [14] Kissinger's early scenario for the progression of U.S.-Soviet accords actually *began* with the negotiation of the most important agreement, the arms treaty, with every other subsidiary issue to serve as a bargaining counter in the initial negotiation only to be settled in its wake. The success of the arms negotiation, in turn, required an improved Soviet attitude toward the West. But did it not seem strange to expect the disappearance of suspicion and animosity to precede concrete policy agreements, instead of the other way around? And was it not equally presumptuous to suppose that the most difficult and complicated negotiation with a suspicious and hostile opponent could be concluded without a prior settlement of subsidiary issues? To be sure, Kissinger would not have wished to prejudice the outcome of the most important negotiation by giving away all of his bargaining counters before the negotiation began. But if the most important settlement demanded that the Soviets first "improve their attitude," on what, other than a sensible liquidation of the subsidiary crises, was the improvement to be based? To take a paramount example, the logic of Nixon-Kissinger linkage would have demanded that the German settlement await the more fundamental agreements on nuclear arms and European security arrangements. It was only through Willy Brandt's initiative that the German issue was settled first, and that the NATO powers were then obliged to confront the problem of Berlin. Yet ironically, it appears likely that the ratification of the treaties on Germany was an important factor in inducing Soviet willingness to host President Nixon in Moscow following the U.S. mining of North Vietnam's harbors.

What fuels Kissinger's policy is a vision of the United States and the Soviet Union reaching a unified settlement which will encompass all trouble spots and crises, a Congress of Vienna solution for each of the areas in which they confront each other throughout the globe. Such a symmetrical situation presupposes that each side will observe the same standards of restraint in international behavior that it would expect of the other. Yet there is a curious one-sidedness in Kissinger's thinking on how to reach a final accord with the Soviet Union, a trait of double vision which enables him to see restraint or legitimate self-defense in a given action if taken by the United States and yet perceive aggression in that same action if taken by the Soviet Union. This has been particularly true of Kissinger's thinking on Vietnam. America's negotiating position on the war became a good deal more moderate in the Nixon administration; rather than demanding the permanent installment of a non-Communist regime in the south, the new President and his advisers sought merely to insure that a "decent interval" would transpire between the U.S. withdrawal and the collapse of the Saigon regime. Seeing their objective as a reasonable one, despite the other side's refusal to comply with it, they did not conceive of their successive escalations — designed, they felt, only to bring about a modest settlement — as threatening and aggressive acts. North Vietnam, however, did so; and though the Soviet Union, which supports Hanoi and the NLF only from a distance, finally chose to withstand a confrontation when the U.S. war effort reached a high pitch last May, there is a real possibility that if a settlement is not forthcoming, Washington might still draw Moscow into the conflict with another escalation of the war. Is Washington violating its own code of conduct by its behavior in Vietnam? Kissinger has described one of the principles of the Nixon Doctrine as follows:

> . . . when a non-nuclear country is threatened by a nuclear country, the United States recognizes special responsibilities. It recognizes these special responsibilities because . . . there is no conceivable way non-nuclear countries can resist, unless there is some implicit backing, at least, from the nuclear countries.[15]

Does Kissinger suppose that North Vietnam, a non-nuclear country, is being threatened by the United States, a nuclear country? Surprisingly enough, he appears to feel sincerely that Washington is not infringing on North Vietnam's sovereignty or its right to survive, that the President is simply attempting to extract a reasonable settlement. Hence, the United States can mine North Vietnam's harbors and still expect that its actions pose no "unacceptable risks" of a confrontation with Hanoi's distant ally, the Soviet Union, that Moscow must simply go ahead with the summit meeting and the signing of the arms agreement. At the same time, if the Soviets had mined Cam Ranh Bay in retaliation, there could have been no doubt that the summit would have been called off by the United States. Kissinger frequently insists that Vietnam is not nearly as dangerous a flashpoint as the Middle East, which he describes in bleak terms:

> We believe that while the war in Vietnam is our most anguishing problem, the situation in the Middle East is our most dangerous problem. The danger of the Middle East situation is that you have two groups of countries with intense local rival-

ries and with an overwhelming concern for their grievances or their security, or both, both backed by major countries, but not fully under the control of the major countries confronting each other. This is the sort of situation that produced World War I.[16]

Yet it does not stretch the imagination to suppose that Kissinger's depiction of the Mideast may one day be appropriate to Vietnam.

These failures of perception raise a number of ominous questions. If Nixon and Kissinger seriously believe that any U.S. action in Vietnam is justified in the pursuit of what they consider a fair settlement, what are the limits of their willingness to escalate further? And if they believe that the Soviet Union will not engage in confrontation with the United States over any development in the war, a belief doubtless encouraged in some quarter by Moscow's non-reaction to the escalation in May 1972, will they be restrained by the fear of risking a reaction from a nuclear country? The conclusion to which we are driven by the logic of events is the possible American use of tactical nuclear weapons in Vietnam. The President and Kissinger have both endorsed in principle the use of such weapons,[17] and although Washington would probably refrain from authorizing a nuclear attack on the North for a variety of reasons, the resort to limited nuclear war is still a possibility, because the most effective use of nuclear weapons would currently be in South Vietnam. These weapons could be used to destroy the North Vietnamese armies if they should mass for ground attacks on South Vietnamese cities. At this stage of their efforts in the war, Nixon and Kissinger might well believe they could effectively justify the use of nuclear weapons in South Vietnam because, presumably, they would be acting with the approval of that country's President and government. And if they believe that the war policy will ultimately yield them increased credibility in other areas of the globe, then their use of tactical nuclear weapons in South Vietnam might even be conceived as a deterrent to Soviet misbehavior in Europe, where Kissinger has frequently speculated that the use of tactical nuclear weapons would first come.

But perhaps the most disturbing aspect of linkage is that it is meant to serve not as a policy of safety or surety but rather as a policy of risk. Nixon and Kissinger cannot satisfactorily demonstrate to themselves or to anyone else that a high degree of "resolution" in one area will have the desired effect in other areas. From a more detached outsider's view, it seems as plausible to say that this approach builds tension by encouraging Soviet toughness as to claim that it relaxes hostility by forcing Moscow to be more reasonable. Kissinger said after the Jordanian crisis of September 1970, "We believe that the action in Cambodia . . . did help establish the credibility of [the President's] action in Jordan. But this cannot be proved. But it is our judgment that it helped." [18] It would be at least as reasonable to suppose that the invasion of Cambodia made the Russians even more intractable in the Mideast, caused them to violate the cease-fire in Egypt, and contributed to the atmosphere of confrontation which produced the turmoil of September 1970 in the first place.

Stated in its present terms, the linkage theory is little more than unreconstructed Cold Warriorism. It is a tired repetition of the idea that the United States must bargain from "situations of strength." For what it means in specific terms is an unwillingness to "give" in any single crisis area until general tensions begin to disappear, and linkage becomes little more than a formula for perpetuating confrontation all over the world. Ironically, the linkage approach has sometimes been prevented from doing serious damage because the Soviets, showing occasional good sense, have shied away from adopting it as well, despite the fact that they have sometimes been provoked outright into doing so. For example, Moscow offered on the day of President Nixon's Inauguration to begin arms limitation discussions immediately. But a few days later, at his first official press conference, Nixon asserted that the opening of the talks would depend on Moscow's assistance on a solution for the Mideast and Vietnam. He said:

> What I want to do is to see to it that we have strategic arms talks in a way and at a time that will promote, if possible, progress on outstanding political issues at the same time — for example, on the problem of the Mideast, and on other outstanding problems in which the United States and the Soviet Union, acting together, can serve the cause of peace.

Bluntly speaking, the White House had assumed that since the United States was strategically superior to the Soviet Union, an arms settlement would be more in Moscow's interest than in Washington's. The President was stating openly that, in exchange for arms talks, the Soviet Union must ease its stand on the Mideast. Soviet leaders subsequently answered through their own press that they would not "pay a price" for SALT; the talks *did* open in November 1969 without abject Soviet cooperation on the Mideast — although, as we will see, the American side had come with other bargaining counters in its position. Similarly, after the U.S. mining of North Vietnam's harbors last May, the Soviets — having clearly suffered sufficient provocation to call off the summit meeting scheduled for later in the month — did not do so, instead taking the approach that an arms control agreement with the United States was a sufficiently high priority in terms of their own national interest that they were willing *momentarily* to ignore the American action.

It would be difficult to demonstrate, however, that these applications of linkage by U.S. officials contributed to improvement or conciliation in Moscow's attitude. Indeed, the opposite seems more likely. It would be surprising, after Nixon's opening statement on arms talks, if the Soviets did not privately toughen their behavior to add to their own bargaining power. And though there are doubtless many in Washington who saw signs of Moscow's weakness in the fact of the summit-cum-mining-of-North-Vietnam, it is more sensible to suppose that the response was tempered by a most unusual occasion: the imminent signing of the first meaningful agreement to limit the use of nuclear arms. After the American action against North Vietnam, the summit came about not as a result of tough, skillful U.S. diplomacy but rather as an unusual exhibition of Soviet prudence. In the face of another U.S. escalation in Vietnam, especially if it involves nuclear weapons, Moscow's reaction is not likely to be so compliant; one can only hope that Washington will not press its luck too far. And hope may be the American public's only recourse in view of the White House's reluctance to heed domestic critics in its pursuit of foreign policy.

Needless to say, this vastly complicated worldwide situation, this delicately woven fabric of action and response, would require an enormous amount of flexibility in U.S. policy. And that, in turn, would demand unlimited freedom of action for American policymakers. If the President appeared hampered in his responses, his credibility would be impugned; the greatest failure of diplomacy was the loss of credibility, and there was a reverence for the honor of a great power that went very deep in Kissinger. American decisions must come quickly, and they must be convincing. In this setting, public opinion, once it gave its assent for a particular individual to become President, must recede into the background. It was the right, even the duty, for the President and his senior policymakers to erect safeguards to insure that popular views could not infringe on their decision-making prerogatives. As Kissinger has said privately:

> We are at a point where we can redefine the American position with respect to the world, where, for whatever reasons, it may be that even the Soviet Union has come to a realization of the limitations of both its physical strength and of the limits of its ideological fervor.
>
> But none of these possibilities can be realized except by an American government that is confident that it knows what it is doing, that can respond to its best judgment, and by an American public that has enough confidence in its leaders so that they are permitted the modicum of ambiguity that is sometimes inseparable from a situation in which you cannot, at the beginning of a process, know completely what all the consequences are.[19]

This attitude does not come new to American policymakers; they have held it before, and they will doubtless adhere to it in the future. What represents a departure is the systematic regularity with which it is embraced, the dogmatic justifications which are summoned — and sometimes even flaunted publicly — to defend it. Witness this remarkable passage from the 1971 State of the World Address: "As their [Asian policymakers'] decisions are made, we will need to adjust our policies to them, not only with flexibility but with virtuosity. And flexibility is not always the strongest virtue of a system dependent upon public participation for its sanction and continuity." [20]

The same rationale is applied with equal force to Congress and the foreign affairs bureaucracy. Members of Congress cannot be expected or allowed to play any meaningful role in policymaking; they lack the training and temperament of the seasoned diplomat, and they remain more responsive to the uninformed concerns of their voters, to the shoddy tug-and-pull of the popular political process, than to the arduous twists and turns of great power relationships. The bureaucracy, too, is an impediment — shallow, unimaginative, composed of mediocre minds which are ever hedging their bets. "With each administrative machine increasingly absorbed in its own internal problems," Kissinger wrote in 1966, "diplomacy loses its flexibility." [21] Again, none of this is particularly innovative; Congress has never really been taken seriously in a foreign policy context, and inside the bureaucratic process, it has always been clear to everyone that the President has the final word. Even the most distinctive bureaucratic phenomenon of the Nixon-Kissinger period, the near collapse of the State Department as an effective foreign policy agency, is really a continuation of something that began well before World War II. But in the past, the White House would take the trouble to go through the motions of procedure; Congress would be implicated, the departments would be consulted before a decision was cast. What talent there was might be assimilated into the process; if there were arguments that could stand the test of their own strength, they sometimes received attention. What comes new with the present administration is the blatancy, the explicit disdain with which each of these constituencies is ignored or scoffed over. And what emerges is a system that is wholly devoid of institutional safeguards or intellectual variety, subject only to the preconceived whims and desires of the President and his closest advisers.

Finally, of course, Kissinger regarded the Presidency as the only force capable of governing American foreign policy. He had long had enormous respect for the strength and power of the office, for the opportunity it offered its holder to forge a stable international structure. If Kissinger felt the importance of domestic consent on a single issue, it was a recognition of the Presidency as the only legitimate agent of America's role in world affairs. And if he had one overwhelming concern about popular dissent in this country, it was that the White House, not one President but the Presidency itself, might be ravaged by waves of public protest, forever to lose its credibility and its capacity to govern. Kissinger's outbursts in response to antiwar demonstrations, particularly those against the invasion of Cambodia, constitute something far more serious and deep-rooted than "a pathetic version of the tyrant's plea," as one observer has glibly put it.[22] They are the haunted dreams of a child of Weimar, the dread specter of revolution and political anarchy, the demise of all recognizable authority:

> When you look around the world you see student riots in Berlin, which have co-determination with the universities. You have student riots in Paris which do not have co-determination. You have student riots in the United States which has a race problem, Vietnam, and slums. And you have student riots in Holland which has no race problem, no slums and no Vietnam.
>
> Therefore, you could conclude that what we are facing in this world is not capricious students — I will not say anything as pat as this — but a resolve against a condition of modern society which is much deeper than any policy issue — a state

of mind which, precisely because it will not grapple with specific issues, and just with a mood, is very hard to deal with — which leads to a rebellion against authority of any kind, not just the authority of this President, but the authority of any President, whether he be president of a university or the President of the United States.

What we have to attempt to do, really, all of us, is to preserve some vestige of authority in this country, if we are ever going to move with confidence and competence toward a better future. What we have to do in Vietnam inevitably has some elements of ambiguity.

We have to convince the American people that we will pull out our troops, but we have to convince Hanoi that the withdrawal is not independent of their actions, so that they have an incentive to negotiate. We have to do many things which cannot be done unless the intermediary leadership in this country . . . will at least support the proposition that there is only one man who can bring peace in Vietnam, and that is the President of the United States. If confidence in him and in all institutions is systematically destroyed, we will turn into a group that has nothing left but a physical test of strength and the only outcome of this is Caesarism.

We suffer from the illusion that by not yielding to this trend we constitute the best protection to the very people who are often out on the streets against us. The very people who shout "Power to the People" are not going to be the people who will take over this country if it turns into a test of strength.

Upper middle-class college kids will not take this country over. Some more primitive and elemental forces will do that if it happens . . .[23]

This conceptualized image of the Presidency must have preoccupied Kissinger when he traveled to the Hotel Pierre in New York City in late November 1968, because the individual who, as President-elect, had summoned him there was not a man for whom Kissinger had a great deal of respect or admiration. He had only met Richard Nixon on one previous occasion, and his secondhand impressions were the ones common to America's intellectual community: Nixon had a politically muddy identity and a second-rate mentality. Worst of all, perhaps, Kissinger then felt that Nixon had no clear-cut view of international affairs, that Nixon, as President, would instead be guided by the transitory whims of popular opinion in the United States. And he feared that, once in office, Nixon would arbitrarily shun the dauntless anti-Communism that he had so frequently expounded in his public utterances.[24] Kissinger's political patron saint of long standing, Nelson Rockefeller, was an interventionist in principle, a far more dedicated Cold Warrior and alliance builder than anyone with earthbound, contingent claims to popularity could ever have been; but with Nixon, how could one tell where the political animal ended and the statesman began? If these were the questions now running through Kissinger's mind, he had scarcely any idea of where his meeting with Nixon would lead.

Nixon had scheduled a brief appointment for Kissinger; the two men talked beyond their allotted time, and Nixon canceled a string of appointments. Kissinger returned several days later, and again Nixon's calendar was reshuffled to add time for their meeting. The preconceptions each man brought to the meetings, and what was said, will never be fully known. One hopes, at least, that some version of these conversations has been preserved for posterity, because they must have been absolutely fascinating. It is clear, though, that the two men emerged from their meetings convinced that they could work together as President and adviser, that Kissinger found in Nixon a man whose instincts and preferences he could accommodate to his own policy outlook.

Politically, what Kissinger found in Nixon was a mature and sophisticated anti-Communist who was willing to adjust his anti-Communism to the domestic and international realities confronting American policy. Nixon's tactical flexibility had long been well developed; one finds in his 1967 *Foreign Affairs* article several admissions — such as the "reality" of People's China and the need to refine America's role as "world policeman" — that do not jibe well with a hard 1950s-style anti-Red line.[25] In his anti-Communism, of course, Nixon was at serious philosophical odds with Kissinger, whose vision of an ideal world order excludes all supranational ideologies, including that of anti-Communism. But while the intellectual differences were sharp, Kissinger felt that the operational styles could be made to converge, that there need be no differences in practice. And Kissinger was determined to submerge the differences between his thinking and Nixon's, to exert his own influence on the shape of American policy. As he had written of Metternich's collaboration with Napoleon: "To co-operate without losing one's soul, to assist without sacrificing one's identity, to work for deliverance in the guise of bondage and under enforced silence, what harder test of moral toughness exists?" [26]

Kissinger also perceived in Nixon something to which he attached great importance, yet something he had never expected to find: that, as a President, Nixon would be an enormously effective bulwark against right-wing forces in this country. His anti-Communist credentials could hardly have been challenged; and yet Kissinger inferred that, privately, Nixon was determined not to be undermined by his electoral constituency in his approach to foreign policy. Kissinger felt that Nixon as President could bring about important modifications in American policy — such as a speedy

withdrawal from Vietnam and rapprochement with China —
without inciting the reaction that a "liberal" in the White
House might have stirred from the ideologists of the right.
"Nixon will save us from the hard-hats," Kissinger would
frequently say to his often incredulous White House assistants
in discussing Nixon's real policy dispositions. And Kissinger's
infatuation with this particular Nixon quality, an infatuation
that could only have characterized an individual who was
obsessively concerned with the threat from the right, was
largely the reason Kissinger was often able, despite his
antipathy to rhetorical excess, to feel so at ease with Nixon's
relative verbal harshness. Once the new administration was
in office, Nixon's public bombast and Kissinger's private
eloquence did not so much spring from contrasting views as
much as they were two sides of the same coin.

Kissinger's major qualm about Nixon, it appears, was the
President-elect's lack of individual assertiveness. According
to a number of colleagues who spoke with Kissinger at
Nixon's New York headquarters, the Hotel Pierre, in the days
following his appointment, Kissinger remarked over and over
again how timid and unstatesmanlike he found Nixon's
demeanor, how weak and undistinguished Nixon's personal
presence was. In his conversations with Nixon, Kissinger
would recount, he found it hard to believe that he was sitting
in the same room with the next Chief Executive of the United
States; there was a perpetual void, no evidence of any commanding presence. Nixon faltered badly in conversation;
Kissinger had to jump in and rescue the dialogue from those
awkward and unpleasant moments of silence. Kissinger
remarked to colleagues on that early occasion that his principal function as Nixon's adviser would be to underwrite the
President's personality and sense of purpose, to impart as-

surance and confidence to Nixon in the enterprise of state-craft. And from the beginning of the administration, there would develop a personal and intellectual rapport between the two men that was deep and profound.

Their relationship deepened even further with a common appreciation of the fact that they would both have a place in history. Indeed, the history-in-the-making rhetoric of this administration's foreign policy has been one of its most striking characteristics. And the tendency to speak and think in terms of ultimate historical judgments is particularly typical of Kissinger who, curiously, appears even more ambitious than is Nixon to make an impact on the historical process. To be sure, once men become Presidents, they immediately become conscious of the fact that they will be read, studied, and analyzed for decades to come. And yet the entire Nixon approach — in public and in private — is so lacking in grandiloquence and in conceptual style that one is impelled to assume that the source of the White House's "history"-laden rhetoric lies elsewhere. Kissinger, on the other hand, is an individual who, even before his arrival in government, was obsessed with making his mark on history. The ruminations about "writing a page in history" or "turning a page in history" in Kissinger's private usages are too persistent to be merely superficial or coincidental. In 1967, when Kissinger, serving as an authorized intermediary between the United States and North Vietnam, felt he had reached a negotiating breakthrough, he exclaimed to startled colleagues, "Look, we have written a page in history." In late 1971, describing his meeting in Peking with Chou En-lai, Kissinger said that the U.S.-China rapprochement was "so great, so historic, that Vietnam will be only a footnote when it is written in history." And so on. "This administration came into office at what really, I am sure, historians will regard as a dividing line in American foreign policy," [27] Kissinger habitually tells newsmen and other visitors at the White House. The dividing line, of course, is between the hysterical, excessive, blindly interventionist period ushered in by the Truman Doctrine, and the subtle, measured, even-handed policy over which Nixon and Kissinger now claim to be presiding. Perhaps most dramatically, even before the arrival of the Presidential party in the Soviet Union for the 1972 summit meeting, Kissinger told reporters that they were on a "threshold of history" — the first nuclear limitations pact. It would not be at all surprising if, besides seeing Nixon administration foreign policy as a historical turning point, and besides conceiving of himself as a notable historical figure — which, no doubt, he does — Kissinger imagines, in his moments of greatest personal self-esteem, that he is one of Hegel's great men, one of those rare individuals, those carriers of mankind's historical spirit, about whom Kissinger's favorite philosopher once speculated so long ago.

How great a historical figure Kissinger is must, of course, be left to the historians of the future to determine. Yet it is probable that Kissinger's estimation of historical judgments is even now having an impact on the exercise of American policy. Nixon, it is clear, has great respect for Kissinger's talent as an intellectual, and likely defers to him on judgments about historical consequences. One can easily imagine Kissinger, armed with his guileful, almost magical charm, shaping Nixon's opinions on foreign policy by expressing the sentiment, "Think of your place in history." And in this connection, one thinks especially about Vietnam, about the brutal and unpopular war that is now being fought largely to serve a number of intellectual principles — credibility and place-in-history being two — and one is tempted to suppose that if Nixon had been advised by someone who favored either leaving Indochina to the Indochinese or even cutting military losses and undertaking a politically pragmatic withdrawal, the outcome would today be vastly different than it is with Nixon constantly being told that if he is defeated, it will not look good for him in history, that his image will be downgraded in the eyes of future men and societies. For above all else, a policy that speaks not to concrete realities or to contemporary concerns, but merely to what its formulators see as the vindication of history, is really a policy that removes itself from all conceivable criticism. It is characterized by a perspective which harshly excludes those human beings who are not living with the historians of the future in mind, a perspective that completely disregards whatever torment and anguish happens to be generated in the here and now. After all, how can the petty whims and desires of popular opinion play any role in so grand a vision?

> Our dramatic departures of the past year — the fruits of our planning and policies over three years — reflect the historical conditions we see today and the historic possibilities we see for tomorrow. They were momentous steps, accelerating the very process of change which they addressed. The world — and we ourselves — are still in the process of adjusting to the developments we have set in train. But we know where we are going. We are moving with history and moving history ourselves.[28]

The President immediately demonstrated himself to be a man intensely, almost exclusively, interested in foreign policy. He had stated many times before, and would repeat since, his belief that the United States could administer itself domestically without a Chief Executive, that the Presidency was necessary only for decisions on America's role in international affairs. Most of his prior government experience had been in the foreign policy field, and before expressing interest in the Presidency this time around, he appeared to many of his associates to be grooming himself as the next Republican Secretary of State. As President, Nixon would be his own Secretary, his own adviser, his own deskman. Kissinger was not speaking lightly when he said of the "options" system, ". . . it is the President who decides and he, therefore, has to feel comfortable with the way his choices are presented to him or indeed whether he wants any choices." [29]

The result is that the presentation of options reflects the President's desires rather than shapes them. Options cover a broad range of tactical possibilities, but do not challenge the more important strategic decisions that the President and his advisers have already made in private. An option for unilateral American military withdrawal is stricken from a paper on Vietnam; the deferral of a decision on an antiballistic missile system does not get written as an option because the President has decided to make a deployment decision *now*. And the revival of President Truman's national security council system, which fell into impotence with the emergence of powers like Acheson and Dulles, serves the purpose in this administration of undercutting the Secretary of State. No longer is it necessary for the Secretary to confer with the President, because the best ideas in his department travel directly via the assistant secretaries through a network which Kissinger administers. The Secretary chosen by Nixon, though a talented and friendly administrator, is completely unschooled in foreign affairs, and falters badly when he confronts Kissinger and the President on serious policy issues. His failure, in turn, demoralizes the assistant secretaries, the operatives in the system, by making them more reluctant to challenge the White House view. It would not be an exaggeration to say that William Rogers has presided over a vast conglomerate of career analysts and foreign service officers who play little if any role in the creation of foreign policy.

In many ways, the Department of Defense is similarly an entity unto itself. "Under the leadership of Secretary Laird," in Kissinger's words, "the Pentagon has not attempted to assert a prerogative in wide areas of foreign policy. It has confined itself more to strictly military considerations than has been the case at least in the two previous administrations." [30] That alone, of course, gives it weighty influence, but subject to the limitation that military and economic matters are predetermined by prior White House decisions on political strategy. Within the "options" framework, Kissinger has employed a clever method of dealing with bureaucratic arguments that is particularly effective vis-à-vis the Joint Chiefs. Their preferences are taken not as fixed recommendations, but rather as "factors to be taken into account." In this manner, the President can dismiss their standard doctrinaire objections on such issues as the Seabeds Treaty and force reductions without unequivocal repudiation; if the military want something, they are told indirectly that they must seriously lobby for it. In the Kennedy White House, this approach was used on occasion with some success; but in the judgment of several senior policy administrators, it was employed so often in the first year of the Nixon administration that it soon lost its effectiveness. It is possible, in fact, that its overuse contributed to a military "backlash" which evidenced itself during the Cambodian crisis of spring 1970.

There is little doubt that the President is the chief opera-
tive in the National Security Council setup. It was he who
decided that the Eisenhower-style bureaucratic "compromise" recommendation was badly outdated, that the choices
should not be presented in a take-it-or-leave-it way. But if
Nixon has drawn the conceptual design, Kissinger has been
the architect. He sees Nixon several times a day, sometimes
for lengthy discussions, and has more contact with the
President, as one White House observer put it, "than all the
members of the Cabinet put together." Kissinger is the only
post-1968 Nixon associate to have emerged as a member of
the Presidential inner circle. If his relationship with the
President is correct and polite, it is also warm; there is an
intellectual attachment between the two men that transcends
their official connection. And if they began their association
with differences of outlook, they have by now fused much of
their thinking into a unified whole, Kissinger often deferring
to the President's thinking but Nixon also adjusting his views
to fit Kissinger's. It would not be too much to say that Kissinger has relinquished much of his intellectual identity
and merged it with Nixon's; even in his private policy recommendations to Nixon, his thinking will never fail to intersect
with what he knows are the President's perceptions. But Kissinger would want it no other way; he does differ with Nixon
on many issues but would not want to diminish Nixon's
strength and authority, even to benefit his own, because he
has a deep and abiding respect for the Presidency of the
United States. And a President openly subverted by his own
adviser would set as dangerous an example as any popular
infringement on White House authority. That Kissinger
until 1971 received no meaningful public attention is no

coincidence; even his background briefings for the press, briefings which are remarkably impressive for their intellectual range and scope, have remained off the record. And his virtual anonymity reflected Kissinger's view that a public identity would diminish the President's prestige as well as make his own job more difficult.

Whatever circumspection Kissinger exercises in his relationship with Nixon does not apply to his treatment of his own National Security Council staff. Besides his deputy, Brig. Gen. Alexander Haig, there is no one on the staff who has any regular access to the President besides Kissinger himself; very few underlings even see Kissinger with any regularity. Kissinger's conversations with the President, the conversations that are most crucial to any foreign policy decision, are strictly confidential, and most of Kissinger's staff assistants have only a very indirect idea of what Kissinger or Nixon is thinking. By any standard, Kissinger is a difficult taskmaster, and he requires that his assistants work long and arduous hours without extending them the recognition they may deserve for their efforts. The enormous turnover on Kissinger's staff is hard testimony to the fact that few foreign policy analysts of any appreciable talent will long stand such treatment. And it reinforces the feeling that Kissinger's approach to the larger bureaucracy is even more peremptory and terse.

Outside the White House, Kissinger is regarded as the President's only authoritative spokesman on foreign affairs. He conducts all the major press briefings; he is sought by ambassadors and foreign governments, all of whom by now have learned that State Department emissaries do not usually reflect the official view. And Kissinger's refusal to testify on the record is a major source of irritation to Congressional

committeemen who are not satisfied by the appearances of
Secretaries Rogers and Laird. The most vehement expression of this anger came in March 1971 when Stuart Sy-
mington, a member of the Senate Foreign Relations Committee, said in a speech on the Senate floor that Kissinger
was "Secretary of State in everything but title," that Rogers'
appearance before the committee had become "a rather
empty exercise." Kissinger's pre-eminence, combined with
his refusal to appear in open session, has cut off Congress
and the public from any meaningful exposure to Washington's foreign policy process.

For his own part, Kissinger has repeatedly disavowed the
assertion that he is the President's chief policy formulator.
Even before he took office, in fact, Kissinger said on several
occasions that he did not aspire to be another Rostow, that
he would never become obsessed with the details of any
specific policy, and that he would not play the role of a White
House Rasputin, withholding from the President and the
National Security Council all of the foreign policy positions
which he himself disliked. It appears that Kissinger sincerely
hoped during this early period to serve as a rather detached,
theoretical critic from within — to be able, in other words,
to play out the policy intellectual's fondest dream. But once
in power, he found that the only way to be effective was to
immerse himself in concrete policy issues, and that is precisely what Kissinger set out to do.

Since 1969, Kissinger has involved himself most deeply in
two subjects: the war in Vietnam, which he identified at
the outset as the major obstacle facing American policy, and
the arms limitation talks, which until the signing of the May
1972 treaty continued to be the central feature of Washington's relations with the Soviet Union. His mastery of

these two issues has given him virtually complete control of Washington's foreign policy process. Great publicity has been devoted to the fact that the Department of State retains its traditional prerogative on Washington's Mideast policy, a prerogative which Kissinger has been reluctant to challenge directly. But even there, when events reach a boiling point, Kissinger has emerged to set the tone, if not the content, of U.S. policy — as when he proclaimed in June 1970 that the purpose of Washington's activity in the Mideast was to "expel" the Soviet military presence. And the "linkage" approach has further consolidated Kissinger's role; by retaining his grasp of the two pivotal issues — Vietnam and SALT — he has been able to control the policy in its entirety because he can insure that a Soviet action on any front will be answered in one of the central arenas.

Yet in spite of his clear predominance, it would be a serious mistake to see Kissinger as a man who is able to work miracles in the exercise of foreign policy. His very centrality has caused a great many of his own efforts to backfire on him. His immersion in the details of Vietnam and the arms talks has often rendered him incapable of dealing competently with sudden crises that arise in areas about which he knows little — such as Cambodia in April 1970 and East Pakistan in late 1971. Yet the handling of crises is especially important in Nixon-Kissinger policy because that policy is a virtual prescription for continuing crisis and confrontation. To function autonomously in his position, Kissinger has had to disregard the bulk of advice and information his office receives from the vast bureaucratic network below it. Yet the successful resolution of foreign policy issues, especially those on which the White House can claim little if any expertise, ultimately depends on the skillful, imaginative use of raw bureaucratic input. To maintain his consistently superior standing, Kissinger must regularly alienate each of the foreign policy agencies, causing them either to lapse into disinterest or inactivity or to gather such strength and momentum for specific occasions that Kissinger's own position is considerably harmed as a result. And, of course, he is always limited by what Nixon is thinking. In fact, there are few better illustrations of Kissinger's strengths and weaknesses in office than his handling of the arms control issue.

Aside from Vietnam, the most important and enduring White House foreign policy decisions have been in the area of the arms race. They have been characterized by virtually complete agreement between the President and his chief adviser, although as on Vietnam, the areas of agreement were not immediately visible. Ever since the early sixties, Kissinger has believed that it would be impractical and dangerous for the United States to strive for unambiguous nuclear superiority vis-à-vis the Soviet Union, fearing that any such situation would inevitably tempt one side to strike first. Before taking office, Nixon did not seem to share this view. Two weeks before his election, he made a speech which eerily recalled Senator John F. Kennedy's "missile gap" attacks on him eight years before; in the speech, Nixon ridiculed "the peculiar, unprecedented doctrine called parity" and pledged that, if elected, he would restore "clear-cut" American military superiority over the Soviet Union. Then, at his first press conference, he answered a question on America's strategic posture by saying, "I think 'sufficiency' is a better term, actually, than either parity or superiority." An ambiguous term, one which drifted between parity and superiority, and rescued his campaign pledge, it nonetheless reflected his actual view that one should never be in a posi-

tion to strike first — a conviction which the President re-
iterated quite strongly in his announcement of the Safeguard
ABM decision that March.

Nixon's decision not to be strategically provocative formed
the essential backdrop for the ABM debate which proceeded
inside the administration during its first few weeks in office.
But other factors prodded the White House in the direction
of rapid deployment. In September 1967, following the Soviet decision to begin constructing a Moscow-area ABM,
Secretary of Defense McNamara, under great pressure from
President Johnson and the Joint Chiefs, announced that
Washington would build a "thin" area defense system to
protect the United States against a possible Chinese missile
attack. It is unclear that U.S. leaders felt acutely threatened
by the ABM being built by the Soviets, who maintained
during this period that they saw nothing destabilizing about
population-defense ABM. In fact, the American decision
appears primarily to have been a domestic political, not a
strategic move; most of the civilian strategists denounced
it as ludicrous. Still others, including Kissinger, saw it as
necessary to convey Washington's intentions to the Soviets,
with whom a verbal dialogue on ABM was still impossible.
McNamara and others hoped that actual deployment would
be made unnecessary by an early agreement in arms limitations talks with Moscow, which were tentatively scheduled
to begin in late 1968. But their hope for talks was dashed
by the Soviet invasion of Czechoslovakia, and a long-standing decision to deploy a "thin" ABM — known as Sentinel
— was the situation inherited by the new President in January 1969.

While Kissinger apparently saw nothing wrong in continuing with the McNamara program,[31] Nixon wanted it changed

for several reasons. He seems to have been concerned fore-most with producing his own missile defense program, one that would be clearly distinguishable from that of the for-mer administration. He had campaigned on a platform of strategic superiority; now, he was under pressure from the military and from many in Congress to act decisively. And from the standpoint of popular opinion, he was interested in "moving the missiles out of the back yard," in eradicating the considerable public pressure that had greeted the Army's plans for ABM sites in the environs of several major Ameri-can cities. Here, in all probability, was the genesis of the switch from a "thin" area to a "hard-point," or missile, de-fense ABM.

These, then, were the major considerations in the ABM review that took place in February and early March. The President wanted to move quickly toward deployment; he and Kissinger both favored some form of ABM. The review incorporated these assumptions; while pretending to con-sider all feasible options, the White House effectively ruled out the possibilities of a no-ABM or a delayed decision. The final options paper prepared at the Department of De-fense ostensibly contained the full range of options: a "thick" population defense ABM, the Sentinel system, a Minuteman defense, or no ABM at all.[32] But in fact, one alternative had been seriously restricted before the National Security Council ever considered it. The no-ABM option had origi-nally been a proposal for no ABM *now*, but Kissinger or-dered it rewritten to exclude the possibility of putting off a decision. In this devious fashion, ex-officials have disclosed to this writer, the case against ABM had been rendered impo-tent. Clearly, it would have been much easier to argue for a delay in deployment than for no ABM at any time. In its final version, in fact, the no-ABM option was a pathetic joke; how could it conceivably be demonstrated that no American missile defense would ever be necessary? As one disgruntled Defense Department official later said of the working of the "options" system as evidenced by the ABM decision, "That is just enough to discourage the Pope in the pursuit of the faith."

All of this was transpiring without apparent relationship to U.S. policy in the upcoming arms limitations talks with the Soviet Union. Yet as 1969 wore on, the connection between ABM and SALT deepened in Kissinger's mind. If the talks had been set up for a single purpose, it was to prevent the emergence of a strategic disparity which, in turn, could lead to nuclear war. And if there was one development in the arms race which seriously threatened to upset the strategic balance, it was ABM. By early 1969, even the Soviets had been made to accept this view. As Kissinger would later put it, "It has become obvious during the course of the SALT negotiations that the one American development that the Soviets seem to be interested to stop, above all, was [sic] the ABM development. That is the area in which they have shown the greatest interest and the greatest flexibility." [33] And the danger of ABM was clear. In the current strategic context, the means of destruction are so plentiful that no potential attacker can possibly think he will escape irreparable damage if he himself should launch a first strike. But an expanded and technologically sophisticated ABM might have made such thoughts possible. [34] If ABMs on both sides were allowed to proliferate, it may one day have happened that, in a moment of crisis, an American or Soviet leader might have felt confident that he could escape significant damage if he struck first; his initial salvo would destroy most of the opponent's offensive force on the ground (or in the sea), and the remaining offensive missiles, when launched in retaliation, would be taken out by his fully developed ABM. It is no exaggeration to state that the arms limitations talks were set up to prevent such flights of imagination, and that, in effectively abolishing ABM as a factor in the arms race, they achieved a crucial purpose.

In fact, the official American attitude throughout the SALT talks was that the central issue would be a resolution of the ABM problem. And according to National Security Council staff members who worked on Washington's negotiating position, Kissinger was almost singlehandedly responsible for its emergence, which came about largely through the rigorous questionnaires which Kissinger has so often used to embarrass or tie up the bureaucratic departments on other policy issues. In this case, the SALT studies were successful in discrediting the doctrinaire, take-it-or-leave-it approach of the Pentagon and in accentuating the role of the more dovish Arms Control and Disarmament Agency. One Kissinger staff assistant said recently of the SALT position, "If it had been left to high-level chit chat, the Department of Defense would have run it. It is largely to Kissinger's credit that a reasonable position was arrived at."

But if the position was sensible in conception — and it is hard to fault a policy which grasps the unique danger of ABM — it often faltered badly in its execution; and its failure is one for which Kissinger was also partly responsible. For here again we encounter the dastardly notion of linkage, without which no Kissinger policy enactment would be complete. It was still the American position that the Soviets, because their strategic posture was slightly inferior, had a greater interest in an ABM settlement and in an overall

SALT agreement than did the United States. And since Moscow refused to make concessions elsewhere as an entrance price into SALT, it was Kissinger's view that they must instead pay the price in terms of the SALT agreement itself. More particularly, the formal U.S. position at the talks was that there could not be an ABM agreement until the Soviets agreed to place a limit on the number of their giant SS-9 missiles, which were allegedly being built for the ultimate purpose of a Soviet first strike against Minuteman.[35] Kissinger stated this position quite succinctly: "If they are worried about our ABM, it is very easy for them to stop it. All they have to do is agree to limit the building of the SS-9s." [36]

It was this conflict which characterized the lengthy and frequent impasses at the arms talks. Moscow pressed for an agreement on defensive weapons only, but Washington insisted that any agreement must link offensive and defensive capabilities. It is difficult to criticize Kissinger's desire for a mutual limitation on offensive weapons. But it is just as reasonable to question the logic of making one limitation a condition of the other. Admittedly, if Washington had acceded to an ABM-only negotiation, Moscow might well have broken off the talks after obtaining an ABM treaty; but that action would not have placed the United States in mortal danger. With its superior submarine force and its highly developed MIRV capability, the United States, far from being at the brink of imminent annihilation, would still have been strategically superior to the Soviet Union. And just as Moscow's strategists became convinced of ABM's destabilizing potentialities, they could have been shown the wisdom of a separate offensive weapons agreement. A conciliatory attitude by Washington on an early ABM treaty, far from selling out to the Red Menace, might have speeded the SALT talks, halted the vicious spiral which has characterized the arms race since the end of World War II, and won concessions from the Soviets in return.

In the treaty of May 1972, the issue was temporarily resolved in America's favor. But unfortunately, the problem with Kissinger's approach goes deeper than the linkage approach at the SALT talks. Kissinger rejects the notion that the problems of arms control and nuclear war transcend other aspects of international relations; to put it another way, he still does not see a qualitative difference between the present era, in which worldwide destruction can come in a single stroke, and that time in the now distant past when a speedy resort to war was merely an extension of balance-of-power diplomacy. And for that reason, Kissinger continuously insisted on a linkage between a SALT agreement and good Soviet behavior in other areas of the globe; in fact, the formal U.S. position at the talks alternately eased or hardened according to Washington's changing perception of Moscow's activity elsewhere. For obvious reasons, this approach was not a safe or prudent one. To begin with, it placed too much of a premium on the stability of Moscow's decision-making structure, a stability about which one can never be sure. And, of course, it placed the SALT talks at the mercy of any sudden crisis in any area of the world, whether that crisis was provoked by Washington or by Moscow. And if Kissinger makes frequent complaints about the Soviet Union's global intransigence, it is still likely that the arms pact was placed in considerable danger by America's spring 1972 escalation of the Vietnam war.

The dangers of the present arms policy are unusually disturbing. And they are underlined by an enormous failure to forejudge the catastrophic possibilities of strategic nuclear war. In four years, Kissinger's office has not energized the bureaucracy to update the Joint Chiefs' strategic war plan (Single Integrated Operational Plan, or SIOP), a plan that has remained essentially unchanged since 1962.[37] And what Kissinger's failure means is that, in the event of any willful Soviet attack, of any size, on the United States, the entire American arsenal will be launched at targets inside the Soviet Union. Khrushchev's 1959 dictum on Berlin, "Our rockets will fly automatically," is strangely appropriate to the American strategic war plan for 1972. It appears that Kissinger's reluctance to challenge the Joint Chiefs on SIOP has sprung not from principle, but rather from expediency; in view of SALT, possible European force reductions and an overall decline in America's worldwide military presence, Kissinger does not want to push the Pentagon one step too far. "Under those circumstances, you can't tell the military that their war plan is corny," one Kissinger staff assistant said recently. "You have to make a judgment of just how much they have to swallow without rebelling." Yet in view of the increased emphasis which Nixon-Kissinger doctrine places on the threat to wage nuclear war, Kissinger's unwillingness to challenge the most extreme and dangerous aspects of America's military planning leads one to the notion that his policy, which was designed to avoid tragedy, has instead had the effect of tempting and inviting it.

Part II

VIETNAM

I F THERE IS any single aspect of U.S. foreign policy that has dominated Henry Kissinger's attention for the past half-dozen years, it has been America's war in Vietnam. Yet his attention has focused on the U.S. effort not as an enterprise to be pursued, but as a debacle to be ended as swiftly as possible. He has sought not to devise a United States victory, but rather to spring America from a trap.

Through all these years, Kissinger has felt that a solution in Vietnam has been the outstanding priority of American foreign policy. Yet his interest in the war has not sprung from any belief that a war policy could be viable or legitimate, or that Vietnam must be viewed as a test of American strength; the contrary notion has always been uppermost in his mind. For he has long felt that Vietnam was an unworthy and inappropriate display of American power and diplomacy, that it would obstruct America's ability to act responsibly elsewhere in the global arena. And if he has remained faithful to a single goal in his contributions to U.S. policy on Vietnam, it is that Vietnam should not be allowed to preoccupy America's pursuit of its worldwide objectives.

Kissinger was among those who supported the American commitment in 1961, but he soon came to fear that the United States would extend itself far beyond that initial display of resolution and become mired in a struggle that was

largely irrelevant to its central concerns. It was here that
his critical instinct about Kennedy-era foreign policy was
most prescient; America was acting without regard to the
lessons of history (in this case, the French experience), it
sought fruitlessly to apply its political and cultural institutions in areas where they were unwelcome and completely
inappropriate, and it pursued its objectives with an optimism
that was at once unquestioned and unjustified. As he said
in June 1968, "I never understood, even before I knew anything about Vietnam, why we thought we could achieve
with sixteen thousand men what the French could not do
with two hundred thousand men." [1] At its comparatively
small, pre-1965 level, the Vietnam war was not one for which
Kissinger had any particular liking; with the huge escalations
in U.S. ground strength and air power, the war became for
Kissinger an exercise in absurdity.

His real experience in Vietnam came only at the end of
1965, when he traveled to Vietnam as a consultant to Ambassador Henry Cabot Lodge. Determined not to be taken
in by the skilled military briefers and other purveyors of the
official U.S. line, Kissinger did not limit his associations to
the "Cercle Sportif" and Embassy Saigon; he found a French-
Vietnamese translator and traveled far into the field. He
made extensive contacts with political dissidents, especially
the then powerful Buddhists; at considerable risk to his own
safety, he visited many areas in the always insecure countryside, talking to buck privates and village dwellers as well
as those in power and command. In the setting of Washington's official liturgy on Vietnam, his observations were
striking: middle-level American officials and their South
Vietnamese counterparts were untalented and corrupt, the

pacification program was unable to address the central political issues, the Americans' military strength was largely
ineffective, and the reporting to Washington was hopelessly
distorted. On returning from his frequent trips to Vietnam,
he gave briefings at the highest government levels, including President Johnson and Secretary of Defense McNamara.
On one occasion, in the spring of 1966, his reporting con-
trasted so embarrassingly with the official military line that
General Westmoreland, then the American field commander,
requisitioned a list of everyone Kissinger had interviewed in
Vietnam and a complete account of what everyone had told
him. That spring, when the Vietnamese Buddhist movement
was at its peak, he asked a number of academic specialists
on Indochina — in a hopeful tone — about the possibility of
the Buddhists sweeping the Saigon regime out of power and,
then, requesting that the United States withdraw. His query
was not unlike the silent wishful thinking of those dissenters
inside the government who hoped and prayed that they
would awake one morning to find the Saigon regime overturned, a non-Communist government unfriendly to the
United States established in its place, and then, the American commitment peacefully ended.[2]

But short of such a deus ex machina, how could America's
involvement in the war be responsibly terminated? For
Kissinger, as for countless others, this question has always
towered over every consideration about Vietnam. And for
as long as he has been conscious of the war, Kissinger's answer has always been the same: the United States must depart in such a way that it does not *appear* to have abandoned
the Saigon regime. For the sake of its global commitment,
and for the morale of its other allies, America must demon-

strate a willingness to "go to the mat," in John McNaughton's colloquial phrase, in defense of its declared South Vietnamese ally.

For if the United States appeared to fail in South Vietnam, Kissinger felt, the domestic and international consequences would be severe. The enemies of American allies would feel carte blanche to resort to arms; and even where they did not, some allies — notably in Western Europe and Japan — might feel pressured into some form of voluntary submission. Domestically, Kissinger feared a right-wing backlash, a resurgence of McCarthyism, which would endanger creative and intelligent foreign policy thinking. And if a precipitate withdrawal were forced on the White House by Congress or by popular pressure, the Presidency would be irreparably damaged as an effective agent of American policy. As it would turn out, these fears were greatly misguided; but they were as real a factor in Kissinger's policy thinking as was his assessment of the power balance in Vietnam itself.

At the same time, Kissinger's position did not stipulate the *permanent* survival of the Saigon regime. Unlike President Johnson and his most influential advisers, all of whom were unmistakably committed to the indefinite perpetuation of a non-Communist government in South Vietnam, Kissinger thought merely in terms of an "interval" between an American withdrawal and what he long regarded as the likely collapse of the government in the South. And in the context of Johnson's Vietnam policy, Kissinger's approach was a remarkably moderate one. As one of the most anguished students of America's Vietnam policy, Daniel Ellsberg, would later remember, "Kissinger had an attitude in 1968 that made him look far more liberal than anyone in government. Literally no public figure had come out for unilateral military withdrawal. Kissinger was saying fairly early that what you wanted was a façade or delay before the Communists took over." [3]

Underlying Kissinger's thinking on Vietnam was his lack of faith in the durability of the Saigon regime. Aside from what he knew of the South Vietnamese government in 1965, his skepticism was informed by the historical failure, typified by the French, to create a viable alternative in the South to the party of Ho Chi Minh — a skepticism which, by and large, characterized even those who had argued years earlier that a more politically astute French approach might have secured an anti-Communist regime in Saigon. Yet why did Kissinger not advocate outright American abandonment of its South Vietnamese ally? Because he felt that, whatever the value of change, the United States could not precipitously alter its stated goals in the world arena. As he expressed it,

> Others judge us — and set their own course — by the steadiness of our performance as well as the merit of our ideas. Abrupt shifts in our policies — no matter how sound in concept —are unsettling, particularly for those who may have committed themselves to past practices at United States urging. For their own political future is involved. If we acquired a reputation for unsteadiness, we would isolate ourselves . . .[4]

In fact, the standards Kissinger applied to American behavior in Vietnam were identical to those which he advocated in U.S. policy toward Europe. And his approach was particularly similar to his own recommendations on the Berlin crisis several years before. The United States must be willing, for the sake of international stability and the collec-

tive morale of her allies, to endorse in theory a goal which
it would not seek to observe in practice (unification of Germany or a non-Communist South Vietnam); its approach
must be ambiguous enough so that its ally interprets American policy as an expression of support, while its enemy sees
restraint and moderation in America's behavior; Washington
would be able, under desirable circumstances, to convey
restraint to the enemy by means of private, bilateral negotiation; and yet, should negotiation fail, America must be
prepared to back up its ally by military action (Kissinger's
proposal to tear down the Wall or renew bombing and
blockade of North Vietnam), action which would ironically
have been undertaken in pursuit of a goal which Washington
understood was at best elusive and, more likely, unattainable. This absurdity, this Quixotic seeking after completely
chimerical objectives, was an outgrowth of the quest for
credibility; and Kissinger understood that the likelihood of
Washington's being drawn into military action over such
falsified issues was indeed considerable. Yet Kissinger's phi-
losophy of confrontation was underlain by his Metternich-
like faith in the efficacy of great power diplomacy; it was
the same faith that would unleash considerable international
violence should negotiations fail.

For many years, Kissinger was uncannily optimistic that
a mutually acceptable settlement could be negotiated in the
Vietnam war. He was an unusually acute and well-informed
critic of President Johnson's Vietnam diplomacy — indeed,
he had a firsthand opportunity to test it. But he thought
that, under ideal circumstances — and, most certainly, that
if *he* ever had a free hand to negotiate on Washington's behalf with the North Vietnamese and the NLF — a settlement
would rapidly ensue. His reason for thinking so, of course,

was that, from his point of view, America and the Vietnamese Communists had a common interest in ending the war. And whatever reservations he might have had about Hanoi's negotiating ability were eradicated by his knowledge that, in the international arena, the North Vietnamese had always behaved in a shrewdly tactical, entirely nonpolemical manner — as evidenced by their negotiations with France in 1946 and with the Western powers at Geneva in 1954. Further, the cause of the Vietnamese liberation movement — national unification — is one to which Kissinger, reared in the European tradition of nationalism, can only have accepted as legitimate. The struggle against the Saigon regime was not an instance of aggression across a recognized international boundary, and Kissinger's position was a tacit recognition of that fact. So free of ideology and political dogma was the Vietnamese revolution that even its leading champion, Ho Chi Minh, made his mark not as a theoretician but as an activist. The great Vietnam scholar, Bernard Fall, once observed that Ho's leftist journal in the Paris of the 1920s

reflected Ho's own inimitable, direct style, hammering away at concrete problems, never bothering with doctrine. As one peruses Ho's writings forty years later, one can only be amazed at how *little* they offer: most of them are polemic tirades about some obscure French official in some remote province who beat up his houseboy, raped the kitchenmaid's daughter, and closed the village school. It would be difficult to pin down the "essential Ho" in a small booklet of his quotations, as was done by the Chinese Cultural Revolution in that best-seller of the millennium, *Quotations from Chairman Mao Tse-Tung;* for Ho, throughout his whole life, did not seek to convert the world to anything — except to accepting the existence of an independent Viet-Nam, united from North to South.[5]

Here, then, was a situation that, in Kissinger's mind, was ideally suited to the traditional remedy of nation-state negotiation, an exchange during which each side would make compromises to insure a fair and balanced outcome. Indeed, one must see along with Kissinger's future willingness to continue the war a deep and unshakable faith, at each step of the way, that serious negotiations would soon begin. This is not to say that the other side ultimately behaved in an intransigent manner; it is only to emphasize the depth of Kissinger's misunderstanding of his opponent's situation, and the stubbornness of Kissinger's refusal to accept the fact that the realities of the Southeast Asian war did not lend themselves to the panacea of great-power settlement.

The perpetuation of the Vietnam war into the 1960s had been cruel testimony to the shortcomings of negotiation. On two prior occasions, the leaders of North Vietnam had agreed to forgo complete independence in return for promises of eventual reunification and national sovereignty. But on each occasion, the West had gone back on its word — in 1946, with the proclamation of an autonomous Cochin China, and in 1956, with the cancellation of nationwide elections. It would have been difficult to induce Hanoi again to give up its aims and bide its time — especially since Kissinger wished to preserve the *appearance* of American success. How, through negotiation, could Kissinger ever hope or presume to convince the other side that, in this case, the appearance was distinct from the reality? After all, he could offer no concrete proof, he could devise no public safeguards. He failed, of course, and the war has continued. But if Hanoi's misperception of Kissinger's motives appears to us as a cruel trick played by history, we must also understand that there is abundant justification for the skepticism of the other side.

With the failure of negotiation, a more open-minded man
— a man less committed to a particular scheme of international relations and less concerned with the role of one particular nation in shaping it — would have supported withdrawal from a war that he himself recognized was fruitless
and unwinnable. Yet, in the end, Kissinger's obsession with
U.S. credibility would prevail. Much as he despised the war
and the regime which it held in place, he clung to the belief
that the United States must never appear to have abandoned
an ally. For years, he felt that the only way to free U.S. policy from Vietnam was to withdraw, because he thought that
Hanoi and the NLF could be induced to accept the temporary existence of the regime in the South. Yet for years during the Nixon administration, he believed that Washington
could extricate itself only by "winning" the war. By the time
he regrasped the soundness of his original vision after the
great North Vietnamese offensive of April 1972, he had already become committed to a policy of continued threats and
increasingly escalated violence. And, trapped by the bureaucratic mind prison he once sought so carefully to avoid, he
could not comprehend how severe a failure of credibility his
policy had suffered.

More Powerful Than the Sword

IF THERE IS PARADOX in Kissinger's policy of prolonging the war as a means of ending it, there is bitter irony in Kissinger's gradual loss of faith that serious discussions could be held with the North Vietnamese. For that loss began on an occasion when Kissinger came closer than had anyone else to engineering negotiations between Washington and Hanoi. An episode begun in the late spring of 1967 was to spell the end of many hopes Kissinger had once had to reach an agreement that would conclude the war.[1]

On Monday, June 5, the day war broke out between Israel and the Arab states, Herbert Marcovich, the French microbiologist and member of the International Continuing Committee of the Pugwash Conference, contacted the secretary general of Pugwash with an urgent request. Could the conference hold a small, private meeting to discuss a possible solution to the crisis in the Mideast? The conference's executive committee members were all agreeable, but the Russian representative insisted that the Vietnam war also be considered. Under that condition, a Pugwash group met in Paris two weeks later, and Kissinger, who happened to be in the city at the time, was also asked to attend.

The group finally decided to press for a Vietnam settlement through the French government. As the Western power most experienced in dealing with North Vietnam,

France was thought to possess special entrée in Hanoi.[2] And the man chosen by Paris to carry out the contact had been a personal friend of Ho Chi Minh. While a rising government official of postwar France, Raymond Aubrac had entertained Ho at his villa when the Vietnamese leader came to Paris in 1946 to negotiate a treaty of independence for his country. Years earlier, in fact, Aubrac had refused a request to mediate with Hanoi on behalf of another government at war with Vietnam, the government of Pierre Mendès-France.[3] For Pugwash, however, Aubrac agreed. Together with Marcovich, he would travel to Hanoi and attempt to discuss a settlement with Ho Chi Minh.

Henry Kissinger turned out to be a good choice for the American contact. He was an intellectual of respected stature, with direct access to some of the highest officials in Washington, a man who had worked extensively on Vietnam and was considered by his Pugwash colleagues to be strongly opposed to the current policy. Most crucial, perhaps, he proved himself able to convey, both to the Frenchmen and to official Washington, a strong sense that he was a man with an important and attentive audience, that his contacts listened to him carefully and would heed anything new and consequential he was given to say. This ability to inspire confidence in one's own words and influence was terribly important at a time when all other communication between Washington and Hanoi had broken down, when neither government was disposed to take the initiative or recognize third parties who claimed to have learned something about the intentions of the other side.

And as the channel to Hanoi began to open, those officials in Washington who had only silently opposed their government's narrow views on talking with Hanoi started to press their arguments on President Johnson with unusual force-fulness. Men who were not ordinarily found to stand fast on an issue, who preferred to connive or to keep their views to themselves, took great pains to argue that the Kissinger chan-nel should be used to the fullest. And their shift on this issue can largely be attributed to Kissinger's remarkable skills of persuasion and mediation.

On returning from the Pugwash Conference, Kissinger in-formed Secretary McNamara, and then Undersecretary Kat-zenbach, of his exchange with Marcovich.[4] Both were inter-ested, but others at State and the White House were not as enthusiastic. Aubrac, after all, had once been a member of the French Communist party; both he and Marcovich were regarded with great suspicion as intermediaries because of their amateur status. As for Kissinger, he was either person-ally unknown or disliked by everyone except McNamara and Katzenbach — and would have been disliked even more if he had made his views on Vietnam more fully known in gov-ernment circles. As a result, Kissinger was initially refused any status as Washington's representative.

The two Frenchmen nonetheless traveled to Hanoi in late July; they spent four hours with Pham Van Dong, and Au-brac alone visited with Ho.[5] What they learned was so sur-prising and so encouraging that they cut short their stay in North Vietnam and returned immediately to Paris. Kissin-ger debriefed them there a few days later, and when he re-ported his findings to Washington the mission took on genu-ine importance. As Marcovich remembered later, "What we brought . . . from Hanoi in July seemed to us very substan-tial." [6]

What Hanoi's leaders had done was to state with unprec-edented clarity their attitude toward direct negotiations with the United States. They had, of course, addressed the issue publicly on several occasions, but the meaning of their formal pronouncements had never been brought so sharply into focus as in the conversations with Aubrac and Marcovich. For instance, in a widely publicized interview with Wilfred Burchett in January 1967, Foreign Minister Nguyen Duy Trinh defined the possibility of talks with Washington in these words:

> Si les Etats-Unis désirent réelement des conversations, ils doivent d'abord cesser sans condition les bombardements et tous les autres actes de guerre contre la République démocratique du Vietnam. C'es seulement après la cessation inconditionelle des bombardements et de tous autres actes de guerre américains contre la République démocratique du Vietnam qu'il pourrait y avoir des conversations entre la République démocratique du Vietnam et les Etats-Unis.
>
> (If the United States really wants talks, it must unconditionally stop the bombing and all other acts of war against the Democratic Republic of Vietnam [DRV, or North Vietnam]. It is only after the unconditional stopping of the bombing and all other American acts of war against the DRV that talks can take place between the DRV and the United States.)

This was Hanoi's official position at the time of the Aubrac-Marcovich exchange, the position with which every Vietnam policy specialist in Washington was intimately familiar.[7] And yet, as the secret negotiations would soon reveal, there were few key decision makers in the American government with any grasp of what the position might mean. In a literal sense, it seemed to say that Hanoi was demanding a bombing halt without promising anything in return. But, as conveyed to Aubrac and Marcovich, the position *did* contain an informal commitment to negotiate in exchange for cessation of the bombing. Hanoi's commitment, in fact, was one that turned not on literal expression but on nuance, not on hard promises but on the subtle idiom of a single word.

The crucial word was *pourrait*. Literally translated, it means "could" and it is less committal than the definite *peut* or "will." In the context of the otherwise sharply worded statement, *pourrait* was taken by Washington as an indefinite commitment; Trinh was thought to have said that if the United States halted the bombing of North Vietnam, then talks *might* begin. To those officials who wanted a solid guarantee that negotiations would open with a bombing halt — and this group included everyone of importance — the formulation was unacceptable. Unfortunately, *pourrait* loses something in literal translation. Idiomatically, it connotes a strong, nearly definite commitment; it is not a word that appears in formal contracts, and it cannot provide the basis for prosecution in a French court of law, but it signifies something far more than "could" or "might," and is commonly accepted as an informal understanding that the act in question will be carried out.

That is the meaning of *pourrait* which Kissinger brought to Washington in August 1967.[8] It signified a major shift in emphasis from what Washington's hard-nosed analysts took to be the North Vietnamese position. And it defined the central issues in the debate which would follow on the content of Washington's response.

As a negotiator, Kissinger impressed officials with his ability to probe deeply and report accurately. His version of the Paris debriefing was not characterized by the verbal excesses often characteristic of third party go-betweens. He did not say that he felt Ho would be responsive *if only* the U.S.

promised thus-and-so; he simply stated the facts. And those few in Washington authorized to hear him came away from their talks with Kissinger feeling he had questioned Aubrac and Marcovich in the most thorough possible manner, that he did not omit facts or miss nuances. It shocked them that a mere academic had succeeded where even an experienced senior diplomat could easily have gone astray. And Kissinger's briefings also conveyed the impression that Marcovich and Aubrac were trustworthy intermediaries.

It now remained to formulate the precise negotiating position for the two Frenchmen to carry to Hanoi. Where previous U.S. positions had not been garbled and confused, they had been relatively hard-line. On the key question of a halt to American bombing of North Vietnam, Washington expected a reciprocal halt in Hanoi's infiltration into the South — a demand for the virtual sacrifice of 50 to 75 thousand North Vietnamese troops. At the same time, the U.S. demanded that Hanoi explicitly guarantee its entrance into talks immediately following a bombing halt — that, in effect, the North Vietnamese agree to appear to have knuckled under to U.S. military pressure. By the summer of 1967, a sizable number of officials had come to understand that, in order to bring about direct negotiations, it was necessary to do away with the elements of reciprocity in the U.S. position, regarding both infiltration and promises from Hanoi that a bombing halt would definitely result in talks. Eliminating preconditions had been a common proposition for many months. What was needed was an advocate at the weekly session where final decisions about the bombing were made — President Johnson's Tuesday Lunch.

Secretary of Defense Robert S. McNamara had probably been a secret doubter of the war for more than a year. In

October 1966, he had broken with the Joint Chiefs for the first time, recommending a cutback in the bombing of North Vietnam. And he had come to learn that the bombing, no matter how much it succeeded in "raising the cost," could not stop the infiltration actually needed by Hanoi to keep up its war in South Vietnam. As he told the Senate Armed Services Committee in January 1967, "I don't believe the bombing that I could contemplate in the future would significantly reduce the actual flow of men and material to the South." [9]

At the same time, McNamara held rather firmly to the Byzantine view that, no matter how strongly he disagreed with official policy, he would never press his disagreements for fear of making the President's job more difficult. And in Washington's tension-riddled atmosphere of summer 1967, when arguments ran deeper and Johnson was being torn between alternatives, it required an unusual ingredient to convince McNamara to do the slightest bit of arm-twisting on behalf of his own position.

Henry Kissinger's role as Washington's contact with Aubrac and Marcovich was the crucial factor in McNamara's decision to insist that the initiative be taken seriously, and that a fundamental change in the U.S. position was needed to make the initiative work. Kissinger was a man whom McNamara knew and respected, a policy thinker whose views on Vietnam he had come more and more to understand and agree with. More important, McNamara trusted that Kissinger would be a precise and skillful emissary, that he would interpret the new U.S. position in the way it had been intended. Kissinger's view of precisely what the position meant was of great concern to McNamara, because the message was to be quite deliberately worded in a manner which left room for varying interpretations.[10]

Following Kissinger's report early in August, McNamara asked his assistant secretary for international security affairs, Paul Warnke, to design a new U.S. position on negotiations and a bombing halt. According to McNamara's instructions, the purpose of the formula should be to do away with *all* conditions which had been set by prior U.S. positions. Only in this way, McNamara felt, could North Vietnam be drawn into talks with Washington, ending the difficult logjam which persisted in Washington's decision-making circles as well as in relations between the warring powers. McNamara thus seized upon the Kissinger mission as a way of locking U.S. policy into a position he had long but quietly favored. At the same time, he went to great lengths to camouflage his role in the drafting of the new U.S. position; few officials seem to have been aware that McNamara was deeply involved in the origins of the initiative.

After sorting out the problem with a member of his staff, Warnke gave McNamara the following paragraph:

> The United States is willing to stop all aerial and naval bombardment of North Vietnam if this will lead to serious discussions. We assume that while discussions proceed, North Vietnam would not take advantage of the bombing cessation or limitation.[11]

Concealed beneath this nondescript language was an unprecedented switch. For the first time, the U.S. position on talks would be simply to stop bombing North Vietnam and wait for Hanoi to join in negotiation. The bombing would be resumed, this position implied, only if time passed and no action had been taken by the North. It was, in effect, the same arrangement which Hanoi accepted in April 1968, except that the bombing cutback which then occurred was not a total one.

The second sentence of Warnke's formula contained other tricks. By warning Hanoi not to "take advantage" of a bombing halt, the formula would not be saying that all infiltration had to stop; for the first time, by not spelling out precisely what was meant by "take advantage," Washington would quietly accede to the continuing flow of men and supplies at the present or "normal" level. In addition, the U.S. would not demand any guarantee from the other side that it would abide by this injunction; Washington would simply "assume" Hanoi's cooperation, reserving the option of future bombing if infiltration were measurably increased.

As set down by Warnke and his staff, the formula would have amounted to a unilateral halt in the bombing of North Vietnam. To be sure, it quietly posed some limitations for the other side; the dry season of fall is when infiltration always reaches its peak, when Hanoi increases the flow to sustain its operations in the South during other periods in which resupply is impossible. To the extent that Washington would ask Hanoi to desist from this seasonal increase, the de-escalation of the war was to have been mutual; but a U.S. announcement of a bombing halt, and the subsequent North Vietnamese acquiescence to talks, would each have been unilateral.

All of these implications would have to be explained clearly and meticulously to the North Vietnamese; it is for this reason that Kissinger, a skilled mediator clearly in sympathy with the switch in the U.S. position, was indispensable to the effort. In fact, the purpose of all the written-in ambiguities was not to confuse Hanoi, but to ease the formula through Washington's own decision-making channels.¹² The ambiguities were later used to justify a more hard-line interpretation of the formula than its authors had intended, an interpretation which contributed to the collapse of the initiative itself. But there was little chance that President Johnson would have approved the formula if those ambiguities did not exist.

Finally, before submitting the formula to Secretary Rusk and the President, McNamara himself made two small changes in it: ". . . if this will lead to serious discussion" now read "if this will lead promptly to productive discussions." ¹³ These changes, whose effect was to make the formula sound slightly tougher without affecting its central message, might be explained in any of several ways: to insure Johnson's approval, to tell Hanoi to move quickly and decisively lest Washington revert to its former position, or, perhaps, to camouflage his own interest in the entire matter.

When the formula arrived at the Department of State at the end of the first week in August, Secretary Rusk was out of Washington, and the formula cleared State with relative ease. Only one change was made: "if this will lead" to negotiations became "when this will lead," a change which Warnke and others associated with the original text felt was a reasonable grammatical adjustment.¹⁴

When Rusk returned to his job, however, his reaction to the formula was not enthusiastic. A man who had long held out for reciprocal arrangements with the North Vietnamese, Rusk was skeptical of the concessions involved in the U.S. change of position. He believed that the bombing should not be stopped as long as supplies continued to reach the South at more than a subsistence level. Along with Walt

Rostow — who was even more emphatically a "pour-it-on" man as far as the bombing was concerned — Rusk appears to have been responsible for a small and almost imperceptible yet ultimately crucial change in the official interpretation of the formula. No longer did the position mean that the United States would halt the raids and wait for Hanoi's response; Washington must first receive a firm guarantee on direct negotiations before the bombing could be stopped. More particularly, North Vietnam would be required to change its private position from *pourrait* to *peut*, a shift it was finally unwilling to make. But at the time, even to Kissinger and others who were most eager for the private contacts to bear fruit, it did not seem too much to ask Hanoi privately to change that one small word.

President Johnson himself was initially wary of the entire venture. Already under massive pressure from military leaders and Congressional hawks to add targets in North Vietnam, highly defensive of the bombing campaign in general and suspicious of Harvard academics in particular, he was not especially disposed to change the U.S. position for the sake of Kissinger's channel. Nor, during this period, did he take very seriously the advice he received from McNamara, who had continued to fall silently out of sympathy with official policy and who was not in any event inclined to dissent strongly from the President's view, no matter how great his disagreement with it. But on this occasion, McNamara argued so skillfully in favor of the change that Johnson momentarily gave in. Along with Nicholas Katzenbach, who chaired the interdepartmental "non-group" in charge of examining possible peace proposals and initiatives, McNamara convinced the President that the Aubrac-Marcovich channel was a viable one and that, in order to make it work, the two men had to be given something new to say to the other side.[15]

In approving the formula, Johnson and his advisers were aware of the ambiguities contained in it and probably reasoned that the ill-defined wording provided an easy escape valve should the North Vietnamese reject the proposal.[16] In contrast to Warnke and others who hoped that the formula would become the new U.S. position regardless of the other side's response, the President reluctantly signed on to the formula with the expectation that it would be withdrawn if it did not succeed in bringing about private discussion between Washington and Hanoi. The U.S. position, in fact, *did* harden later on; when Foreign Minister Trinh stated publicly on December 29 that his government would definitely sit down with the United States after a bombing halt — thus fulfilling Hanoi's obligation under the old formula — the raids on the North continued.[17] With this understanding of the formula's deniability — and in the absence of opposition from General Wheeler, who typically abided by civilian political judgment — Johnson officially approved the formula; about two weeks later, Kissinger delivered a written statement of the formula to Aubrac and Marcovich, who then handed it to the North Vietnamese representative in Paris on August 25.

Unfortunately, the President was then speaking with two voices and thinking with different minds. On August 8, feeling pressured by the Senate Armed Services Committee's hearings on the bombing which were scheduled to open the following day, the White House quietly authorized raids on several new targets inside North Vietnam. One of these targets — the Paul Doumer Bridge on the outskirts of Hanoi — was destroyed by U.S. planes three days later. The only bridge crossing the Red River, this structure had been a vital link in North Vietnam's transportation and communication networks. The bombing of it outraged North Vietnam's leaders, and probably contributed more than any other single factor to the collapse of the Kissinger initiative.[18] After the incident, Washington prohibited all American air strikes within a ten-mile radius of Hanoi, a prohibition which lasted until the final collapse of the negotiation in October. Yet the officials who carried out the bombing of the North, the U.S. Pacific Command, were apparently uninformed of the reason for this limitation[19] and merely diverted their planes to sensitive targets around the port cities of Haiphong and Cam Pha. When Aubrac and Marcovich delivered the U.S. note in Paris on August 25, the North Vietnamese replies were rude and suspicious in tone. Chester Cooper, the special assistant to Ambassador Harriman who accompanied Kissinger to Paris late in August, has a terse recollection of the exchanges:

> There are more pleasant ways of spending an afternoon than negotiating with the North Vietnamese. You say to them, we want to play baseball, and they say, all right, let's play baseball. You say, nine men on a side? Okay, nine men on a side. Nine innings in the game? Fine, they agree, nine innings in the game. Only by the time you finish, there are six men on each team and you're playing hockey.[20]

After other prolonged communication, the private talks floundered on the distinction between *pourrait* ("almost definitely will talk") and *peut* ("definitely will talk"). The distance between the two words is admittedly small, but it was reinforced by deeper and more pronounced differences in the negotiating styles of Washington and Hanoi.

Virtually all U.S. officials — especially those such as Kissinger who favored an early negotiated settlement of the war — believed that it was necessary in private talks with the other side to take positions which departed significantly from their public pronouncements. This belief has been a central feature of U.S. negotiating methods, and it has underscored explicit statements by successive American administrations that the public sessions in Paris can by themselves accomplish nothing. It has been particularly characteristic of those policymakers, such as Kissinger, who believe that the United States should salvage the *appearance* of success in its departure from Vietnam while relinquishing the reality of a non-Communist government in the South. And of course, the primary assumption of those who were willing to present an entirely different U.S. position in private talks was that the other side should be similarly willing to compromise its public stance.[21]

Kissinger's hopes that North Vietnam would be more conciliatory in private were bolstered by his knowledge that Hanoi's leaders had long been men of unusual tactical flexibility. The North Vietnamese have a reputation in this country for being stiff and dogmatic negotiators, but the most cursory glance at their history would illustrate that they have observed extraordinary circumspection in talks with Western powers. A political spirit that is always tempered by practical wisdom, what Lacouture felicitously calls "the mixture of conviction and technique," [22] comes easily and naturally to them. In March 1946, six months after the Communist takeover of northern Vietnam, Ho signed a treaty with Paris placing his country inside a French Union, his vision of ultimate independence intact nonetheless. And again, in 1954, after the victory at Dienbienphu, he abandoned a promising military situation and agreed to "temporary" partition. True, neither agreement was conceived by

Ho as an agreement in principle; each was conceived as the more palatable of unfriendly alternatives. But then, how else is flexibility to be defined? These settlements are striking proof that the North Vietnamese, in spite of their superior power position, have traditionally inclined toward negotiated solutions instead of protracted and bloody war.

What Kissinger failed to recognize is that the North Vietnamese would learn from their historical mistakes. Highly as he regarded his own intentions, Kissinger did not take the necessary step of putting himself in his opponent's position and asking himself how he would behave if he were an official in Hanoi who had been a party to North Vietnam's earlier negotiations with the West. By 1967, after yet another deceitful escalation by a Western power in their country, Hanoi's negotiators could not possibly face their American counterparts with the same good faith and willingness to compromise that had dictated their earlier relations with the West; instead, they would see at the other end of the conference table the ghosts of Paris in 1946 and Geneva in 1954, and they would be obsessed with the memories of having been tricked so often into negotiating away their independence. "You know, Raymond," Ho had said to Aubrac in July 1967, "I have been fooled many times. After each time, it gets harder to fool me." [23] After receiving a strong indication that talks would take place after a bombing halt, was it now too much to ask that the United States, as a sign of its own good faith, stop the raids even in the absence of absolute assurances that Hanoi would respond in kind?

It would be wrong to say that *pourrait*, the North Vietnamese position of fall 1967, was inflexible. In view of the fact that Hanoi had decided in July to launch the Tet offensive the following February, [24] a decision which would have been made impossible by an acceptance of the U.S. position, North Vietnam's very entrance into this private discussion with Washington — not to mention the very liberal meaning of the word *pourrait* — is itself a sign of willingness to compromise. But while Hanoi had clearly consented to elucidate its public position in private talks with the United States, it was not prepared to subvert its formal stand outright, and that is what the use of the word *peut* would have required.

To that extent alone, North Vietnam can be said to have been inflexible. But North Vietnamese officials had a great deal less room for maneuver, even in private, than did the United States. Because they were revolutionary leaders, their acts carried the added burden of ideological commitment; as a people who verged on physical devastation at the hands of the United States, they understood that one mistake for them would mean death. If they accepted the formula with the conditions it entailed, and then if talks should collapse, might the United States not resume the bombing, perhaps to destroy North Vietnam's irrigation dikes or raid Hanoi and Haiphong? Strong hints of a response were one thing, but Hanoi could never firmly agree to talks after a bombing halt because the principle of firm agreements with the United States was a principle Hanoi was afraid to admit.

What of America's behavior during this negotiation? Doubtless there were some who fought the good fight in Washington for conciliation with the other side, but as a corporate unit the United States cannot be said to have been truly flexible. How does one explain the destruction of the Paul Doumer Bridge? Or, when the limitation of strikes in the Hanoi area was later put into effect, the drastic escalations around Haiphong and Cam Pha? "My conviction,"

Marcovich says today, "is that the White House was not pre-pared to discuss." [25] And history may demonstrate that the President was not the only guilty party. Even the valiant doves, Kissinger included, would finally agree that firm, ex-plicit guarantees should be sought from North Vietnam — guarantees that could be whipped around and used against Hanoi to justify a further resumption of U.S. raids. More imaginative and compassionate men, hearing the word *pour-rait*, would have stopped the air strikes with the hope that Hanoi could be taken at its word. The evidence now avail-able indicates that if Washington had done so, North Viet-nam would have entered talks and stabilized its levels of infiltration, *with the result that the massive onslaught of Tet 1968 would not have taken place.* But, as it happened, the result of Washington's failure of imagination was the tragedy of Tet 1968. And, even more tragically, Kissinger drew from this episode the conclusion that an acceptable end to the war could not be worked out with North Vietnam by purely ver-bal means.

In Kissinger's view, the only realistic Vietnam policy avail-able to the U.S. government in 1967 was the policy of the "decent interval." Put simply, the decent interval meant that the fall of the South Vietnamese government — which Kis-singer regarded as highly likely, if not inevitable — would have to be delayed for a sufficient period of time following an American withdrawal so that Washington would not ap-pear to have failed in the defense of an allied regime. In this context, the key issue of the Vietnam war — political control of the South — was really a moot point, to be subject to sec-ondary considerations of timing and appearance but suscep-tible of only a single outcome. To Kissinger, the crucial question was not whether, but how and when, to disengage.

If Kissinger had erased from his mind the possibility of further escalation and victorious withdrawal, so had he dismissed the possibility of an immediate, precipitous withdrawal. He knew that, even in the event of instant disengagement, a period of time would pass before a Communist or Communist-dominated government arose in the South; after all, the Hanoi regime and the National Liberation Front had political imperatives of their own to observe, one of which was that the takeover in the South should appear to result from widespread political involvement and approval, rather than from physical force alone. Kissinger understood in 1967 that, with a maximum of military effort and expenditure, the North Vietnamese could probably have engineered the fall of Saigon or brought it to a state of near collapse; such a campaign, however, would surely have caused a diminution of Hanoi's political prestige, as well as risked the kind of military retribution from the United States that followed the offensive of April 1972. Thus, Kissinger's conception of the decent interval was cast not primarily in terms of a chronological lapse, but in the *appearance* of effective political and military assistance to the Saigon regime.

Under ideal circumstances, Kissinger felt, U.S. officials could simply convey this message to Hanoi in private bilateral discussions, order an appropriate redeployment of U.S. troops in the Vietnamese countryside, and then stage the withdrawal. For despite surface appearances, the decent interval settlement would be non-antagonistic in character, acceptable to the North Vietnamese, and bearable to a non-victorious United States. With the crux of the issue already determined, the war could be brought to a mutually agreeable end. At the same time, such a bargain could not be consecrated by treaty or by any other formal meas-

ure, because an open arrangement would reveal the blow
that had been dealt the United States; the treaty ending
the war would *embody* a decent interval, but it could
not state it in explicit terms. It seems clear, for example,
that the U.S. proposals of May 1969 were designed for negotiation on a decent interval basis. American and North
Vietnamese forces would have withdrawn from the South,
and an "internationally supervised" election would have kept
in power Thieu's regime. But his survival would be only
temporary; after a U.S. departure, Saigon's tottering government and army would eventually succumb to a rearmed
and politically strengthened NLF. Nevertheless the decent
interval agreement could never be acknowledged in the
treaty; the agreement would instead have to be reached in
sustained verbal exchanges between the two sides.

In return for political control of South Vietnam, Hanoi
would agree to acquiesce in the illusion that Washington had
successfully, if only temporarily, given life to the Saigon
regime. In concrete terms, this would mean a lower NLF
political and military profile for twelve or at most eighteen
months following the U.S. withdrawal, after which time the
insurgents would be free to resume their full activity. This
settlement would have to be arranged with great care and
subtlety, and even in private would probably not be recorded
in its naked terms. Nonetheless, even more than the contacts
which would have been necessary to obtain North Vietnamese agreement on the Defense Department formula in late
1967, any talks leading to a decent interval would have had
to consist of genuine dialogue and understanding between
the negotiators.

Kissinger's conception of a "decent interval," quirkish as
it may sound, was no abstract device; on the contrary, it was

very much in keeping with the historical tradition of negotiated settlements on Vietnam. In its general aspect, the
decent interval bore a remarkable similarity to the agreements arrived at between the Viet Minh and various Western powers in 1946 and 1954. Each of the earlier agreements
had been undertaken by Ho and his colleagues to preserve
their essential gains and avoid a costly continuation of war;
each was designed to permit their Western opponent a
peaceful and gradual, or "honorable," departure from Vietnam. These were precisely the objectives that Kissinger felt
in 1967 would have to embody any negotiated settlement of
the war. Yet Kissinger's position so eerily resembled the
offer that Hanoi had twice before accepted, only to be
tricked each time, that it is hard to see in retrospect how
Kissinger believed a decent interval could again be negotiated with the other side.

Consider:

The agreement of 1946 stated that France would "recognize the Republic of Vietnam as a free state having its own
government, its own parliament and its own finances, and
forming part of the Indochinese Federation and the French
Union." Hanoi would administer its internal affairs, and
would coordinate its foreign policy and trade with the wishes
of France. French troops would be garrisoned in the country, their status subject to further negotiations on the future
relationship between France and Vietnam. Most important,
the fate of Cochin China, or what is now most of South Vietnam, would be determined by popular referendum. There
seems little doubt that the Viet Minh leaders felt the French
would one day leave them as their own sovereign master,
"perhaps," as Ho said soon afterward, "within five years." [26]

Within three months, the agreement lay in tatters. On

June 1, high-ranking French officials in Saigon proclaimed the "autonomous republic" of Cochin China, and Paris offered no objection. After sporadic fighting throughout Vietnam, an incident in Haiphong Harbor led to a French shelling of the city, which caused several thousand civilian casualties. With the Viet Minh attack on Hanoi in December, the first Indochina war was on.

Almost eight years later, when the Viet Minh joined the talks at Geneva after Giap's triumph at Dienbienphu, they again negotiated on the basis of a decent interval. Under considerable pressure from the major Communist powers, they proposed to relinquish momentarily the fruits of their military victories over the French and offered partition at the seventeenth parallel. Again they sought to achieve independence and reunification by peaceful means. To be sure, their safeguard was now spelled out in a most explicit manner; the Southern regime of Bao Dai, consecrated in Paris five years before, must agree to a nationwide election. And the interval would be shorter; in 1946, Ho talked of five years, but now, the nationwide election must take place in two years. There was little doubt in anyone's mind that Ho would win in that election; and the Soviet Union, as coguarantor with Britain of the Geneva Conference, pledged to insure that the election would in fact take place. Moscow, of course, did no such thing — a point that would never be lost on Hanoi — because the United States, in the years following the conference, succeeded in undermining the agreement by giving aid to the regime of Ngo Dinh Diem.

Was it likely that the North Vietnamese would again be willing to negotiate with a Western power on the basis of a decent interval? In 1967, Kissinger thought they would; and whatever other conclusions Kissinger drew from his experience as Washington's intermediary in the Aubrac-Marcovich exchange, it is clear that he came away from these talks with the impression that, under the best of circumstances, North Vietnam's leaders were still prepared to be flexible, an impression that can only have been confirmed in Kissinger's mind when he understood, after the Viet Cong attack on Saigon in January 1968, that the other side had earlier expressed a willingness to negotiate on a basis that would have made it impossible for them to carry out an offensive in the South. But the failure of the 1967 negotiation — and the manner of its failure — convinced Kissinger that the war could not be settled by negotiation *alone*.[27] For Kissinger recognized that something far more fundamental than the bombing of the Paul Doumer Bridge lay behind the obstinate North Vietnamese refusal to make the transition from *pourrait* to *peut*. By August 1967, Hanoi's fear of acknowledging America's right to resume bombing probably would not have disappeared even if all the raids on the North had stopped during the entire course of the secret talks. And if the other side was unwilling even to guarantee its entrance into negotiations, what chance was there that once the talks began, it would willingly promise, for a long period, to give up its activity in the South?

In view of the outcome which Kissinger — and, doubtless, others in the government — hoped would emerge from negotiations with Hanoi, the success of the 1967 initiative would have been the necessary first step. Aside from the fact that continued bombing made *any* direct talks impossible, an incorrect reading of the U.S. message by the other side would have meant that the further, more complicated understandings needed for a verbal settlement were hopelessly out of reach. And again, though not everyone in the small circle of U.S. officials aware of the Kissinger initiative was in sympathy with the new U.S. position, the meaning of that position, as presented to the North Vietnamese, was quite clear: Washington had grown skeptical and weary and was willing to make concessions to end the war on palatable terms. Tacitly, it also posed the threat that, if negotiations failed, the U.S. would resume the bombing, probably with greater force and at more targets than ever before. This corollary reflected the widely held view in Washington that the *threat* of renewed bombing was now a more effective political weapon than a continuation of the bombing campaign that had already failed. And, ironically, it is precisely this threat which Kissinger himself later made, and enforced, when the Nixon administration's talks with the North Vietnamese broke down.

As it turned out, the only fixed point in Kissinger's thinking on Vietnam — as it had been on the confrontation over Berlin — was the need for credibility in the U.S. pledge. Diplomacy might fail, and the military debacle could grow to monstrous proportions, but American claims must be upheld at any cost. Kissinger's early faith in the possibility of negotiation with Hanoi was rooted in his belief that the war was an aberration, a dreadful historical accident, not in the mold of great power contests where fundamentally divergent interests had to be reconciled by difficult and complicated means. Yet at the same time, he felt that grotesque errors of past American decisions had elevated the war to a higher plane of policy. As he would write in January 1969:

. . . the commitment of five hundred thousand Americans has settled the issue of the importance of Vietnam. For what is involved now is confidence in American promises. However fashionable it is to ridicule the terms "credibility" or "prestige," they are not empty phrases; other nations can gear their actions to ours only if they can count on our steadiness . . . In many parts of the world — the Middle East, Europe, Latin America, even Japan — stability depends on confidence in American promises. Unilateral withdrawal or a settlement which, even unintentionally, amounts to it could therefore lead to the erosion of restraints and to an even more dangerous international situation.[28]

Of all possible methods of bringing the war to a close, the one which Kissinger clearly preferred as he undertook the transmission of the Defense Department formula to the North Vietnamese was private, closely held discussion. But the failure of such discussion, in Kissinger's mind, did not preclude a resort to military means; rather, it demanded it. And it is evident, in retrospect, that Kissinger would lean heavily on his 1967 experience in any further negotiations he might undertake with the other side. He realized that the circumstances in which negotiations opened were crucial in determining what rapport there could be once the discussion actually began. And he was quite aware that an inability to carry on private verbal exchange would complicate a decent interval settlement and force U.S. policymakers to consider other routes of disengagement. As Kissinger later put it in his discussion of the Paris talks, *"The way negotiations are carried out is almost as important as what is negotiated. The choreography of how one enters negotiations, what is settled first, and in what manner is inseparable from the substance of the issues."* [29]

Kissinger's experience in the 1967 negotiation convinced him that it would be impossible to end the war by verbal means alone. An incurable suspicion of American intentions, combined with a refusal to compromise its public position in private talks, would make Hanoi a difficult and intractable partner in negotiation, ruling out a simplified, nonantagonistic settlement. This did not rule out the discussion of relatively simple matters, such as the precise modalities of U.S. withdrawal and prisoner exchange, with the other side; nor did it exclude the usefulness of communicating with Hanoi on a unilateral basis, such as when a U.S. negotiator would say that a particular policy was about to take effect, and that it was being adopted with certain expectations in mind. Kissinger's attitude, however, was that the flux of political and military interaction between the two sides would have to resolve itself before meaningful bilateral contact could take place. As Marcovich put it, "The level of distrust was so high that verbal commitments, especially from the White House, were not enough." [30] At this stage of his evolving consciousness, Kissinger then made a choice between two alternatives: unilateral withdrawal, or the extraction of a "decent interval" by threatening Hanoi with less palatable consequences than those a decent interval would bring. Because of his concern for U.S. "prestige," Kissinger chose the second alternative, and became committed to a policy of threat. It is less than clear that U.S. prestige in early 1969 would not have been better served by a quick withdrawal, along with an announcement from Washington that it no longer wished to obstruct national liberation movements that did not directly infringe on American interests. But Kissinger believed, wrongly, that the threat of military pressure might succeed where negotiation had failed, that Hanoi would "flex" once again in deference to a power from the West.

None of this is to say that Kissinger had ever been naive

about how easy communicating with the other side would be. In fact, even before the San Antonio episode, his awareness that the gap between the two sides would be difficult to bridge, that "history and culture combine to produce almost morbid suspiciousness on the part of the Vietnamese," [31] was probably deeper and more acute than that held by most other critics of the war. But, hopeful that verbal negotiations could somehow be made to work, he did not suffer this realization until he himself had experienced it. Never again would Kissinger's attitude toward Hanoi be as hopeful and conciliatory as it was in August 1967. He began to believe after that time that a period of *tacit communication* between Washington and Hanoi would have to precede substantive talks. And in simple strategic practice the easiest method of tacit communication would be the calculated deployment of military forces in Vietnam for the purpose of conveying a particular message to the other side, a message that could also be enunciated verbally and unilaterally to Hanoi.

The inability to communicate openly did not mean to Kissinger that a final settlement with the other side would be impractical or unattainable; in fact, the evidence is ample that Kissinger retained great hopes for years afterward, and had more faith than any other major figure in the Nixon administration that such a settlement would be reached. After all, tacit communication was historically the prevalent mode of interchange in great power relationships, and Kissinger's world view was one in which international stability thrived on such accommodation. He did recognize, however, that the absence of bilateral discussion would prolong the final settlement and make it more difficult, and he understood that by the time the two sides sat down for serious talks, all but the most insignificant of their differences would

already have been resolved. And what he meant by negotiation — never the most well-defined of terms — was
the mopping-up of the conflict once the pieces had fallen
into their final place. As he would tell reporters, in a striking display of candor, in September 1969, "We have been ex-
changing ideas with Hanoi at the conference table now for
many years. One of the problems is that words tend to be,
in many respects, the least useful means of communication." [32]

But how would the North Vietnamese and the NLF respond to tacit communication, which, in its more sinister
aspect, was actually a policy of threat? If, as Kissinger felt,
Hanoi could appreciate the U.S. position, if it could be
brought to believe that Washington would one day accede
in the collapse of the Saigon regime, then the American
signals — whether de-escalatory or threatening — would be
read correctly. But if the other side did not privately share
Washington's perceptions — and the evidence is ample that
it did not — the only signs to which it would be responsive
were those that pointed toward a withdrawal; a pattern of
escalation would appear to the other side not as an inducement to compromise, but as proof that the United States was
really following in the footsteps of colonial France, that it
aspired to establish a lasting non-Communist regime in South
Vietnam. Had the Vietnamese fought so bravely and fero-
ciously for twenty-five years only to perceive an American
escalation as a willingness to strike a balance? It would soon
become clear that Washington could only negotiate fruitfully
with Hanoi in the context of its own de-escalation and withdrawal.

The closing events of Johnson administration Vietnam
policy bore out this reality. On April 3, Hanoi accepted a

partial bombing halt as an inducement to enter talks,[33] though it stated then that it would only discuss the complete termination of raids on the North. The cutback, advanced in the President's speech of March 31, was, in fact, a less sweeping concession than had been offered in the San Antonio formula seven months earlier, but it differed from the former position in an important respect: it was completely unilateral, acceptable to a Hanoi which was hardly unmindful of the resumption that might ensue in the absence of a reply. And the total halt of November 1 was similarly unilateral, with caveats about the DMZ and the cities in the South carefully spelled out to, and later observed by, the other side. It was this full cutback which corresponded precisely to the offer Henry Kissinger brought to Paris in August 1967. And it is no small quirk of history that a major effect of Nixon administration policy on Vietnam would be to unravel even this understanding with the other side, an agreement which Kissinger himself had proposed to Hanoi years before.

Interlude: 1968

IT IS A SCHOLAR's peculiar grace to feel prescient on a given subject and, consequently, be bullheaded at the same time. True to his intellectual roots, Henry Kissinger did not change his thinking on Vietnam in the learning process which exploded over the United States in the aftermath of Tet 1968.

More than any other event of the war, Tet caused a massive public re-examination of Vietnam policy in the United States, and it set off a hard-fought, wide-ranging internal government debate which ultimately fell to Kissinger to resolve. Yet, through it all, the crux of his position on the war remained the same: before disentangling itself from Vietnam, the U.S. must insure the immediate safety of the Saigon regime.

If any change of policy direction within the government could be discerned in the months following Tet, it was a movement toward reducing American involvement in the war. Arguments for unilaterally withdrawing U.S. troops from the combat zone, and from South Vietnam itself, were aired for the first time; and, beginning that spring, a number of officials began developing a scheme for conducting mutual withdrawal negotiations with North Vietnam in sessions which would virtually exclude the Saigon regime. Most significant of all, a full-fledged debate had begun to emerge on negotiating with Hanoi a cease-fire "in place," a concession of NLF-held areas which would cut directly at the political and territorial base of the South Vietnamese. Even if the President and his closest advisers were unmoved by Tet, and they apparently were, a way had been opened for the dissenters to state their reservations more clearly and to see some of those reservations adopted as policy.

By contrast, Kissinger's position hardened slightly as the Presidential election edged closer. He no longer believed that the war could be settled by direct verbal means; he thus sought a more circuitous and riskier "carrot-and-stick" approach in bargaining with the other side. The essence of this strategy, as it emerged in mid-1968, was to exert indirect diplomatic influence on Hanoi through the Soviet Union and People's China,[1] and to speak directly with North Vietnam through varying deployments of U.S. forces in the South, deployments which would either loosen or increase the military threat as the case required. On yet another level, the Sino-Soviet split might be useful in weakening Hanoi's morale; as Kissinger would later say to reporters of President Nixon's trip to Rumania, a trip which was clearly calculated in part to influence events in Vietnam, "In dealing with the Communist world, it is important to find methods of communication that are believable and that can be put in a framework that others understand."[2]

The outlines of this strategy were clearly discernible in the withdrawal plan which Kissinger prepared for Presidential candidate Nelson Rockefeller. The plan, which Rockefeller announced in New York City on July 13, was based on the assumption that, between the warring powers, there existed "a lack of mutual trust about ultimate aims."[3]

As a first move, the Rockefeller plan stated, the two foreign armies would disengage and withdraw to different areas of the countryside, the North Vietnamese to the border regions and the Americans to the cities. Simultaneously, the U.S. would withdraw 75,000 troops from the South "as a token of its good faith." (The idea for the small withdrawal was taken directly from a proposal which Ambassador Harriman had earlier advanced inside the government.) Then, to avoid the possibility of any misunderstanding between the two sides, "an international peace-keeping force composed of neutral nations — Asian, if possible — would be interposed as a security buffer between American and allied forces on the one side and North Vietnamese on the other." This force would be constituted by multilateral negotiation among the 1954 Geneva Conference powers or some other group including Washington, Hanoi, Moscow, and Peking.

As a next step, the NLF would surrender its arms and "abide by the Democratic process," after which "it will be guaranteed participation in the political life of the country." U.S. and North Vietnamese would withdraw from the South, and the international force would remain to supervise a national election. Finally, Saigon would negotiate directly with Hanoi on whether to reunify Vietnam or keep the two capitals separate. After this discussion, the buffer force would leave the South.

The thrust of this plan was to provide for mutual withdrawal and a temporarily secure regime in Saigon, while minimizing the degree of direct discussion between Washington and Hanoi and confining that discussion to the most perfunctory possible matters. In a less explicit way, it rendered Saigon's part in the process virtually meaningless. To be sure, the plan would be enacted only after "consultation" (not a highly meaningful word) with the South Vietnamese; further, the Thieu government would remain in power during the voting, and despite the presence of foreign observers, the regime's internal security apparatus would serve as a quiet guarantee of Thieu's re-election. Nonetheless, in Kissinger's mind — and his perception of the plan must certainly have differed from Rockefeller's — all of this support for Saigon was strictly in the realm of appearance. Before the agreement on a peacekeeping force, Washington would privately tell Hanoi through Moscow and Peking that it would not object to Communist rule in the South at some future date, and could then put pressure on the intermediaries to hold Hanoi to this understanding. If such pressure were to fail, Washington could threaten to stall on arms talks or recognition of Peking. Meanwhile, the political future of the South, whatever its outcome, could publicly be laid to the Vietnamese.

As was true of so many of Kissinger's grandiose schemes, the Rockefeller plan had a distinct air of unreality about it. In retrospect, it was clear that the North Vietnamese, aware of having been tricked by the West in previous negotiations, would be unlikely to risk the pain and indignity of a recurrence; and, as Kissinger would discover in early 1969, the Soviets — whose influence was hardly unlimited in Hanoi — would not be willing to stake what influence they did have on a peace proposal from the United States. Further, the Thieu regime would demonstrate by its refusal to come to Paris in November 1968 that it would not stand idly by as its destiny was being mediated by Washington and Hanoi. In view of Kissinger's feeling that an allied government must be treated with ostensible respect and care, Saigon's intransigence alone would rule out an easy settlement.

At the same time, the lines of Kissinger's approach had been neatly drawn by November 1968. Any Vietnam settlement would have to involve the participation, witting or otherwise, of the major Communist powers. And if Moscow and Peking did not cooperate, their aid might be enlisted by more tacit means. As Kissinger was well aware, North Vietnam was the only sovereign state in the world which depended directly on the continued cooperation of the Soviet Union and People's China. If tension between the centers of Communist power could be exacerbated, the reverberations would be felt in Hanoi. Should the U.S. threaten to exalt one power at the expense of the other, the potential victim might willingly compel the North Vietnamese to negotiate on Washington's terms. In this way, the Nixon administration would elevate Vietnam to its major foreign policy priority, set in a context that Moscow and Peking, intentions aside, could easily "understand."

As for direct negotiations among the warring powers, Kissinger finally adopted — and described in the January 1969 issue of *Foreign Affairs* — a plan which had been developed earlier in 1968 by analysts in the State Department and the international security affairs division at Defense. Popularly known as the "two-track" method, it envisioned two lines of discussion which would proceed in parallel, but entirely distinct, directions. On one level, North Vietnam and the United States would agree to a mutual withdrawal of their forces from the South, and would confine their exchanges to the modalities of the withdrawal: cease-fires, safe departures, and so on. At the second level, and at the same time, Saigon and the NLF would also agree to a cease-fire and negotiate a political settlement.

The stated purpose of the two-track scheme, as set down by its authors, was to achieve mutual withdrawal and, more important, to divorce the ongoing military contest from whatever political outcome emerged in the South. The primary *motive* of the two-track proposal, however, was quietly to prod the Thieu regime into serious discussion with the NLF. Those who supported it were fearful that, if the South Vietnamese had to be dragged screaming into negotiations with the other side, President Johnson and his closest advisers would not care to make the effort. In this case, then, the principle of confining discussion of a political settlement to the South Vietnamese was invoked not for reasons of "self-determination," but rather to insure that Saigon could be made to assume ultimate responsibility for that settlement. As the leading supporter of the two-track scheme, Secretary of Defense Clark Clifford, would say of the proposed negotiations, "I did not think that the two lines should touch each other. If they did, we would create an obligation on our part to see that the political agreement was adhered to, and that would keep us there forever." [4]

If Saigon still refused to join in the discussions, Washington could then continue its negotiations with impunity in the absence of the South Vietnamese. Kissinger implied this threat when he later wrote that if the Thieu regime participated, "direct negotiations between the United States and the NLF would be obviated." [5] A similar commitment would be expected of Hanoi. At the same time, the clear implication of the plan was that the U.S. and North Vietnam should under any circumstances refrain from discussing the political settlement for South Vietnam. But when, in January 1969, the NLF representatives in Paris refused to meet privately with Saigon, President Nixon and Kissinger quickly dropped the two-track idea and immersed themselves in the political future of the South.

The two-track approach, ironically enough, *did* move far

in the direction of Hanoi's demands, although it did so in a typically oblique manner. The United States would withdraw all its troops, and, more important, by forcing the Thieu regime to face the NLF alone in direct talks, Washington would quietly undercut the authority and morale of Saigon. The two tracks nonetheless posed important drawbacks for Hanoi. The principle of *mutual* withdrawal, which was at the heart of the two tracks, was a principle North Vietnam was not willing explicitly to admit; its longstanding public position, after all, was that there were no Northern troops fighting in the South. Here too, it appeared, tacit mutual example, not direct negotiation, was the only way to conclude the fighting on the ground.

But more fundamentally, the two-track scheme did not go far enough for Hanoi in effecting an American repudiation of the Saigon regime. To the other side, the two tracks seemed to imply the opposite of repudiation; it demanded, in practice, that the NLF recognize Saigon as the legitimate governing authority in the South. For while Saigon could meet with the NLF as it would meet with just another protest group — and, in fact, Saigon was willing to talk with the NLF in Paris in early 1969 — the NLF could never sit down with Thieu's emissary without implicitly acknowledging Saigon's claim to authority and risking the erosion of its own movement. The NLF's reluctance to accede in a settlement which demands any measure of recognition for Saigon has not changed in almost four years of the Vietnam negotiations.

Yet Kissinger would not endorse any arrangement that made Washington appear to have deserted the South Vietnamese. This attitude would shape Kissinger's reaction to another proposal which a number of officials felt should be offered to Hanoi in conjunction with the two tracks, a proposal which went much further in the direction of publicly undercutting America's recognition of Saigon's sovereignty — whether to suggest a cease-fire "in place" to the North Vietnamese at the Paris talks, a proposal that was being urged primarily by Washington's deputy negotiator, Cyrus Vance.

The cease-fire contemplated by Vance would not have been a standstill cease-fire in which the NLF would have to surrender its arms and give Thieu's army and police free run in the South Vietnamese countryside, but rather one in which the other side would have been ceded whole areas of the country in a way that reflected the already established patterns of territorial control. Such a cease-fire in Vietnam would have involved unusual difficulties; in a war with no lines, what did a cease-fire mean? But that was not the point. In Vance's view, the cease-fire proposal was essentially a device to get at the more fundamental issue of political rule in the South. The immediate outcome of it might well have been some form of nationwide NLF-GVN coalition operating in Saigon, but, more likely, it would have accomplished the simpler purpose of forcing the Thieu regime to take a serious attitude toward resolving its political differences with the NLF. The cease-fire would have locked Saigon into the position of having to recognize that it was not the only legitimate political force in South Vietnam, and, as the armies of Washington and Hanoi withdrew from the country, the Thieu regime would have been obligated to confront the sharing of political power with the other side. If the South Vietnamese had arrived in Paris for the scheduled November 2 meeting with Hanoi and the NLF, the cease-fire proposal, Vance said later, was "one of the first items we hoped to discuss." [8]

The internal government debate on the cease-fire proposal had not yet reached cabinet level by early November, and there was considerable doubt that the President would have approved it. The Joint Chiefs, who had always been suspicious of political limitations on their prerogatives, would have been implacable foes of any such scheme. It is also unclear, if the cease-fire had been proposed in late 1968, that Hanoi would have accepted it. Such an arrangement would have demanded that they expose their entire guerrilla infrastructure, a move that could have proven fatal should the United States and the Thieu regime have later decided to violate the cease-fire. It is quite possible that the extraordinary degree of mutual mistrust would eventually have made the entire settlement unworkable on *both* sides. Yet, at the same time, the areas of NLF predominance were generally acknowledged to include the Mekong Delta, many of the northern provinces, and large areas of the Central Highlands. And in late 1968, even after the debacle suffered by the NLF during the Tet uprising earlier in the year, the degree of NLF control was considerable; according to most reliable estimates, it amounted to nearly half of the country's population. Despite their mistrust of America and the Saigon regime, Hanoi and the NLF may well have seized on the cease-fire proposal in order to consolidate their gains in the aftermath of Tet and prepare for a final struggle against Saigon.

The cease-fire proposal was indicative of a pronounced tendency in the Harriman-Vance negotiating style: to remain visibly independent of the South Vietnamese, to be explicit in distinguishing Washington's concerns from those of Saigon, to insist that Washington prod Thieu and his advisers into cooperation with the U.S. position and hit them over the head when necessary. To Kissinger, this posture of disdain toward the South Vietnamese was inexcusable, albeit for lack of subtlety alone. Angrily, he would assail the denigration of the Saigon regime by Secretary Clifford, Ambassador Vance, and others, frequently comparing it to President Kennedy's mistreatment of de Gaulle. And one of Kissinger's first acts in preparing for office in late 1968 was explicitly to rule out the offer of a cease-fire in place to the other side. His stated reason for doing so was that the proposal, and the coalition rule of the South which might follow it, were highly unworkable. His real reasoning, more likely, was that the U.S. should not attempt directly to impose such a settlement on Saigon; thus, his judgment that "a tacit *de facto* cease-fire may prove more attainable than a negotiated one." [7]

In this setting, Kissinger began a top-to-bottom review of Johnson administration Vietnam policy shortly after his appointment by President-elect Richard Nixon in early December. And when he embarked on the review, he had already reached firm conclusions on how to handle the central issues. As a problem that had consumed his deepest thoughts and energies since late 1965, the war had already etched a clear, precise image on Kissinger's mind; as the only concrete obstacle which stood in the way of the construction of the new world order, it would demand his immediate and lasting attention. Vietnam was the area that preoccupied Kissinger the most, and it was in that area that he decided to concentrate his bureaucratic strength and cast his strongest possible influence.

Kissinger was fortunate enough to have the new President's private concurrence on most of his thoughts about Vietnam. As the evidence unfolds, it has become clear that Nixon's early pronouncements on the war did not correspond at all to his actual assessment of America's potential for victory and of Saigon's capacity to govern its own people. By far the most interesting and reliable such evidence has come from Richard Whalen, an adviser and speechwriter for Nixon during his 1968 Presidential campaign. In a recently published memoir, Whalen quotes Nixon as having said in March 1968, "I've come to the conclusion that there's no way to win the war. But we can't say that, of course. In fact, we have to seem to say the opposite, just to keep some degree of bargaining leverage." [8] It is more likely, then, that Nixon and Kissinger, sharing a largely fatalistic view of the war, were agreed that they would aim for the *façade* of an honorable withdrawal, and it appears that their initial private strategy for ending the war was a version of Kissinger's decent interval scheme.

Publicly, the two men talked about Vietnam in markedly divergent fashions. Nixon's rhetorical arena on the war was one of "pitiful, helpless giants," "the forces of totalitarianism and anarchy," "the councils of those great powers who have not yet abandoned their goals of world conquest" — in short, what one generally expected of the "old Nixon," an apparent reversion to the linguistic devices of past American administrations which had pitted the Free World against the Communist Bloc, placing the United States in a position of perpetual combat with an opponent that was more fluid if not completely illusory. By contrast, Kissinger's statements on the war were quiet and subtle, and his discussion of the "enemy" was respectful, at times almost reverential, in tone:

The chief problem in negotiations is not lack of ingenuity on our part in coming up with a formula. The chief problem in negotiations is that we are confronting a country that has fought for 25 years with great courage, but whose very quality of courage may not make it capable of visualizing a compromise.[9]

Yet the differences in their rhetoric did not reflect a disparity of opinion so much as they concealed a joint purpose. Each man appealed to a distinct constituency: Nixon, the President and politician, assuaged Middle America, the conservative wing of the electorate which had given him his most loyal and effective support. Kissinger, the diplomatic operator, spoke primarily to Hanoi, attempting in private to create an atmosphere of mutual understanding and willingness to compromise. Working in tandem, both men sought to convince the other side that if negotiation failed escalation would surely follow, and that the American people would support increasing applications of force to achieve an "honorable" settlement.

At the same time, Nixon's ideas posed a small but significant limitation on Kissinger's diplomatic activity. While both men were doubtful of America's ability to win the war, Nixon was measurably more concerned about the well-being of the Saigon regime. As a devout anti-Communist, the President was more deeply and ideologically committed to the survival of Thieu, a commitment that Kissinger, a non-ideologue and a cynical pragmatist, could never really have shared. It is improbable that Nixon authorized Kissinger to negotiate a decent interval in its most exposed and naked terms; indeed, it may even be that Kissinger — who, after all, was new in his position and unsure of his fledgling relationship with the President — did not dare state the decent interval to Nixon in such terms. As a result, it seems likely that, in his private discussions with the North Vietnamese, Kissinger did not explicitly spell out his version of the decent interval in his descriptions of the U.S. position. There could be subtle hints and nuances — indeed, there were — but Hanoi could never receive official assurances, even privately, that the U.S. would one day acquiesce in the collapse of the Saigon regime. In view of Kissinger's prior negotiating experience with Hanoi, this limitation was not a difficult one for him to accept. U.S. positions would simply convey to Hanoi the possibility, or threat, that Thieu would continue to receive substantial American support unless the other side consented to end the war on Washington's terms — a threat that was merely an implicit part of Kissinger's earlier position. As Kissinger himself would later put it:

> The reason we believe Vietnamization can have some impact on negotiations is precisely because we believe that as this happens, at least to some extent, Hanoi faces the prospect of having to deal with Saigon rather than with us, and we believe they would rather deal with us . . .
>
> The other side has fought with courage and great dedication for 25 years. They are not going to be talked out of their struggle. Unless we can create objective conditions such that [it] will look more attractive to them to settle than not to settle, there will be no negotiation.[10]

Nixon and Kissinger were completely agreed on a secondary, but nonetheless quite essential, factor of the policy: the need to neutralize antiwar sentiment in the United States. For they feared that if Hanoi seriously believed that the White House could be constrained by public opinion in this country, that if the other side felt the pattern of the French Indochina war, of crumbling spirit and demoralization in the homeland, could be repeated, then no settlement on Washington's terms would take place. The NLF would simply wait out Vietnamization, looking toward some point in the future when the American war effort would collapse of its own weight. Kissinger and the President both recognized that their first move on Vietnam must be to convince the opponent that internal criticism of the war would pose no limitations on the conduct of official policy. The early escalations in the spring of 1969, the incrusion into Laos by a contingent of U.S. Marines (Dewey Canyon I) and the first bombing of eastern Cambodia with B–52s, were conceived not only as military acts, but also as signals to Hanoi that Vietnamization and other acts of war could be made tolerable to the American public. And these escalations occurred under conditions of extreme secrecy, without arousing the domestic opposition which would have canceled the value of the signals.

With these considerations in mind, the President-elect and his adviser had thought through their ideas on Vietnam well in advance of the full-scale review Kissinger was soon to initiate. And that review was undertaken not to provide policy alternatives — the range of which Nixon was well aware — but rather to cope with the problem of bureaucratic overkill. Both Nixon and Kissinger were acutely fearful of how easily they could become immersed in enervating battles over technical detail; both of them, by nature withdrawn and instinctively insecure, were determined to be masters of their policy, to keep the bureaucratic lions at bay. In preparing the first Nixon White House record on Vietnam, Kissinger was intent on exposing the administrative apparatus which had blundered so badly under Nixon's predecessor. And the effect of the review was not only to subordinate the bureaucracy, but also to disembowel it.

Tet 1968 had left Washington's foreign policy agencies in a state of raging controversy. Rusk and Rostow, along with the Joint Chiefs, consistently argued that the opponent's offensive had been a last dying gasp, that the failure of an earlier guerrilla strategy had caused Hanoi to "throw the Little Red Book out the window" and "go for broke." The military collapse of the insurgents was imminent, these officials argued, and a breakthrough in Paris was only months away. Rigid and unbending in their attitudes, they nonetheless consituted the only group of men with regular access to the President, and their conversations with him were not apt to reflect the opposing point of view.[11]

Virtually the entire body of middle- and lower-echelon officials, on the other hand, felt strongly that Tet had been a setback for both sides, and that the overall stalemate had not changed; they cited substantial evidence to indicate that the low North Vietnamese profile was deliberate, that the guerrillas were regrouping forces and growing stronger all the time. To a certain extent, this group of officials also held a position that had hardened through years of extravagant military promises followed by no results; even if a major strategic shift had really occurred after Tet, many in this group would clearly have tended to disbelieve it. But their view, by far more accurate, had been so grossly under-represented in previous years that the consultants whom Kissinger had asked to structure the Vietnam study were particularly anxious to uncover this view and expose it to the new President.

His advocacy of the "options" system aside, Kissinger understood that the mere listing of policy alternatives was itself a stale exercise; no matter what the situation, such listings inevitably conformed to the syllogism of "blow up the world, scuttle and run, or continue the present policy." At the prod-

ding of one consultant, Daniel Ellsberg, Kissinger agreed
that in addition to an options paper on Vietnam, the new
White House staff would distribute a list of questions to be
answered separately by each foreign policy agency, questions which, in the cases of most departments, fell far outside their area of primary responsibility. In this way, Ellsberg felt, the new decision makers could confront the prevailing bureaucratic view.[12] And under scrutiny from their
institutional rivals, the most convinced hard-liners in the
government would be forced to recast their earlier views.
Even before the distribution of the questionnaire, one could
almost have written a script of the interagency battles that
would occur, such as one which took place in the Pentagon
between an army officer and a colonel from international security affairs:

> OFFICER: "I see here that you describe the South Vietnamese
> army leadership as 'cowardly.'"
> COLONEL: "That's right."
> OFFICER: "General Abrams doesn't have that in *his* answer to
> the question."
> COLONEL: "So?"
> OFFICER: "Do you think you know more about ARVN than a
> four-star general in the field?"
> COLONEL: Well, yes, as a matter of fact, yes we do."

And in its answers to the questionnaire, the military command first abandoned the "attrition" rationale for continued
American ground troop deployment in Vietnam.[13]

At the same time, the completed questionnaire did not
reach the White House until well after the execution of Vietnam policy had begun; it arrived in a large crate box early
in March, and Kissinger did not read further than the sum-
mary. The major effect of the questionnaire, instead, was to

tie up and discredit the bureaucracy itself. As a result of it Vietnam specialists in every department were tearing at each other's throats; whole agencies were in outright conflict over simple facts. Untouched by the raging conflict below, the President and his national security adviser forged ahead undaunted in pursuit of a policy that had been affirmed in private several weeks before. And from that time on, whatever studies they needed were undertaken not through the bureaucratic wrangling that had produced the first Vietnam papers, but rather within the quiet isolation of the National Security Council staff. The larger body of officials outside the White House had, by and large, been cut adrift.

As for considering the options themselves, Kissinger kept the discussion within close range of Nixon's views, reasoning that any other approach would unnecessarily complicate the formal policy decisions. And as the more limited experience of option-gathering under President Johnson had amply demonstrated, the choices to be presented would *reflect*, not *dictate*, policy preferences at the highest official level; as if to seal any doubts that this practice would continue, Kissinger decided in early 1969 to strike a unilateral withdrawal option from the document that would be considered at the first meeting of the National Security Council.[14]

In so doing, of course, Kissinger borrowed a familiar rationale; the military, after all, were already putting pressure on Nixon to revoke the Manila formula of 1966, and were similarly set against arguments for *any* troop withdrawal.[15] Yet here was an opportunity, for the first time, to make the options system work, to present a widely held but unenunciated view at the highest decision-making level, and Kissinger threw that opportunity away. Never would the new policymakers question the war-torn assumptions of U.S. intervention, never would they see Vietnam in fresh perspective. As if twenty-three years of history had suddenly been swept aside, Nixon and Kissinger were determined, anew, to salvage the appearance of a regime in Saigon.

"Another Foolish Westerner Come to Lose His Reputation to Ho Chi Minh"*

SOME TIME AFTER assuming the Presidency in January 1969, Richard Nixon spoke to a White House gathering of the National Security Council staff. After heaping abuse on the Department of State, he told the group that their job was to "watch the world." Then, turning to Henry Kissinger, Nixon said, "You and I are going to end this war."

If any foreign policy issue in the past four years has been monopolized and hoarded by the President and his national security adviser, it has been the conduct of the war in Vietnam. At the outset, no issue had been as pressing, as demanding of resolution, as the war; and since that time, no policy has been nearly as crucial to the prestige of the Presidency as well as to the international impact of the United States. It was on the war that Nixon and Kissinger staked their greatest effort and influence, and it is to the perpetuation of it that they must now answer.

There was once a time when the war was not a Nixon-Kissinger enterprise, when it was something the new administration had inherited and — so it seemed — was publicly committed to dissolve. But with the extension of American groundfighting into Cambodia, Laos, and — briefly — North Vietnam,[1] as well as the drastic escalation of air attacks all

---

* I am indebted to Neil Sheehan (quoted in David Halberstam, *Ho*) for this chapter heading.

over Southeast Asia and the mining of North Vietnam's harbors in May 1972, the war has become the central ingredient of Nixon-Kissinger policy. And it is a policy that originated not in the depths of the Pentagon, not in an overbearing bureaucracy's forward thrust, but in the clearly visible diplomatic ambitions of the President and his aides.

It is, of course, an open question whether, in early 1969, the President and Kissinger would have resolved to insure even the temporary survival of the Thieu regime if they could foresee then what they know and understand now, that their policy would unleash the political chaos and human destruction which it has caused during the past four years. Yet it was a question, curiously enough, that seems never to have occurred to them. Both men believed that a negotiated solution on moderately favorable terms was within their instant grasp, and they derived great satisfaction from the fact that their position on the war was far more reasonable than that of their immediate predecessors. After all, they did not demand that Hanoi agree to the permanency of the regime in the South; they asked simply that the regime be kept in place long enough so that its eventual collapse could not be imputed to the United States.

And they felt that by posing the double-edged threat of Vietnamization and protracted war, the United States could induce North Vietnam to make that one concession. "It just cannot be," Kissinger said after the U.S. invasion of Cambodia, "that the North Vietnamese are the first people in history that are immune to any sort of material consideration." [2] Here, in essence, was the early Nixon-Kissinger strategy: to communicate the two alternatives of settlement or endless war in such a way that the other side would give in on U.S. terms.

The President and Kissinger both believed that any increase in the Sino-Soviet rift would induce Hanoi to become more cooperative. In the early days of 1969, this consideration was instrumental in Nixon's decision to make diplomatic overtures to the People's Republic of China, a decision whose impact was not lost on the Soviet Union. And as for getting Moscow to exert pressure directly on Hanoi, Nixon and Kissinger repeatedly threatened non-cooperation on arms control and on the Mideast unless the Russians chose to intervene in their behalf. As Kissinger himself succinctly put it:

> In fact, if these people are logical at all, if one looks at the pressures on Hanoi, it isn't that Hanoi is a free agent, but when Hanoi looks at the Sino-Soviet dispute, for example, they have now fought for six years. They are completely at the mercy of the Sino-Soviet dispute. If Communist China and the Soviet Union should clash, for whatever reason, Hanoi would be finished, and everything they had fought for would be down the drain.[3]

In addition, Kissinger himself was particularly sensitive to the threat which Hanoi felt from the People's Republic of China. A sense of their history, of a millennium of Chinese occupation, has long compelled the North Vietnamese to be relentlessly suspicious of Peking; Kissinger thought the real danger perceived by North Vietnam's leaders was not encroachment by the United States, a power located 10,000 miles away, but domination by their fearsome neighbor to the north. "It is better to smell the French dung for a while," Ho had said before signing the Paris treaty of 1946, "than eat China's all our lives." [4] And Kissinger knew that Peking's emergence on the world scene, an emergence that would be ushered in by increased diplomatic contact with the United

States, would further intimidate Hanoi. After assessing all these factors, Kissinger assumed the North Vietnamese could be induced to give in to the temporary existence of an alien regime in the South.

The shortcomings of this logic are, in retrospect, particularly glaring. The North Vietnamese leaders are a group of men who have fought side by side for some forty years in pursuit of a single objective, and it should have been evident to any intelligent observer that, barring an extraordinary circumstance, they would continue with the same determination and ferocity to wage anti-imperialist war. It was fruitless to think of them as being responsive to diplomatic plaints from Moscow or Peking, because by training and temperament they are above all Vietnamese nationalists, and they have learned through long and arduous experience that they cannot depend on the major Communist powers to provide the means of their own salvation. And if they fear Peking the most, their treatment at the hands of successive Communist regimes in Moscow does not instill much more faith in them either. Their memory of having to give up their struggle against the French in the late thirties for the sake of Stalin's "united front," and their betrayal by Bulganin, who did not raise a whimper at the cancellation of the 1956 elections provided for by the Geneva accords, are still very much with them. If Hanoi's leaders now understand anything, it is the need for self-sustenance and self-reliance in their struggle against the United States, and no amount of diplomatic pressure from Moscow or Peking will change this essential fact.

If even this had been lost on Washington, it is so much simpler to see the striking naiveté of Kissinger's notion that this same group of men could again be insinuated into signing away reunification with the South, if only for two or three years, for the sake of their enemy's prestige. They could never have viewed America's involvement in their country with the same cynical, almost wry, detachment that Kissinger did; for them, the war was not something that could just be intellectualized out of existence. Kissinger may indeed have had a greater sense of the past, a more profound appreciation of world-historical forces operating in Vietnam, than any of his new-found colleagues in Nixon's retinue; but the men who led his enemy were by now themselves historical figures, men who embodied the past and who, by their very survival, reaffirmed their decades of struggle with each passing day. It was hard to imagine that these men, who had been long buffeted by conquering colonial giants and repeatedly jaded by the major powers of the Communist world, could again be shown the wisdom of compromise. But under the terms of Kissinger's strategy, Hanoi's failure to envision compromise would only lead to greater U.S. escalations and further threats of force.

There was another crucial element in Hanoi's decision-making calculus that Kissinger, quite revealingly, did not take into account: the fact that the struggle of North Vietnam and the NLF was fueled not primarily by high-level policy figures, but by broad sectors of Vietnamese society, by the committed insurgents and by those among the population who provided them with sustenance and support. Theirs was, in fact, a revolutionary war of independence, fought not by paid mercenaries but in many ways by the people themselves. Unlike the United States and Saigon, which fought their war not because of public opinion but in spite of it, the war of the Vietnamese revolutionaries was directly dependent on popular participation and involve-

ment. And even if Hanoi's leaders viewed their struggle
in a completely cold-blooded way — as a few U.S. policy
analysts would surely maintain — they could not have arbitrarily decided in early 1969 to abandon their publicly proclaimed goal of some twenty-five years' standing if only because their people would likely have been deeply resentful
of the reversal. On the two previous occasions when North
Vietnam's rulers had renounced some of their military gains
in the hope of peaceful reunification, they had encountered
considerable opposition among their own people for having
done so;[5] and, following the collapse of the Geneva agreements, they only hesitatingly decided to resort to armed
struggle once again,[6] their hesitation doubtless due in part to
their reluctance to commit their land and people to what
might evolve as another fruitless war. Now, ten years later,
after the war against the Americans had wreaked such devastation and horror in their country, after it had imposed
such overwhelming sacrifices on the Vietnamese people, was
it really possible for the leaders in Hanoi to end the war on
American terms and still live to fight another day? Would
their people again support them in waging an armed struggle for reunification with the South? Even more ominously,
would their people tolerate such manipulation from their
leaders without attempting to effect fundamental changes
in the way their society was ruled? Might the North Vietnamese leaders not risk their own overthrow by suddenly
deciding, for reasons unexplained, to give up a long and
costly struggle that they themselves had started?

Yet Kissinger did not comprehend the complexity of his
opponent's position. He did not see North Vietnam as a vast
and intricate society to whose will its leaders were in some
way responsive: in the tradition of nineteenth-century bal-

ance-of-power Europe, he saw the Vietnamese revolution as a diplomatically unitary factor, an entity whose entire foreign policy lay in the hands of a single minister of state. Much as Kissinger liked to think of himself as being free of Congress and popular opinion, unfettered by cantankerous generals and bureaucratic politics, he attributed the same simplicity of rule and response to the other side. His approach to the secret Vietnam negotiations often reflected the view that the war could be ended as soon as he successfully won over his negotiating partner from Hanoi. Yet, ironically, even if the men in the North Vietnamese politburo had grasped and sympathized with the U.S. position, and it is extremely unlikely that they did, the war would have continued because in many ways it was out of even their control. Pham Van Dong was not speaking lightly when, in a formulation that must have struck his American opponents with a feeling of bitter irony, he said, "Never Munich again, in whatever form." [7]

The only possible outcome in such a situation would be mutual and increased levels of destruction, the physical embodiment of the widening gyre, with no end in sight. The United States, of course, had wanted to wage a limited war, but their opponent was obliged to fight total war, and the thrust of Washington's strategy, should negotiations fail, was to deny that totality by increasing its own effort.

Yet initially, as does any "slow squeeze," the new administration's Vietnam policy began at a relatively low key. In view of his respect for Hanoi's tenacity on its home ground, Kissinger did not believe that Washington's principal thrust should be blindly to increase its military strength in Vietnam; he had never believed in the possibility of a "classical" military victory, and he believed now that the United States had already demonstrated its ability to prevent such a victory by the other side. He felt, instead, that it was of paramount importance to demonstrate to the North Vietnamese that the U.S. could maintain its massive presence in Vietnam for an indefinite period of time, and he thought that Hanoi, once aware that Washington was capable of an indefinite presence, would negotiate a compromise. Kissinger then decided, in complete accord with the President's views, that American domestic opinion, as the only force that could conceivably dislodge the U.S. military machine from Vietnam, was the crucial obstacle facing the new administration in early 1969. The casualty-reduction strategy which the President ordered put into effect, a strategy which called for phasing out U.S. combat missions, withdrawing large numbers of American ground troops, and beefing up the army and police of the Saigon regime, was not inspired by pure military necessity; it took place amid the stringent objections of the Joint Chiefs. Rather, it was adopted in response to the political threat which American war critics posed to the chances for compromise negotiation with the other side. Nixon and Kissinger both realized that the American public would not continue to tolerate large-scale U.S. participation in the ground war for a prolonged period of time, that casualty reduction alone could preserve their freedom to keep a sizable military force in Vietnam. Otherwise, as Kissinger would later put it, there remained the danger that public opposition to the war might flare up and "domestic dissent in this country [reach] a point where Hanoi believes that no matter what the local situation it need simply await the collapse of our domestic position . . ." [8]

Kissinger assumed, in turn, that Hanoi would relent if faced with a seemingly interminable U.S. presence, which

Washington could spice with tacit threats of escalation to insure the reception of its message. The most obvious such threat — and the one undoubtedly felt most keenly in Hanoi — was a resumption of bombing in the North; in 1969, Kissinger still felt this threat was more potent in unstated form than in its utterance, and thought it was likewise more effective when exercised unpredictably, at random, than if undertaken with any frequency or regularity. It would be difficult for Americans, who took note of these air strikes only when they occurred, to understand the terror felt by the North Vietnamese, who lived every day with the fear that the bombs might without warning fall on them again. And it was remarkable how little of this quiet blackmail would be stated publicly by U.S. leaders, who were consistently curbing their verbal behavior to avert a mass outbreak of public opposition. "I believe it is far more effective in international policy to use deeds rather than words threatening deeds in order to accomplish objectives," Nixon said at his press conference of March 5, 1969. Indeed: Four days earlier, in a move ordered by the White House without any consultation of its foreign policy departments, a move whose announcement was withheld three weeks for "security reasons," a combined force of U.S. and South Vietnamese troops began a prolonged sweep of the Ashau Valley *inside Laos*.[9] The sweep was ordered in response to a series of small Tet attacks begun six days earlier throughout South Vietnam by the other side, attacks which an NLF spokesman described as a "stern answer" to Washington's earlier proposals for mutual withdrawal. As early as the opening months of 1969, it was clear that serious talks would not begin until a fundamental shift of perspective had occurred; the new administration was set on a course of protracted war, and threats to escalate, outside the public eye. And where the White House decided to verbalize its threats, it did so privately, as in the case of a threat that preceded the invasion of Cambodia. The communication of these most important messages would occur only tacitly or privately, free of popular view.

Nixon and Kissinger clearly hoped that, after weighing the possible consequences of U.S. policy, Hanoi would break the negotiations deadlock by consenting to talk on Washington's terms. After stating their position of mutual withdrawal, American negotiators would put forward no other proposal; they would simply wait for North Vietnam and the NLF to accede to their point of view. It is true that, beyond the public relations arena, the administration did not want to lead the North Vietnamese to expect one U.S. concession after another as time passed without any movement or response from them; at the same time, Nixon and Kissinger were strangely hopeful that Hanoi's leaders would one day take stock of their efforts and decide suddenly that it was time for them to give in. Kissinger quite bluntly stated this view to the White House press corps in December 1969:

> When we talk about negotiations and the success and failure of negotiations, we tend to look at it from an Anglo-Saxon legalistic point of view; that is, we think negotiations are successful when there is a protracted period of give and take leading towards a settlement. This for better or worse is not the way the Vietnamese negotiate. The Vietnamese negotiate, or Hanoi negotiates, by adopting a posture of implacable ferocity and wanting to be paid — they consider it a concession to enter that process of give and take.
>
> Not that they don't look at that process for the place at which you make the concession. If you look at the negotiations that have taken place with the Vietnamese, over the years, you will see that every negotiation that succeeded has been pre-

ceded by a protracted stalemate that looked almost hope-
less . . .

Now, I won't insult your intelligence by saying the fact there
is a deadlock proves that they are going to settle. I am saying
that the fact that there is a deadlock does not prove that they
are not going to settle . . .[10]

But the other side would hold unswervingly to its own
position. The NLF proposal presented in Paris on May 8
was that "During the period intervening between the resto-
ration of peace and the holding of general elections, *neither*
party shall impose its political regime on the people of South
Vietnam." (Italics mine.) Dropping their earlier position
that the U.S. flatly overthrow the Saigon government, the
other side proposed that South Vietnamese groups of all political persuasions convene and set up an interim coalition
government to supervise the elections. The plan demanded
unilateral U.S. military withdrawal, and effectively called
for Washington's acquiescence in the dismantling of the
Thieu regime.

The distance between these two positions should not preclude an objective judgment of their merits. The American
proposals suggested that South Vietnam's election occur under a regime which Washington, an alien power, had in-
stalled and shored up. North Vietnam, taking a nationalist
view, insisted that the United States has no right to intervene
in the political affairs of the South, that a settlement of the
conflict must be arrived at by the Vietnamese themselves,
Northerners included. If Hanoi's terms had been met in
early 1969, the Thieu regime would have disappeared into
history; under the conditions of an all-Vietnam settlement,
the odds of success would not have favored the United
States. Yet it is difficult not to sympathize with the integrity

of Hanoi's position; it is easy to imagine that most Americans, after hearing a balanced presentation of the facts, would agree with the North Vietnamese minister, Xuan Thuy, when he said of the NLF peace plan, "Is there any formula more logical, more reasonable, more equitable, and more appropriate than this one? Is there any one more flexible?" [11]

Kissinger's objection to a coalition government reflected his own understanding that the Communists in the coalition would quickly gain predominance. True, the other side had said repeatedly that it did *not* wish to impose Communism on the coalition or on the people of the South, that their "government of national concord" would be a many-sided government in practice as well as in conception. Kissinger was extremely skeptical of this claim, and his skepticism derived from his perception that, "It is beyond imagination that parties that have been murdering and betraying each other for twenty-five years could work together as a team giving joint instructions to the entire country" [12] — in other words, that the obstacle to effective coalition rule was that basic quality of mutual antagonism and mistrust which had ruled out so much else in the Vietnam negotiations. It *was* likely that the Communists would emerge as the prime movers in the coalition rule; after all, they are the only political force in modern Vietnam that has been able to mobilize and maintain enduring support from broad segments of the population, and not one Vietnam expert, not even among those working for the government, would deny it. Why not acknowledge this reality? Because the entire purpose of U.S. policy was to show that America could defy reality, that its power would enable it to have its way in spite of the enormous political and psychological forces pitted against it. Hence the grotesque non sequitur in Kissinger's approach;

coalition was unworkable because of understandable mutual mistrust, and so America's policy should be not to withdraw but to shore up its client regime, a regime which Washington knew had even less popular support than the one which opposed it.

Here again, the principle of the decent interval won out. Kissinger's objection to coalition was not that it would obstruct legitimate political representation, but that it was too insufficient a fig-leaf to cover a U.S. withdrawal. Ironically, Hanoi and the NLF may well have offered coalition to serve as just such a fig-leaf. The other side had long held to the position that it entered the Paris talks not because it had suffered setbacks and grown weak — as many U.S. policy analysts would have had it — but because in doing so it would provide America with an "honorable" way out of the war. It appears that Hanoi and the NLF viewed their offer of a coalition government as precisely that, a convenient mask behind which the United States could extricate itself in good conscience from the war. To be sure, it was not a "decent interval" solution in Kissinger's sense of the term because it called for a visible modification in U.S. policy; and where the decent interval would have presented the other side with uncomfortable ambiguities, the coalition was a sure-fire device to guarantee NLF predominance and eventual reunification with the North. And yet, in the first few months of office, when they were most able to effect some change in the prior direction of U.S. policy, if Nixon and Kissinger had consented to coalition, there seems in retrospect a real chance that the American people and the rest of the world would have seen Washington's consent to the arrangement, and her efforts to insure its fair observance, not as a dishonorable retreat but as an adept and courageous recognition of political realities. Yet Nixon and Kissinger rejected the proposal, not because it was unjust, but because it did not provide them with *enough* of a cover. In his explanation of the President's decision to mine North Vietnam's harbors in May 1972, Kissinger spelled out the White House's objection to coalition in a most revealing fashion:

What is it that the other side is asking of us that we have rejected? The other side has asked of us . . . that the following steps must be taken:

The President of South Vietnam must resign. What is called by the other side "the machinery of oppression of the government" must be disbanded. Pacification must be stopped, which means the end of American military and economic aid. All persons who have been arrested on political grounds must be set free. Then a government should be formed which is composed of all those who favor peace, independence, neutrality and democracy, presumably, by definition, including the Communists.

In that government, in other words, the Communists would be the only organized force, since all the organized non-Communist forces would have been disbanded by definition. [To maintain that the Thieu regime constitutes "all the organized non-Communist forces" in South Vietnam is an exercise in absurdity; it cannot have escaped Kissinger's attention that Thieu has jailed or exiled many of his most popular non-Communist opponents, including his runner-up in the 1967 Presidential election, and has otherwise stilled many of the most eloquent non-Communist voices in the South.]

. . . Then this government is supposed to negotiate with the Communists a final solution. In other words, *this is only the thinnest veneer;* this government, which already contains the Communists, is then supposed to negotiate with the Provincial Revolutionary Government, which at that moment will be the only force in the country which has an army. It will be the only force in that country that has any physical strength, and it is supposed to negotiate with them a final settlement . . .

This is what we have rejected. This is what we call the imposition, *under the thinnest veneer,* of a Communist government . . . [Italics mine.] [13]

What Nixon and Kissinger objected to in the coalition proposal, then, was not the "imposition . . . of a Communist government," but the thinness of the "veneer." And to thicken the veneer, they demanded instead that the other side recognize, for the time being, the Saigon regime as the only legitimate political authority in South Vietnam.

If the President and Kissinger have done well in diplomatic gamesmanship and fancy footwork, they have been absolutely inflexible on the central issue: Nguyen Van Thieu. And the North Vietnamese, who are equally inflexible on the same issue, have shown their ability to compromise on everything else: cease-fire to follow a political settlement, safe departure for U.S. troops, even an expressed willingness to negotiate with anyone in the current Saigon regime except Thieu himself. Ironically, the crux of the current negotiations stalemate is a man for whom Kissinger privately has little, if any, respect.

True, it has been Hanoi's consistent failing to take a position which cannot be encompassed by the most "flexible" of U.S. approaches. But if extreme tactical flexibility seems a small price to pay for an end of the war, there is now another item at stake. Suspicion and distrust of U.S. motives aside, it is clear that Hanoi places a great premium on the illusion of its own prestige. For the appearance of victory is a far more important ingredient in the survival of a revolutionary power than in the continued well-being of an established colossus like the United States. The success of liberation movements in Southeast Asia and elsewhere depends far less on tangible qualities, and far more on hope and vision, than most officials in Washington can begin to imagine. It was because of his concern for U.S. credibility that Kissinger sought to deprive the Vietnamese revolutionaries of their image and prestige; yet through that denial, the American effort in Vietnam became not simply a quest for "honorable" peace, but, more essentially, a war of repression.

With the conflict so clear-cut, mutual trust and understanding between Washington and Hanoi were not in excessive supply. Yet it was largely to foster an atmosphere of understanding, it appears, that Kissinger, with the full authority of the President, began secret talks with the North Vietnamese in August 1969. It was he who, through Jean Sainteny, a personal friend and the negotiator for Paris in 1946, set up the first meeting with Xuan Thuy; and it was he who, at what associates now say was considerable bureaucratic and domestic political risk, encouraged and nurtured these contacts with the other side as well as carried them out. With the opening of these talks, Kissinger became the principal, indeed the only real actor in Washington's Vietnam diplomacy; with carte blanche from the President, he gained an independence and an autonomy that few American negotiators have ever had. It would be surprising if he did not use that autonomy to the fullest. And the available evidence indicates that he often tried very much to convey his decent interval notion to Hanoi's negotiators, that by his participation in the negotiations he sought to impress upon them that he and the President sought a quick departure from the war and were not particularly interested in the

permanent survival of the Thieu regime. He probably did
not state any of these things directly; instead, he employed
the guile and innuendo that are often the skilled diplomat's
most useful tool. To wit: One of his techniques was to begin
each meeting with the same adulatory phrases which he
would use to describe the North Vietnamese to newsmen
and friends in Washington — that they were epic people,
heroic fighters who had struggled so long and so coura-
geously, that they would be there long after the United
States had left, and that it was they who would ultimately
shape the future of Vietnam. In making these remarks, he
attempted not to be personally friendly or to convince the
other side that he was a decent fellow — we would never
hold Kissinger to something as banal and simplistic as that
— but instead to convey to Hanoi's negotiators the fact that
these sentiments were very much a part of the President's
policy. Yet in his treatment of these negotiations, Kissinger
seems to have operated under the mistaken assumption that,
if only he could convince Le Duc Tho of America's official
good will, then the war could be brought to a speedy halt.
It does not seem to have occurred to him that factors other
than Tho's esteem for his and the President's sincerity would
have entered into Hanoi's reaction to the American proposals. Our impressions must remain incomplete until the full
record becomes available on both sides, an event that does
not seem in the immediate offing. But a PRG official in Paris
told this writer that Kissinger's remarks failed to convince
the Vietnamese of his good intentions. Instead of building
confidence in the United States, these remarks would more
often cause the Vietnamese representatives to wonder about
this man Kissinger, to ask themselves how he could utter these
words and yet continue to support and represent the position

of the United States; they would simply suppose that if Kissinger meant what he said, then Washington ought to pull out of Vietnam immediately without making any demands because, really, the American client regime in Saigon was Vietnamese in name only; it represented not the best and most heroic, but the ugliest and most despicable segment of the Vietnamese.[14]

By the time of the first secret Paris meeting, U.S. policymakers were carefully watching a potentially hopeful trend in the South Vietnamese countryside: the decline in guerrilla operations and the adoption of a low military profile by the other side. As might be expected, American military leaders and other hard-liners interpreted this trend as a sign of weakness; at the same time, Kissinger and others in the White House held out the possibility that Hanoi had quietly taken a first step toward mutual withdrawal and, ultimately, some form of temporary rapprochement with Saigon. Kissinger's next move, then, was to initiate reciprocal military action which might communicate the idea of restraint or withdrawal to the North Vietnamese. At his first meeting with the North Vietnamese in Paris, Kissinger disclosed that the United States was cutting back by 20 per cent all of its bombing operations in Indochina in response to the North Vietnamese-NLF de-escalation, and urged that mutual de-escalation continue.

Yet through the fall of 1969, the ground war in the South, already at low ebb, failed to de-escalate further, and Kissinger came to the conclusion that the North Vietnamese standdown was not meant to be a reduction at all; on the contrary, he felt, the other side had made a conscious decision to "wait out" Vietnamization by blending with the populace and conserving its strength for the inevitable battle against Saigon.

And in the absence of any cooperation from the opponent, the thrust of Washington's policy would be aimed at military success; as Kissinger himself had written, "If Hanoi insists on total victory, the war must continue." [15]

The outcome of this evaluation was Nixon's speech of November 3, a highly charged emotional appeal to the nation in which he attacked Hanoi for its alleged inflexibility on negotiations and called for public support of his war policy. In effect, the speech was a declaration of continued U.S. military action in Vietnam, laced with the threat of "strong and effective measures" if the other side should broaden its own combat efforts. Aside from a reference to an unspecified withdrawal deadline, Nixon mentioned no new plan for ending the war; instead, he chided his domestic opponents in familiar jingoisms that would be overshadowed only by his near-hysterical tirade announcing the invasion of Cambodia the following May. "North Vietnam cannot defeat or humiliate the United States," he said. "Only Americans can do that." And though the rhetoric was the President's own, the intellectual rationale of the policy contained in his speech had been carefully laid out by Kissinger and two members of his staff.

It seems evident, in retrospect, that both Nixon and Kissinger felt certain during this period that their threats against North Vietnam would succeed, and that the United States would be able to withdraw completely from Vietnam within a year or slightly longer. At a press conference September 26, Nixon had said, "Once the enemy recognizes that it is not going to win its objectives by waiting us out, then the enemy will negotiate and we will end this war before the end of 1970." At a background press briefing accompanying the

November 3 speech, Kissinger answered a reporter's question about further possible U.S. troop withdrawals with the strong implication of a one-year deadline:

I would like to stress this, ladies and gentlemen: We will not be justified before the American people by the numbers we withdraw and the date we withdraw them, *but by how it will come out a year from now.* We will withdraw the number of forces we responsibly can over as short a period of time as we responsibly can. But we are not going to engage in a numbers game or in a competition in escalation of estimates . . . [Italics mine.] [16]

With the use of such innuendo, the President and Kissinger deceived the public, and, perhaps more dangerously, they also deceived themselves. Given their open-ended policy, it was ludicrous to imply possible withdrawal dates unless they were absolutely sure, which they could never have been, that their threats would work. And as a result of their extravagant predictions, large numbers of Congressional and public critics, who would not have tolerated a plan for endless involvement, were willing to withhold judgment. The result, as events unfolded the following spring, was that the United States became more deeply mired than ever in a war that even Kissinger recognized it could not possibly "win."

Yet the President, who had always disliked the idea of considering Vietnam a "lost cause," began to depart from his earlier cautionary thinking on how effectively America could control events in the war. As 1970's dry season opened with an increase of North Vietnamese activity in Laos and South Vietnam, Nixon appears to have grown irascible and frustrated at the opponent's determination to continue fighting. At the same time, his earlier perception of the war seems to have been worn away by the internal bureaucratic propaganda so typical of Washington's assessments on Vietnam, the pacification statistics and the "kill" ratios that are impressive when measured against their own criteria but are largely irrelevant in the concrete circumstances of the war. It also seems that Nixon committed that fatal error so common in Washington's tortured perceptions of its opponent in Vietnam — in thinking that the stand-down of the previous fall and winter was really a sign of weakness, that the other side had been irreparably defeated at Tet and that, contrary to his own thinking in March 1968, the other side was increasingly vulnerable and was continuously losing ground. And, if that was so, then a breakthrough in Paris *could* be brought about by quick and decisive American military pressure. Nixon became increasingly isolated from that body of opinion within the government which argued for a withdrawal deadline or some other like measure to make the Paris negotiations work. And Kissinger, as one who believed in a policy of threat, upheld Nixon's position even though he and the President envisioned vastly different outcomes, for the policy of threat acknowledged a willingness to resort to the same measures that Nixon would have been somewhat quicker and more eager to use. In that sense, Kissinger provided invaluable intellectual support for the President, and made possible Nixon's isolation.

There is a group of officials who feel that Washington's remaining internal resistance to escalation collapsed completely in early March, that Cambodia really crystallized a month and a half in advance, when North Vietnamese troops began an assault on the Plain of Jars in Laos. Kissinger immediately convened the Laos subgroup of the Washington Special Action Group — the body chaired by Kissinger that meets constantly during crisis situations — and asked the officials in it to consider sending the artillery battalions of the Royal Thai Army to the aid of General Vang Pao's CIA-supported Armée Clandestine, which had fallen under considerable pressure in the area of Lon Chenh. Through eight meetings on Laos, the WSAG line held; all the departments — State, Defense, CIA, even the Joint Chiefs — were united in opposition, for varying reasons, to the use of the Thai artillery battalions in Laos. At the ninth, a tough, beleaguered Kissinger left the meeting, dashed into the President's office, reappeared, and proclaimed, "The President has ordered that they go."

The sudden overthrow of Prince Sihanouk in Cambodia on March 18 threw Washington's policy into a state of unremitting turmoil. It seems evident that the White House had little if any warning that the coup would take place, that, as Kissinger said the day after the President's April 30 speech, "these are developments which we, A, did not plan, and B, did not foresee, which puts us into good company, because Hanoi also did not foresee this." [17] And perhaps the most important asset for the White House in those days after the coup would have been a degree of expertise on the political and military situation inside Cambodia, expertise which the President and his advisers sorely lacked. Yet no clear-headed thinking ever developed in the White House on Cambodia because Kissinger, assessing the coup and its aftermath a "crisis" matter, placed it in the hands of that highly unreflective decision-making body, the Washington Special Action Group.

Hanoi, it turned out, did not act on Cambodia in a crisis context, although it did proceed with unusual caution. For years, the neutralist regime of Prince Sihanouk had permitted the North Vietnamese to make eastern Cambodia a staging area for their operations in the South, and to use the port of Sihanoukville for the resupply of their forces in and around the Mekong Delta. But Sihanouk was also a fierce nationalist, and in the year preceding the coup he had clamped down on Hanoi to limit its territorial prerogatives in his country. He was primarily interested in eliciting a firm commitment that North Vietnamese forces would leave Cambodia at the conclusion of the war, and in pursuit of that commitment, he had begun negotiations with Hanoi and closed Sihanoukville, hoping to use it as a bargaining chip in the talks. Nor did he register a protest when U.S. planes began to bomb North Vietnamese emplacements in Cambodia in March 1969.

After the coup, the North Vietnamese made efforts to sustain these contacts with Sihanouk's successor, Lon Nol. They appear to have been primarily interested during this period not in overthrowing the new government, or even in joining with Cambodian Communists, but in ascertaining whether Sihanouk's arrangements with them would be allowed to continue.[18] At the same time, they feared, correctly, that Lon Nol, an unreconstructed right-wing strongman, would be more interested in dealing with Saigon or Washington than with Hanoi; they also understood that the U.S. military command in Vietnam, which had long and obsessively argued that it should be allowed to assault the North Vietnamese sanctuaries inside Cambodia, might now be given permission to do so. Underlying Hanoi's concern was the fact that its military strength in the delta had seriously declined in recent months, that an American sweep of its Cambodian sanctuaries would cut its remaining supply lines and render its physical posture in the South increasingly untenable. As a result, the North Vietnamese decided to firm up their position in Cambodia by making their border areas contiguous and, then, by expanding their lines slightly westward. The opponent had no unmistakably discernible ambitions in Cambodia other than to insure its own safety; true, North Vietnamese forces fought Lon Nol's army fifteen miles from Phnom Penh, but their movements occurred entirely within a border context, as well as in response to a series of attacks which Lon Nol almost immediately launched against them.

Even if Hanoi's actions were not known in crystal clear detail, its general posture was quite familiar to Cambodian specialists in the State Department and intelligence analysts at State and elsewhere. But little of this was known to Kissinger; he had become so immersed in details of other issues that, with Cambodia, he lost his ability to arbitrate and became a victim of the events themselves. Throughout March and early April, he struggled furiously to acquire knowledge of the ripening crisis, but he had already sown his predicament by failing beforehand to anticipate the possibility of it. And with that failure, he lost a control of the process that he never quite regained. His depiction of the coup five months later is a striking illustration of how shallow his grasp of the Cambodian situation really was:

> First of all, let's understand who Lon Nol is. The Lon Nol Government is the Sihanouk Government minus Sihanouk. This is not a group of outsiders who came in there and overthrew the existing government; this is the government that Sihanouk appointed, that he left behind when he went off to France for two months, and Lon Nol and Matak, the two key people, are his appointments. They are not usurpers.[19]

Sihanouk minus Sihanouk indeed: the only differences being that, where peace once existed, war now raged throughout all of Cambodia's territory, that Phnom Penh now dealt with Washington, Saigon, and Taipei instead of with Peking, Hanoi, and the NLF, that in contrast to the minimal American presence in Sihanouk's Cambodia, the new national government was virtually dependent for its survival on massive U.S. military and economic aid, and on all the amenities — CIA agitation, strong "internal security" measures, a nationwide police apparatus, etc., etc. — which extensive American involvement frequently brings with it to that general area of the world. Beyond the gross misrepresentation in this statement, one wonders how Kissinger would react to the proposition that if Nguyen Van Thieu were suddenly deposed from South Vietnam's Presidency, the result would be a Thieu government minus Thieu.

President Nixon, too, felt pressures that egged him on toward drastic escalation. The opponent had begun an offensive in Laos and, by early April, had stepped up its activity in South Vietnam. At home, Congressional majorities had slighted him on the Family Assistance Plan and the Supreme Court nomination of Judge Harrold Carswell. In Moscow, the Soviet government had decided to send Russian pilots into Egypt, and had deadlocked the United States in the strategic arms talks. Whipsawed by this hostile environment, Nixon was more inclined than usual to see North Vietnamese activity in Cambodia as a threat to Saigon's western flank. And Kissinger, ill-informed about the crisis and already in broad agreement with the President's strategy, was not prepared to disabuse Nixon of his thinking. One senior State Department official characterized Kissinger during this period as

. . . not a man who appeared to be in a situation so fluid that he could weigh in on one side; he was importantly curtailed. He still demonstrated confidence that, within that limitation, he could be objective. But he was under the lash because he *knew* how the President thought. He really wasn't interested in spending a lot of time on the political side, not a lot on the restraint side. At most, he was willing to consider limiting the most extreme kind of military actions . . . On anything, he should talk with the President for five months before the thing reaches a crisis point, so he could plan some of his own ideas, his own restraints, and get them into the President's mind as his own. But now, he seemed to be acknowledging the conclusion that things had already gone far, that the President had a strong mind-set.

In an important sense, Cambodia grew out of the flaws in the decision-making structure that Kissinger himself had evolved. By isolating and demoralizing the civilian bureaucrats who favored unilateral withdrawal or something approximating it, Kissinger insured that they would not fill the role on Cambodia which they might otherwise have played. And by having cast aside since 1969 all recommendations of the Joint Chiefs as "factors to be taken into account," he made certain that if they wanted something badly enough they would *really* fight for it. A passive, disinterested civil service abdicating to a forceful and united military ushered in the decision to invade Cambodia.

The decision arose in a frightfully limited period of time. Soon after the coup, Washington had suspended all military activity in Cambodia; but by mid-April, the North Vietnamese were fighting Cambodian troops, and the U.S. command resumed its Cambodian operations, this time in Lon Nol's support. On April 20, Nixon announced the withdrawal of 150,000 American troops to take place over a period of one year, giving himself the opportunity to suspend withdrawals in the coming months should he so desire.[20] Even then, the final crisis had not really yet begun: Kissinger told reporters in a briefing before the April 20 speech that

> . . . our expectation is that the Viet Cong and the North Vietnamese will be operating on the basis of a more protracted warfare strategy with occasional high points and less of the massive onslaughts of the Tet offensive. So, we will not be surprised if there are occasional high points over the next few months, but we do not expect the massive, Tet-like attack.[21]

This calm, measured assessment did not jibe well with Kissinger's claim eleven days hence that the North Vietnamese, shortly after the President's speech, "debouched out of these sanctuaries in a totally unambiguous manner and penetrated more deeply into Cambodia . . ."[22] It seems plausible, in fact, that Kissinger did not believe the later judgment as fully as the President, that he realized the military had seized this opportunity to press its Cambodian proposals on the White House with greater conviction than ever before. But he and Nixon had already turned a trick that few other officials, even at the highest levels, were told of at the time. Shortly after the April 20 speech, the President's warning of "strong and effective measures" was elucidated privately to the other side;[23] several officials have told this writer that the warning was carried to the North Vietnamese in Paris by Kissinger himself. No matter what the extent of the opponent's "debouchery," both Kissinger and the President felt strongly that the U.S. had to respond; and in view of Nixon's strong preference for the ground action, Kissinger was inclined to go along.

But it is still not enough to say that Kissinger's commitment to some form of action, combined with the appeal to Nixon of the military's views, induced Kissinger to agree passively with the plan to invade. Kissinger knew that an invasion would mark a qualitative departure from the more low-key policy of threat he had long advocated, that it would commit the South Vietnamese and the United States to some degree of long-term military responsibility inside Cambodia, that Vietnamization would have to be extended and America's involvement in the war prolonged. He feared that all of these outcomes, once recognized by the American public, might lead to the destruction of public morale at home. Yet his stepping aside at the end of April did not stem from powerlessness. After all, he had successfully concentrated his major efforts on Vietnam policymaking since the very beginning of Nixon's Presidency, and he would have asserted himself quite effectively if he had disagreed with policy he saw evolving toward the April 30 speech.

The answer to this perplexing question may never be found. Yet the likeliest clue lies in the private threat which followed the President's April 20 speech. It would be surprising if the North Vietnamese responded in a civil and restrained manner to the threat which Kissinger uttered to them. And it would be equally surprising if Kissinger emerged from an acrimonious negotiating session confident that U.S. policy was sufficiently coercive in tone and effect, or that *any* meaningful verbal rapport existed with the other side. To Kissinger, the real answer to the private U.S. threat came not at his meeting with the North Vietnamese in Paris, but in declarations by Prince Sihanouk and others of a Cambodian government in exile — declarations which were also broadcast by Radio Hanoi to North Vietnamese troops inside Cambodia. One such declaration came at the Summit Conference of the Indochinese Peoples held on April 24 and 25 in "a locality of the Laos-Vietnam-China" border area. The conference, attended by Prime Minister Pham Van Dong, Prince Sihanouk, and the leaders of the NLF and Pathet Lao, sealed Hanoi's recognition of Sihanouk as the legitimate Cambodian head of state. It asserted:

> The Cambodian, Lao, and South Vietnamese parties affirm that their combat objectives are independence, peace, neutrality, the prohibition of the presence of all foreign troops and military bases on their soil, nonparticipation in any military alliance, prohibition of the use of their territories by any foreign country for the purpose of aggression against other countries . . . The people of the Democratic Republic of Vietnam fully respect these legitimate aspirations and unreservedly support the struggle for these lofty objectives.[24]

Were these declarations a blueprint for protracted Southeast Asian war? Almost certainly. Were they proof that the purpose of the North Vietnamese troops in Cambodia in April 1970 was to overthrow Lon Nol? That, of course, is far from clear, but Kissinger took them that way. Personally piqued at again being rebuffed in negotiations with the North Vietnamese, Kissinger accepted these declarations as tangible proof of Hanoi's motives:

> . . . We did not make the decision to go into the base areas until we were persuaded on the basis of intelligence reports *and our analysis of the situation* that they had made the decision to go deeper into Cambodia to set up a contiguous territory in which they could establish the National Liberation Front; in other words, that they were acting for purposes that were relatively independent of our action.
> We have rather conclusive evidence that this decision — in fact, we had overwhelming evidence — had been taken.[25] If

you look at the fact that they had moved toward establishing a provisional government before we moved, and if you consider that it is inconceivable that they would establish that unless they were imagining getting some contiguous territory with some provincial capital from which it could operate, I think their public actions support what we have really overwhelming independent evidence for. [Italics mine.] [26]

With Cambodia, Nixon-Kissinger policy became not one of simple threat, but one of coercion and brute force. The decision of April 1970 laid the groundwork for the U.S.-South Vietnamese invasion of Laos in February 1971, as well as for the drastic escalation of air attacks all over Southeast Asia, and, finally, the mining of North Vietnam's harbors in May 1972. But retrospectively, Kissinger viewed the invasion as a brilliant success. Internal government studies would confirm his early impression that the invasion had seriously hampered North Vietnamese operations in the delta and throughout southern Vietnam. He also conjectured, several weeks later, that "Cambodia seems to have exacerbated the division between Communist China and the Soviet Union," [27] causing Peking to condemn Moscow's "adventurism" in the Mideast and further undermining Hanoi's resolve. And what emerged from these impressions was a man who had become, like the Black Moor, more Venetian than the Venetians, an intellectual whose last vestige of independence in thought and judgment had been subverted by the relentless inner logic of Washington's giant propaganda machine:

In Cambodia, the South Vietnamese Army, to everybody's surprise, actually defeated the North Vietnamese Army whenever they fought against each other. So in a conventional war the South Vietnamese Army has now become quite good . . .[28] if the South Vietnamese develop and continue to develop the governmental vitality of which they are capable, then I think they have a reasonable chance. And if, in turn, Hanoi recognizes that it faces at least a protracted war, and at worst perhaps an indefinite and inconclusive one, then a situation may develop very similar to the Middle East, in which both parties decide that however much they dislike each other, some sort of a modus vivendi has to be found . . .[29]

And after Cambodia, the policy became one of a five-year decent interval,[30] which cannot in political or military terms be considered an interval at all. As Washington's acquiescence — to state it mildly — in Thieu's "re-election" of October 1971 demonstrated clearly, Nixon and Kissinger were dedicated beyond all bounds of cost or political decency to the preservation of the current Saigon regime. Even during this period, Kissinger would vastly have preferred to end the war by negotiation — but negotiation on American terms. Otherwise, the war would rage onward: "What is the fallback position if negotiations do not work or the fallback position if Vietnamization doesn't work?" Kissinger once asked rhetorically. "We don't believe that is going to happen." [31]

With this unabashedly optimistic assessment of America's power position in the war, there began a new phase of Vietnam diplomacy, a phase during which the U.S. negotiating stance continued to harden until Washington's confidence was shattered by the great North Vietnamese offensive of April 1972. This period took shape with the proposal in October 1970 of an Indochina cease-fire in place — *the very course of action that Kissinger and the President had rejected almost two years before.* And their willingness to propose it in late 1970 reflected their feeling that, with their aid, Saigon's rule had become firmly entrenched throughout South Vietnam's major cities and throughout most of the countryside. Ever since the proposal was made, Kissinger has stressed repeatedly that he had great hopes for its success, that he felt there was a real chance that the Indochina cease-fire was a proposition in which Hanoi might show interest; indeed, the proposal of the cease-fire followed its private urging and endorsement by influential critics of the war — including Cyrus Vance, who, as deputy negotiator in 1968, had originated the proposal — critics who told Kissinger and other officials that they were convinced the cease-fire was something the other side could accept. And, if accepted, it would have enabled the United States to withdraw with the sure knowledge that Saigon would not collapse in the aftermath of the withdrawal.

Yet what seemed an ideal solution for Kissinger confronted the other side with even greater drawbacks than had Washington's earlier proposals. Linked as it was to a one-year mutual withdrawal, and lacking any promise of a political settlement beyond a call for the reconvening of the Geneva conference, the proposal demanded in effect that the other side also temporarily recognize the Saigon regime. Even at times when their power position in the South had been greater, the North Vietnamese had always rejected any proposal — and that meant *every* proposal — which had called on them to legitimize the Thieu regime; and now, with their strength in the South at an all-time low, could they realistically have been expected to stop fighting, surface their entire guerrilla infrastructure, and accede to the provisional authority of Saigon?

By asking the other side to expose its networks of communication and control along with recognizing Saigon, at a time when it was still feeling the effects of the supply shortage resulting from the U.S. invasion of Cambodia the previous

May, the United States was not easing or liberalizing its negotiating approach; it was hardening it. And Washington
fully understood that, at the time of the proposal, the North
Vietnamese were at a unique power disadvantage; as Kissinger himself conceded days after the public offer, "The
reason we could not do it before was because our studies
showed that the results of a cease-fire under the conditions
obtaining six months ago might have been catastrophic." [32]
Hanoi's long-standing position was that a cease-fire must
follow a political settlement; for that reason, in fact, they
may well not have accepted the cease-fire in late 1968, even
though a cease-fire proposal at the earlier date would have
gone much further than the 1970 proposal in implicitly defin-
ing a political settlement that was favorable to Hanoi. Now,
at a moment of extreme weakness, the North Vietnamese
were being asked to accept a cease-fire *in advance of* a political settlement. For these reasons it is tempting to suppose
that the White House made the offer simply out of malice,
because the proposal had the effect of making a mockery of
the negotiations and adding to the President's domestic and
international support in his continuation of the war.

Yet the proposal more likely reflected Washington's continued inability to comprehend the unusual nature of Hanoi's
situation. In traditional power politics, an accretion of
strength bestows the right to toughen one's demands and add
weight to one's negotiating position so that the other side
will find it more burdensome. Yet such an approach only
compounded Hanoi's mistrust and animosity. And by the
time the President and Kissinger had grasped the hardness
of their own position, and proposed a scheme that implied
political gains for Hanoi — a cease-fire in exchange for a
four-month withdrawal — a North Vietnamese offensive had

seized control of many key territories in South Vietnam and verged on winning even more. And even at that late hour, Nixon and Kissinger left unclear what kind of a cease-fire — a cease-fire in place or a requirement that Hanoi's troops withdraw back into North Vietnam — they were offering. As a result, in order even to explore the offer, the other side would have had to halt its offensive and engage in prolonged discussions simply to understand what kind of cease-fire was meant. Yet throughout the period following the 1970 proposal, Kissinger simply would not understand that the notion of a cease-fire was acceptable to Hanoi not in the context of who was up or down in the power struggle, but in the context of a political settlement, that a cease-fire could not be used as a device to solve the basic negotiating differences of the two sides; it could only take effect once those differences had been settled. Kissinger's assertion that "the cease-fire is not in itself an issue in the negotiations, the principle of a cease-fire," [33] was symptomatic of his inability to understand that Hanoi would not stop fighting without some guarantee of an equitable settlement; if it had, it may never have been able to start fighting again should it have been betrayed. In his assertion about the non-controversiality of the cease-fire, Kissinger might just as well have said, "self-determination is not itself an issue in the negotiations, the principle of self-determination."

From late 1970 until the North Vietnamese offensive of spring 1972, the White House concentrated on bolstering the South Vietnamese regime in the absence of its ability to negotiate an end to the war. Some of its methods were quite violent: the heavy bombing and abortive prisoner rescue raid in North Vietnam in November 1970, the tragicomic South Vietnamese operations in Laos in early 1971, and the air strikes against the North which began en masse last December and have continued at a huge level up to the present day. Another, and probably the most meaningful, expedient was a diplomatic one: the rapprochement with the People's Republic of China, which accelerated rapidly after the beginning of 1971 and burst on the public scene with Nixon's speech of last July 15. Certainly a major goal of the Peking summit was to demoralize Hanoi by widening the Sino-Soviet split, but even if this were to fail, Kissinger had another object in mind. As he told a group of visiting reporters at the White House last September, "What we are doing now with China is so great, so historic, that the word 'Vietnam' will be only a footnote when it is written in history."

On the same occasion, Kissinger said that the Vietnam negotiations as yet showed no sign of working, that he and the President would give negotiations only a few more months' chance for success. The result, and the admission, of their failure was Nixon's speech of last January 25, when the President disclosed the fact of the secret negotiations and stated the last offer the United States had privately made. The offer was a barely disguised rehash of a position the North Vietnamese had repeatedly turned down: internationally supervised elections in South Vietnam with President Thieu resigning four weeks in advance, plus a cease-fire in place and a guarantee of U.S. withdrawal after the reinstatement, we may suppose, of the Thieu regime. And the only real innovation in the proposal was that it reflected some awareness of Hanoi's domestic position; if they had decided to accept the offer, North Vietnam's leaders could at least have told their people that they had succeeded in forcing Thieu's prior resignation. But again, the only effect of the disclosure was a public relations victory for the White House — "composing the domestic disharmony," as Kissinger expressed it in his press conference the following day.

As late as February 1972, the administration clearly felt that the war had been won, and Kissinger was confident that the goal he once set for America's Vietnam policy some six years before had finally been met. The 1972 State of the World Message proclaimed without a trace of modesty, "Vietnam no longer distracts our attention from the fundamental issues of global diplomacy or diverts our energies from priorities at home." [34] And as a last ritual, the President withdrew his representative from the sterile public sessions at Paris, berating the other side for making the talks a "propaganda" forum and asserting they would not be resumed until Hanoi and the NLF had pledged "serious" talks — which, presumably, meant talks on American terms.

North Vietnam's answer to this year-and-a-half phase of Washington's Vietnam diplomacy was the spring offensive of 1972. Within the span of a few weeks, Hanoi had achieved what Washington's three-and-a-half-year war policy had been designed to prevent: the seizure of several large cities including the provincial capital of Quang Tri, entrenchments around Kontum in the Central Highlands and An Loc near Saigon, amounting to the critical demoralization and near destruction of the Saigon regime. Washington's only response was one that, besides being militarily ineffective, had been rejected even in the previous administration as being dangerously provocative toward the Soviet Union: the mining of North Vietnam's harbors, coupled with renewed bombings on Hanoi, Haiphong, and the rest of the country.

The action posed considerable risks of a confrontation with Moscow at a time when a scheduled U.S.-Soviet summit was only two weeks off; and although Moscow's leaders finally decided that the signing of the long-awaited strategic arms limitation agreement with Washington was too high a priority to sacrifice in protest against a humiliation that was a humiliation in name only, the events of May had nonetheless demonstrated that the Vietnam war was still very much a factor in U.S. policy, and that, if the war continued, it could well "distract our attention from the fundamental issues of global diplomacy or divert our energies from priorities at home." And the effectiveness of the North Vietnamese attacks suggested that if Washington did not quickly withdraw, it might be driven out of Southeast Asia when the Saigon regime was destroyed by force.

In the weeks following the U.S. mining operation and the heavy renewed bombings in Vietnam, the opponent's offensive ground to a sudden halt, and many American observers began to say what had so frequently — and so mistakenly — been said through so many years before; that the "enemy" had really gotten it this time, that he had finally sustained a fatal military blow and that there would at last be "peace" in Vietnam, a peace that had been bought with the blood of a generation of Vietnamese. But there was still another possible explanation for Hanoi's sudden inactivity, an explanation that would be by far the more realistic in the context of past history: that the other side was merely lying in wait, preparing to strike once again. The possibility of another offensive in the fall of 1972 became increasingly credible amid newspaper reports late in June that Nixon had sent a message to President Thieu on a matter that concerned him greatly: rumors of a North Vietnamese attack in October, weeks before the American Presidential election. And Thieu's answer, according to the reports, was that he could not rule out the possibility of an October offensive.

Yet what of President Nixon's repeated assertions that the United States would never suffer defeat? What means would Nixon and Kissinger turn to if all their earlier measures failed and North Vietnamese success seemed imminent? Leveling Hanoi and Haiphong? Bombing the North's irrigation dikes? Such acts would cause mass murder and enormous destruction, but they would not stop the war in the South. There would be only one alternative left: the use of tactical nuclear weapons to rout the North Vietnamese armies from positions in South Vietnam.

Kissinger had observed frequently during his career that tactical weapons could be effective in destroying conventional armies that massed for attacks on the ground. He had also postulated that if their use were circumscribed by clearly defined territorial limitations, it probably would not lead to a general nuclear war. One can now almost hear President Nixon rationalizing the use of limited nuclear weapons to defend the South: "This action is being undertaken in full consultation and with the full approval of President Thieu and the government of the Republic of Vietnam. This is not an aggressive action; it is a defensive action to protect seventeen million people from having a Communist government imposed on them by the international outlaws of North Vietnam. We seek no wider war . . ."

Would further American escalation in the war again risk confrontation with the Soviet Union? If that escalation involves the use of nuclear weapons, there can be little doubt that it would. And if history serves as any guide, the current military measures in effect against North Vietnam will not bring the war to an end. Of this, there is even less doubt;

the goal of a forty-year revolution will never be abandoned, and it would strain one's credulity, as well as one's sympathy for a just and human cause, to believe the struggle will now be given up by a people whose leader once wrote, in a moment of supreme anguish:

> Without the cold and desolation of winter
> There could not be the warmth and splendour of spring.
> Calamity has tempered and hardened me,
> And turned my mind into steel.[35]

Conclusion

HENRY KISSINGER'S FAILURE of perception on Vietnam transcends the collapse of a single policy. It strikes at the heart of Kissinger's approach to international relations. And his failure is only a dramatic expression of all the mistakes and unjustified assumptions which have flawed Kissinger's view of the modern world.

Despite his rapid appreciation of Vietnam as a fruitless and unwinnable war, Kissinger insisted that an "honorable" departure — or something resembling it — was essential to preserve American credibility. In pursuit of that mirage, the United States has actually shattered much of its credibility as a rational and sensible operator on the world scene. Despite Kissinger's declared objective of a non-ideological American policy, Vietnam has demonstrated how a supposedly non-ideological quest for credibility has translated quickly to an obsessive and fanatical rigidity that can only be captured in ideological terms. And despite Kissinger's expectation that the Nixon administration's Vietnam policy would demonstrate America's continued ability to act as the guardian of international politics, the paramount lesson of Vietnam continues to be that America must modify its global objectives, must recognize that it cannot have its way on every occasion in every area of the world. And Vietnam demonstrates forcefully that if America does not recognize this herself, then the recognition will be inflicted by others.

In a human sense, it is no less tragic that a victim of Nazi Germany has helped implicate America so deeply in her present plight, that a man who, like Ivan Karamazov — a figure for whom he could not but have harbored sympathy — was heartbroken at a young child's undeserved tears, and wished to see the lion lie down with the lamb, has now come full circle and administers a system that for many, such as the Vietnamese, is as grotesque and brutal as was that from which he himself once escaped so long ago. Yet it is the essence of tragedy that the circle cannot be halted and, if that is so, then by his actions Kissinger will have devalued the very concepts he once wished to uphold, and he will have exploded the very balance of forces that he had long sought so fervently to defend.

Afterword

FOUR MONTHS after these last words were set down, the Vietnam negotiations entered their final and most Byzantine stage. By all accounts, the bargaining began in earnest when Hanoi agreed to drop its demand that Thieu be removed before substantive talks took place. Clearly, the other side was influenced by what it perceived as a forthcoming Nixon landslide and decided in late summer 1972 to strike the best available compromise with Washington so that the war would not continue four more years. Yet Hanoi would settle only if the final agreement were to leave the political future of the South completely ambiguous; only if, in other words, the U.S. were correspondingly willing to drop its demand for the perpetuation of the Saigon regime.

Since the U.S. position had long contemplated the eventual overthrow of Saigon, the way toward a negotiated agreement was open at last—or so it seemed to Nixon and Kissinger. The nine points were worked out in Paris providing for U.S. withdrawal, omitting mention of Hanoi's troops in the South, permitting Thieu to remain in power but establishing a joint political body—the Natonal Council of Reconciliation and Concord—to assume many vital governmental functions, including the all-important mandate to set up elections for a new government. With some perfunctory tidying up—American POW's to be released immediately, Veitnamese prisoners to be freed by negotiated agreement within roughly 90 days—Kissinger could almost have declared with justice that, as he said in his now-famous declaration of October 26, "peace is at hand."

But not quite. Kissinger and the President had not yet enunciated any concessions. Despite the obvious steps toward compromise made and acknowledged by Hanoi, the White House was still saying that no corresponding adjustments had been made in Washington. It did not want to "admit" any failure. Kissinger described the nine points, in his October 26 news conference, not as a compromise pact but as a virtual surrender by the North: "We believe that an agreement is within sight on the May 8 proposals of the President and some adaptations of our January 25 proposals, which is just to all parties." These two sets of proposals had both been made to Hanoi in the President's characteristically insulting fashion—one along with Nixon's self-serving disclosure of Kissinger's top-secret talks with Le Duc Tho, and the second along with Nixon's announcement that North Vietnam's waters were being mined. Each set of proposals had earlier been loudly rejected by the other side. And yet here was Kissinger telling the nation that the North Vietnamese were going to settle on precisely those terms!

Very few observers clearly understood the proposed agreement that Kissinger described on October 26—a circumstance which later enabled the White House to perpetrate a clever charade. The nine-point draft was not a hard-and-fast set of terms, but rather a vague statement of principle which deliberately left many of the central issues unresolved. As Kissinger himself acknowledged, the nine points were based on a separation of political and military matters; in that way, each party could set aside certain of its fixed objectives and "agree not to agree" on the irreconcilable differences of principle that had fueled the war.

On the central issue, political power in the South, Hanoi and the NLF were dropping their long-standing insistence that Thieu be removed before a settlement was signed; the U.S., in turn, would not demand that Thieu remain in power for longer than 90 days. The political arrangements in the South would be ambiguous; if Thieu were later to be overthrown, Washington could say that the old Saigon regime, and Saigon alone, was to blame. And if the U.S. carried out its promised withdrawal, along with its tacit pledge not to commit itself further to the maintenance of Saigon, Hanoi and the NLF would later have an excellent chance to realize their own long-standing goal: the removal of Thieu and the birth of an independent, united Vietnam.

After November 7, however, Nixon and Kissinger significantly toughened their negotiating position. The ambiguities in the accord must be done away with, they decided; and if the other side refused to cooperate, then Washington, now clear of the election, could employ vast military means to enforce its objectives. This strategy took shape when Kissinger returned to Paris in November and reverted to his rigid stance of earlier years. There were TWO Vietnams; Hanoi must cease support of the NLF even as Washington continued its assistance to Saigon; this was to be no makeshift solution, but, as

Kissinger would announce, "a peace that had a chance of lasting." These changes in the U.S. position became evident when Kissinger reappeared before the press on December 16 to explain the recent collapse in Paris; this he did, of course, by placing full blame on Hanoi. Regardless, it was clear that Washington, not Hanoi, had backtracked from the October document. The ambiguities about political power in the South would have to be removed if the treaty were to be signed; " . . . we wanted some reference in the agreement, however allusive, however indirect, which would make clear that the TWO PARTS of Vietnam would live in peace with each other and that neither side would impose its solution on the other by force" (emphasis mine). Despite a prior U.S. pledge to cease interference in the internal affairs of Vietnam, Kissinger announced that Washington was still committed to a non-Communist government in Saigon; ". . . we will not make a settlement which is a disguised form of continued warfare and which brings about, by indirection, what we have always said we would not tolerate." Kissinger even went so far as to say that Hanoi must refrain from any involvement, political or military, in South Vietnam; ". . . we cannot accept the proposition that North Vietnam has a right of constant intervention in the South." Confronted with these proposed changes, Hanoi followed suit and began to back away from the agreed-on document—standard diplomatic procedure when the other party to negotiations has already done the same—and the dismal result was the Christmas bombing of Hanoi with hundreds of B-52's.

The December raids were the most extreme escalation of the war Nixon and Kissinger had ever undertaken;

yet they were decidedly a political and military failure. Hanoi emphatically refused to capitulate; Washington faced mutinies by men in the B-52 crews; domestic and world opinion loudly berated the Administration and rendered its action useless. The bombing stopped, and in January 1973 American and Vietnamese envoys in Paris signed an agreement similar to the one envisioned on October 26.

Nevertheless, almost a year after the treaty signatures, the situation in Vietnam remains uncertain. War rages through neighboring Cambodia; the National Council of Reconciliation and Concord is in shambles; the White House, despite the Senate vote to stop its grotesque Cambodia bombings, is constantly ready to re-intervene. If the history of the past four years stands as a lesson, it cannot be supposed that Nixon and Kissinger have successfully ended the war; it is still true that they have done more than anyone else to perpetuate it.

October 1973

Notes

SLOUCHING TOWARD WASHINGTON

1 The *New York Times* magazine, November 14, 1971, p. 107.
2 Henry Kissinger, *The Troubled Partnership*, p. 23.
3 The *New York Times* magazine, November 14, 1971, p. 107.
4 Boston *Evening Globe*, May 3, 1972, p. 2.
5 See Kissinger's undergraduate thesis, "The Meaning of History: Reflections on Spengler, Toynbee, and Kant."
6 Text of background briefing, Hartford, Connecticut, October 12, 1970, p. 21.
7 Text of background briefing, San Clemente, June 26, 1970, p. 13.
8 Henry Kissinger, *A World Restored*, p. 322.
9 Ibid., p. 153.
10 Ibid., pp. 195, 318.
11 Many critics have misconceived Kissinger's view on Bismarck and on German unification. Doubtless, Kissinger admired Bismarck's penchant for getting things done, but he regarded Bismarck as a tragedy for history. To Kissinger, Bismarck represented the apotheosis of the revolutionary miscreant — the gifted and well-intentioned usurper whose achievements were unraveled by less gifted successors. And though Kissinger approached Bismarck with genuine fascination and admirable scholarly objectivity, he could not help regretting the man's ultimate historic influence. The most cursory reading of Kissinger's essay on Bismarck (in *Daedalus*, summer 1968, but apparently written a good many years earlier) makes this attitude clear.

   Kissinger also understood quite well that a strong, united Germany posed unspeakable dangers for the Continent, and that it flew in the face of hundreds of years of history. One of the central features of the Metternich system, in fact, was its elaborate provision for keeping Germany divided. Kissinger's views on German unification magnified in importance (that is, in relation to his own political experience) at the time of the Berlin crisis of 1961 (see below).
12 Henry Kissinger, *American Foreign Policy*, p. 57.

13 Text of background briefing, Lahore, West Pakistan, August 1, 1962, p. 12.
14 Kissinger, *American Foreign Policy*, p. 79.
15 Ibid., pp. 46–47.
16 At his White House press conference in which he explained President Nixon's decision to mine North Vietnam's harbors two weeks before the scheduled U.S.-Soviet summit, Kissinger told newsmen that the risks of a confrontation with the Soviets posed by the President's decision were "not unacceptable."
17 *The Pragmatic Revolt in Politics: Syndicalism, Fascism, and the Constitutional State.*
18 Hamilton Fish Armstrong, interview with the writer. New York City, October 5, 1971.
19 Ibid.
20 George Franklin, interview with the writer. New York City, October 4, 1971.
21 Letter from Henry Kissinger to George Franklin, shown to the writer by George Franklin.
22 George Franklin, interview with the writer. New York City, October 4, 1971.
23 Ibid.
24 Ibid.
25 Henry Kissinger, *Nuclear Weapons and Foreign Policy*, p. 155.
26 Ibid., p. 224.
27 Ibid., p. 229.
28 Ibid., pp. 193–194.
29 Ibid., pp. 317–318.
30 Ibid., p. 202.
31 Henry Kissinger, *The Necessity for Choice*, p. 85.
32 Robert Osgood's *Limited War: The Challenge to American Strategy* is commonly regarded as the definitive work in the field.
33 This paraphrase is adapted from working papers of the Rockefeller Special Studies Project.
34 Ibid.
35 See especially Bernard Brodie, "Nuclear Weapons: Strategic or Tactical?," *Foreign Affairs*, January 1954, and James M. Gavin, *War and Peace in the Space Age*.
36 See Herman Kahn, *On Thermonuclear War*, and Thomas Schelling, *The Strategy of Conflict*.
37 Kissinger, *The Necessity for Choice*, p. 365.
38 Kissinger, *American Foreign Policy*, p. 93.
39 Arthur Schlesinger, Jr., interview with the writer. New York City, October 27, 1971.
40 Based on interview material. The source wishes to remain unnamed.

41 Henry Kissinger, "The Unsolved Problems of European Defense," *Foreign Affairs*, July 1962, p. 525.
42 Ibid., pp. 530, 531.
43 Ibid., p. 530.
44 Jack M. Schick, *The Berlin Crisis 1958–1962*, p. 9.
45 Arthur Schlesinger, *A Thousand Days*, p. 362.
46 Kissinger, *The Necessity for Choice*, p. 167.
47 Ibid., p. 169.
48 Ibid., p. 144.
49 Kissinger, *The Necessity for Choice*, pp. 163 ff.
50 Ibid., p. 142.
51 Kissinger, *The Troubled Partnership*, p. 70.
52 Daniel Ellsberg, interview with the writer. Cambridge, February 25, 1972. Ellsberg, then a RAND consultant, was a friend of Kissinger and learned of this recommendation from Kissinger himself in a conversation at Harvard in the fall of 1961. Other officials also knew of the Kissinger recommendation. It remains unclear whether Kissinger ever put this recommendation into writing, or whether he addressed it directly to the President. The only individual who knows the answers to these questions is McGeorge Bundy, who declined an interview with this writer.

THE SALAD DAYS OF HENRY KISSINGER

1 Joseph Kraft, "In Search of Kissinger," *Harper's*, January 1971, p. 57.
2 William W. Kaufmann, "The Crisis in Military Affairs," *World Politics*, July 1958, pp. 598, 603.
3 Text of White House background briefing, September 25, 1970, p. 18.
4 The Harvard *Crimson*, May 19, 1970, p. 4.
5 Ibid., p. 4.
6 Ibid., pp. 4–5.
7 Ibid., p. 5.
8 Ibid., p. 5.
9 Text of background briefing, San Clemente, August 24, 1970, p. 11.
10 Text of background briefing, Chicago, September 16, 1970, p. 5.
11 Ibid., p. 41. Kissinger may, or may not, have been referring obliquely to the earlier dismissal of an Arizona State professor, Morris J. Starsky, who apparently was fired for his activity in various left-wing causes.
12 One of the group, Richard Neustadt, said later of Kissinger, "He's told me personally he's not the source of such rumors." (The Harvard *Crimson*, February 9, 1971, p. 1 ff.)

13 Kissinger's predecessor, Walt Rostow, a former M.I.T. professor, was turned away from M.I.T. when he reapplied for a professorship at the end of his term in Washington. Several of Rostow's friends claimed the decision had been a political one, and this allegation is said to have caused Rostow's fate to weigh on Kissinger's mind. It is widely acknowledged in the academic world that M.I.T.'s decision was *not* political, that by 1968 Rostow was considered to be a mediocre scholar, and that M.I.T.'s Political Science Department — not one inclined to find Rostow an ideological embarrassment but under no particular obligation to rehire him — decided against him for legitimate reasons. It is reasonable to suppose, however, that on this as on many other subjects, Kissinger's paranoia knew no bounds.

14 The Boston *Sunday Globe,* January 17, 1971, p. 8.

15 The *New York Times,* January 14, 1971, p. 41.

16 The Harvard *Crimson,* January 15, 1971, p. 1.

17 The Boston *Sunday Globe,* January 17, 1971, p. 8.

THE NIXON-KISSINGER POLICY

1 Daniel Ellsberg, interview with the writer. Cambridge, February 25, 1972.

2 A striking exception, of course, has been Washington's recent mishandling of its most formidable Asian ally, Japan. The failure even to inform Tokyo of Kissinger's secret trip to Peking before the public announcement, the clear lack of consultation preceding Nixon's new economic policies of August 1971, and the repeated postponements of Kissinger's trip to Tokyo throughout early 1972 — all of these slights served to traumatize Japan.

3 *United States Foreign Policy for the 1970's: Building for Peace* (1971), p. 106.

4 Ibid., p. 105.

5 Text of background briefing, San Clemente, August 24, 1970, p. 10.

6 The *New York Times,* May 31, 1972, p. 8.

7 Text of background briefing, San Clemente, June 26, 1970, p. 9.

8 Ibid., p. 10.

9 *United States Foreign Policy for the 1970's: The Emerging Structure of Peace* (1972), p. 57.

10 Witness this remarkable passage on a "one-and-a-half-war" posture:

"The choice of this strategy was based on the following considerations:

"The nuclear capability of our strategic and theater nuclear forces serves as a deterrent to full-scale Soviet attack on NATO Europe or Chinese attacks on our Asian allies.

"The prospects for a coordinated two-front attack on our allies by Russia and China are low both because of the risks of nuclear war and the improbability of Sino-Soviet cooperation. In any event, we do not believe that such a coordinated attack should be met primarily by U.S. conventional forces.

"The desirability of insuring against greater than expected threats by maintaining more than the forces required to meet conventional threats in one theater, such as NATO Europe.

"Weakness on our part would be more provocative than continued U.S. strength for it might encourage others to take dangerous risks, to resort to the illusion that military adventures could succeed."

("U.S. Foreign Policy for the 1970's: A New Strategy for Peace, February 18, 1970." From the *Department of State Bulletin,* March 9, 1970, p. 322.)

11 *United States Foreign Policy for the 1970's: The Emerging Structure of Peace* (1972), p. 51.

12 E.g., text of background briefing, San Clemente, August 24, 1970, p. 38.

13 Text of background briefing, San Clemente, June 26, 1970, pp. 23–24.

14 *United States Foreign Policy for the 1970's: The Emerging Structure of Peace* (1972), p. 20.

15 Text of background briefing, San Clemente, August 24, 1970, p. 11.

16 Ibid., p. 14.

17 For Kissinger's attitude, see pp. 61–62. For Nixon's, see Richard J. Whalen, *Catch the Falling Flag: A Republican's Challenge to His Party,* p. 27.

18 Text of background briefing, Hartford, Connecticut, October 12, 1970, p. 39.

19 Text of background briefing, New Orleans, August 14, 1970, p. 16.

20 *United States Foreign Policy for the 1970's: Building for Peace* (1971), p. 110.

21 Kissinger, *American Foreign Policy,* p. 24.

22 Kraft, "In Search of Kissinger," *Harper's,* January 1971.

23 Text of background briefing, San Clemente, June 26, 1970, p. 19.

24 George Gilder, speechwriter for Nelson Rockefeller during the 1968 Republican Presidential campaign, interview with the writer. Cambridge, September 27, 1971.

25 Richard Nixon, "Asia After Viet Nam," *Foreign Affairs,* October 1967, pp. 114, 121.

26 Kissinger, *A World Restored*, p. 19.
27 Text of background briefing, San Clemente, June 26, 1970, p. 9.
28 *United States Foreign Policy for the 1970's: The Emerging Structure of Peace* (1972), p. 236.
29 Text of White House background briefing, December 18, 1969, p. 12.
30 Ibid., p. 18.
31 One of Kissinger's staff assistants later recalled: "The one part of ABM Henry was convinced made sense was the thin area defense. The part he was always skeptical about was the Minuteman defense part of it. What got retained was the Minuteman defense."
32 The *New York Times*, March 19, 1969, p. 22.
33 Text of background briefing, New Orleans, August 14, 1970, p. 24.
34 Although the American ABM is set up to defend offensive missile sites, it is constructed with population-defense ABM radar and equipment and can therefore be expanded into a "thick" system without excruciating strategic adjustments.
35 Official statements on this point have varied in strength and intensity.
36 Text of background briefing, New Orleans, August 14, 1970, p. 25.
37 The 1972 State of the World Message notes rather stoically (page 176) that "No President should be left with only one strategic course of action, particularly that of ordering the mass destruction of enemy civilians and facilities . . . This problem will be the subject of continuing study."

VIETNAM

1 Richard M. Pfeffer, ed., *No More Vietnams?*, p. 13.
2 Daniel Ellsberg, interview with the writer. Cambridge, April 11, 1971.
3 Ibid.
4 *United States Foreign Policy for the 1970's: Building for Peace* (1971), p. 15.
5 Bernard Fall, *Last Reflections on a War*, p. 73.

MORE POWERFUL THAN THE SWORD

1 Three months after the following account was written, the U.S. government's internal record of the 1967 Kissinger negotiation leaked to the American press. This record, contained in the 47-

volume *History of United States Relations with Vietnam, 1945–1967,* popularly known as the Pentagon Papers, had been withheld from the press when the rest of the Defense Department study leaked in June 1971. At no time did I ever obtain access to this part of the study before its public release. The Pentagon account of the Kissinger negotiation, though it contains the texts of all the diplomatic notes and many other valuable documents besides, suffers from a lack of information on the unrecorded aspects of the negotiation. Most critically, the writers of the study did not do interviews with many of the key participants — especially the French intermediaries — and, as a result, their work sometimes reflects a one-sidedness, a tendency to see the negotiation through Washington's rose-colored glasses. I did not have their documentation, but I did do interviews — including one with Herbert Marcovich, one of the intermediaries — and my account differs on several points with the Pentagon's. I will list a few of those differences in subsequent footnotes. Otherwise my original text of April 1972 (which may be found in the Archives of Widener Library at Harvard University in the form of an undergraduate honors thesis for the Department of Government) remains essentially unchanged.

2 Herbert Marcovich, interview with the writer. Paris, March 4, 1972.

3 Ibid.

4 Nicholas Katzenbach, interview with the writer. Armonk, New York, November 24, 1971.

5 Herbert Marcovich, interview with the writer. Paris, March 4, 1972.

6 Ibid.

7 The disclosures of June 1972 reveal that Kissinger, surprisingly, did not know about this interview at the time that Aubrac and Marcovich told him Pham Van Dong had referred to it. Kissinger's initial report to Washington quotes Dong, and then contains Kissinger's own parenthetical bafflement, as follows: "We have made clear [Dong said] our position in our four points and in the interview of January 28, 1967. [Pham Van Dong did not explain what this interview was; Aubrac and Marcovich did not know, nor do I (Kissinger adds).]"

8 Based on interview material. The source wishes to remain unnamed, but there are two public sources which indirectly confirm this statement. In *The Vantage Point* (page 266), Lyndon Johnson writes of the July debriefing: "The Frenchmen told Kissinger they thought Hanoi would negotiate as soon as the bombing of the North ended." In Kissinger's report on the Aubrac-Marcovich conversations with Pham Van Dong, the latter

is quoted as saying, "We want an unconditional end of the bombing and if that happens, there will be no further obstacle to negotiations." In other words, talks *would* ensue after a bombing halt, though in this as in subsequent exchanges, Hanoi would not supply a *literal* guarantee.

In general, the Pentagon account fails to focus in any discernible fashion on the major breakdown in the negotiation — whether Hanoi would flatly guarantee an entrance into talks — and, therefore, fails to analyze it. It does record the annoyance of Hanoi's representative in Paris, Mai Van Bo, at the words "prompt" and "productive" which accompanied Washington's demand for a promise of negotiations, but explores the issue no further.

9   Henry L. Trewhitt, *McNamara*, p. 236.
10 Nicholas Katzenbach, interview with the writer. Armonk, New York, November 24, 1971.
11 Based on interview material. The source, who at the time was a senior Defense Department official, wishes to remain unnamed.
12 Nicholas Katzenbach, interview with the writer. Armonk, New York, November 24, 1971.
13 Based on interview material. The source, who at the time was a senior Defense Department official, wishes to remain unnamed.
14 Ibid.
15 Nicholas Katzenbach, interview with the writer. Armonk, New York, November 24, 1971.
16 As Katzenbach said, "He [the President] probably wanted to have those, even if he wasn't going to use them, if only to keep his own house in order." (Phone conversation with the writer, February 25, 1972.)
17 This time, Hanoi used a different verb. Trinh said, "Après la cessation des bombardements et de tout autre acte de guerre contre la République démocratique du Vietnam, Hanoi entamera des conversations avec les Etats-Unis sur les problèmes intéressant les deux parties."
18 The Pentagon account implies strongly that the U.S. bombings in the Hanoi area of August 21 and 22 led to a breakdown in the talks. I believe that implication is mistaken, because my information is that the bombing of the Doumer bridge on August 11 was by far the more disruptive.
19 Admiral U.S.G. Sharp (U.S.N. Ret.), former Commander-in-Chief, Pacific (CINCPAC), interview with the writer. San Diego, December 30, 1971.
20 Chester Cooper, interview with the writer. Arlington, Virginia, January 10, 1972.
21 In a speech at San Antonio, Texas, on September 29, President

Johnson stated the U.S. position in the precise wording used privately the month before. He did not stop to explain the subtleties. Henceforth, the position came to be known as the San Antonio formula.

22 Jean Lacouture, *Ho Chi Minh: A Political Biography*, p. 135.

23 The Pentagon account, drawing on Kissinger's report, quotes Ho as saying, "Remember, many people have tried to fool me and have failed. I know you don't want to fool me." I believe that my informant, not the Pentagon chronicle, has the correct version, one reason being that my informant's version makes more historical sense. Ho had, in fact, been tricked many times before in negotiations with the West, and he would have been the first to admit it. At any rate, this discrepancy raises an interesting possibility: that Kissinger misquoted Ho.

24 Don Oberdorfer, *Tet!* pp. 41 ff.

25 Herbert Marcovich, interview with the writer. Paris, March 4, 1972.

26 Lacouture, *Ho Chi Minh: A Political Biography*, p. 136.

27 In the report of his last contact with Aubrac and Marcovich — made public in June 1972 — Kissinger made clear his frustration with Hanoi's reticence in the private talks. "If Hanoi wanted to negotiate," he wrote, "it should be able to find some way of expressing this fact by means other than subtle changes in tense and elliptical reference full of double meanings."

28 Kissinger, *American Foreign Policy*, p. 112.

29 Ibid., p. 111.

30 Herbert Marcovich, interview with the writer. Paris, March 4, 1972.

31 Kissinger, *American Foreign Policy*, p. 114.

32 Text of White House background briefing, September 16, 1969, p. 7.

33 Ironically, it is doubtful that Washington expected the partial halt to draw Hanoi into talks; it appears to have been primarily intended to assuage domestic public opinion. See especially John B. Henry, Jr., "March 1968: Continuity or Change?"

INTERLUDE: 1968

1 While in Moscow in late 1967 and early 1968 attending a conference on arms control, Kissinger privately urged his Russian colleagues to press their government to act as a mediator between Washington and Hanoi.

2 Text of White House background briefing, December 18, 1969, p. 17.

3 The Washington *Post,* July 14, 1968, p. A-22.
4 Clark Clifford, interview with the writer. Washington, December 15, 1971.
5 Kissinger, *American Foreign Policy,* p. 133.
6 Cyrus Vance, interview with the writer. New York City, November 24, 1971.
7 Kissinger, *American Foreign Policy,* p. 124.
8 Whalen, *Catch the Falling Flag: A Republican's Challenge to His Party,* p. 137.
9 Text of background briefing, New Orleans, August 14, 1970, p. 15.
10 Text of background briefing, San Clemente, June 26, 1970, pp. 17, 18.
11 A partial exception here was Secretary of State Dean Rusk, a man who by any standard defies easy categorization. See John B. Henry, Jr., "March 1968: Continuity or Change?" for a full view of Rusk.
12 Daniel Ellsberg, interview with the writer. Cambridge, April 23, 1971.
13 The texts of answers to the questionnaire — known as National Security Study Memorandum No. 1 (NSSM 1) — appeared in several newspapers during the spring of 1972.
14 Daniel Ellsberg, interview with the writer. Cambridge, April 23, 1971.
15 The Manila formula was agreed on by President Johnson and Marshal Ky at their meeting in the Philippines in October 1966. It stipulated that U.S. forces withdraw from South Vietnam within six months after a North Vietnamese withdrawal.

"ANOTHER FOOLISH WESTERNER COME TO LOSE HIS REPUTATION TO HO CHI MINH"

1 The prisoner rescue operation at Sontay, November 1970.
2 Text of White House background briefing, May 9, 1970, p. 11.
3 Text of background briefing, New Orleans, August 14, 1970, p. 28.
4 Paul Mus, *Vietnam: Sociologie d'une guerre.* Cited in Lacouture, *Ho Chi Minh,* p. 119.
5 See, for example, Jean Lacouture's recounting of the reaction by Hanoi's population to the 1946 accords with France, in *Ho Chi Minh,* pp. 135–136.
6 Jean Lacouture, *Vietnam Between Two Truces,* p. 54.
7 Bernard Fall, *Last Reflections on a War,* p. 161.
8 Text of White House background briefing, May 9, 1970, p. 11.
9 The *New York Times,* March 24, 1969, p. 1 ff.

10 Text of White House background briefing, December 18, 1969, p. 11.

11 Xuan Thuy, speech at July 31, 1969, session of the Paris Conference on Vietnam, cited in Jim Blum, unpublished paper of November 10, 1969, pp. 26–27. Blum is currently (fall 1972) a junior at Harvard College.

12 Kissinger, *American Foreign Policy*, p. 126.

13 Kissinger press conference, May 9, 1972.

14 Ly Van Sau, spokesman for the PRG delegation to the Paris Conference on Vietnam, interview with the writer. Verrières-le-Buisson, France, March 6, 1972.

15 Kissinger, *American Foreign Policy*, p. 134.

16 Text of White House background briefing, November 3, 1969, p. 4.

17 Text of White House background briefing, May 1, 1970, p. 5.

18 See especially David E. Brown, "Exporting Insurgency: The Communists in Cambodia," in Zasloff and Goodman, *Indochina in Conflict*. Brown is an official in the State Department's Bureau of Intelligence and Research.

19 Text of background briefing, San Clemente, August 24, 1970, p. 35.

20 See especially the account of the internal government deliberation leading to the Cambodia decision in the *New York Times*, June 30, 1970, p. 1.

21 Text of background briefing, San Clemente, April 20, 1970, p. 4.

22 Text of White House background briefing, May 1, 1970, p. 10.

23 Kissinger stated the following to reporters on May 1:
". . . Within several days of the President's speech and his explicit warning, and *a warning that was conveyed also through other ways*, these forces debouched out of their sanctuaries in a totally unambiguous manner and penetrated more deeply into Cambodia and raised the explicit prospect that we thought we could control through the things which the President said in his San Clemente speech." [Italics mine.]
A reporter then asked: "This is several days after the speech, are you saying, or before?"
"After." (Text of White House background briefing, May 1, 1970, p. 10.)
The precise nature of the threat itself is unclear. It is possible that Kissinger specified a land invasion of Cambodia as Washington's response to an expansion of the sanctuaries, but it seems more likely that he left the threat open-ended to imply other possibilities, such as renewed bombing of the North.

24 Wilfred Burchett, *The Second Indochina War*, p. 73.

25 What kind of evidence could anyone have considered truly re-

liable during this period? Military reporting? Even CIA estimates? The writer can only express bafflement at this assertion.

26 Text of White House background briefing, May 9, 1970, p. 7.

27 Text of background briefing, San Clemente, June 26, 1970, p. 26.

28 A notion that was violently disproved by the patent failure of South Vietnamese operations in Laos and Cambodia, with U.S. air support, the following February.

29 Text of background briefing, New Orleans, August 14, 1970, p. 27.

30 Kissinger said on August 14, 1970, of a withdrawal from South Vietnam, "After we have done everything we can to develop a governmental structure, after we have put them into the best possible shape that we can, and after we can tell ourselves in good conscience that we have done it in a way that is not a cop-out, if then, after five years, it turns out that they can't make it anyway, I think we are facing different consequences from the consequences of simply packing up and pulling out." (Text of background briefing, New Orleans, August 14, 1970, p. 26.)

31 Text of background briefing, Chicago, September 16, 1970, p. 42.

32 Text of background briefing, Hartford, Connecticut, October 12, 1970, p. 20.

33 Kissinger press conference, January 26, 1972.

34 *United States Foreign Policy for the 1970's: The Emerging Structure of Peace* (1972), p. 236.

35 Ho Chi Minh, *The Prison Diary.* The poem is entitled "Advice to Oneself."

Bibliography

PRIMARY SOURCES

(Note: The final three listings are President Nixon's State of the World Messages, of which Kissinger has been the principal author. I have omitted most of Kissinger's numerous magazine and newspaper articles because, aside from the ones listed here, they have been incorporated in substance or in their entirety in his books.)

Kissinger, Henry A. *A World Restored.* New York: Grosset & Dunlap, 1964.

———. *Nuclear Weapons and Foreign Policy.* New York: Harper & Brothers, 1957.

———. *The Necessity for Choice.* Garden City, N.Y.: Doubleday Anchor Books, 1962.

———. *The Troubled Partnership.* Garden City, N.Y.: Doubleday Anchor Books, 1966.

———, ed. *Problems of National Security.* New York: Praeger, 1965.

———. *American Foreign Policy.* New York: Norton, 1969.

———. "The White Revolutionary: Reflections on Bismarck." *Daedalus,* summer 1968.

———. "The Unsolved Problems of European Defense." *Foreign Affairs,* July 1962.

———. "Military Policy and Defense of the 'Grey Areas.'" *Foreign Affairs,* April 1955.

United States Foreign Policy for the 1970's: A New Strategy for Peace. The White House: Febuary 18, 1970.

United States Foreign Policy for the 1970's: Building for Peace. The White House: February 25, 1971.

United States Foreign Policy for the 1970's: The Emerging Structure of Peace. The White House: February 9, 1972.

SECONDARY SOURCES

Barnet, Richard J. *Who Wants Disarmament?* Boston: Beacon Press, 1960.

Bowie, Robert R. "Tensions Within the Alliance." *Foreign Affairs,* October 1963.

Brandon, Henry. *Anatomy of Error.* Boston: Gambit, 1969.

Brodie, Bernard. *Strategy in the Missile Age.* Princeton: Princeton University Press, 1959.

———. "Nuclear Weapons: Strategic or Tactical?" *Foreign Affairs,* January 1954.

Burchett, Wilfred. *The Second Indochina War.* New York: International Publishers, 1970.

Cahn, Anne Hessing. "Eggheads and Warheads: Scientists and the ABM." A doctoral thesis, Massachusetts Institute of Technology, 1971.

Chayes, Abram, and Wiesner, Jerome B., eds. *ABM: An Evaluation of the Decision to Deploy an Antiballistic Missile System.* New York: Signet Books, 1969.

Cooper, Chester L. *The Lost Crusade: America in Vietnam.* New York: Dodd, Mead, 1970.

Destler, I. M. "Can One Man Do?" *Foreign Policy,* winter 1971–1972.

Devillers, Philippe. "The Struggle for the Unification of Vietnam." *The China Quarterly,* January–March 1962.

———. "Vietnamese Nationalism and French Policies." In *Asian Nationalism and the West,* edited by William L. Holland. New York: Macmillan, 1953.

Ellsberg, Daniel. *Papers on the War.* New York: Simon & Schuster, 1972.

Evans, Rowland, and Novak, Robert. *Nixon in the White House: The Frustration of Power.* New York: Random House, 1971.

Fall, Bernard B. *Last Reflections on a War.* Garden City, N.Y.: Doubleday, 1967.

Gavin, James M. *War and Peace in the Space Age.* New York: Harper & Brothers, 1958.

Gelb, Leslie H. "Vietnam: The System Worked." *Foreign Policy,* summer 1971.

The Senator Gravel Edition of the Defense Department History of United States Decisionmaking on Vietnam. Vol. IV. Boston: Beacon Press, 1971.

Grosser, Alfred. *French Foreign Policy Under de Gaulle.* Boston: Little, Brown, 1967.

———. *The Colossus Again: Western Germany from Defeat to Disarmament.* New York: Praeger, 1955.

Halberstam, David. *Ho.* New York: Vintage, 1971.

Halperin, Morton H. *Defense Strategies for the Seventies.* Boston: Little, Brown, 1971.

———. "The Decision to Deploy the ABM: Bureaucratic and Domestic Politics in the Johnson Administration." An unpublished paper, 1971.

Henry, John B., Jr. "March 1968: Continuity or Change?" An undergraduate honors thesis, Harvard University, 1971.

Ho Chi Minh. *The Prison Diary*. New York: Bantam Books, 1971.

Hoffmann, Stanley. "Vietnam: An Algerian Solution?" *Foreign Policy*, spring 1971.

Hoopes, Townsend. *The Limits of Intervention*. New York: McKay, 1969.

Johnson, Lyndon Baines. *The Vantage Point*. New York: Holt, Rinehart, and Winston, 1971.

Kahn, Herman. *On Thermonuclear War*. Princeton: Princeton University Press, 1960.

Kellen, Konrad. "Adenauer at 90." *Foreign Affairs*, January 1966.

Kleiman, Robert. *Atlantic Crisis*. New York: Norton, 1964.

Kraslow, David, and Loory, Stuart H. *The Secret Search for Peace in Vietnam*. New York: Vintage, 1968.

Lacouture, Jean. *Vietnam: Between Two Truces*. New York: Vintage, 1966.

——. *Ho Chi Minh: A Political Biography*. New York: Vintage, 1968.

McAlister, John T., Jr. *Vietnam: The Origins of Revolution*. Garden City, N.Y.: Doubleday, 1971.

Nixon, Richard. "Asia After Viet Nam," *Foreign Affairs*, October 1967.

Oberdorfer, Don. *Tet!* Garden City, N.Y.: Doubleday, 1971.

Pfeffer, Richard M., ed. *No More Vietnams?* New York: Harper Colophon Books, 1969.

Schelling, Thomas C. *The Strategy of Conflict*. New York: Oxford University Press, 1963.

Schick, Jack M. *The Berlin Crisis 1958–1962*. Philadelphia: The University of Pennsylvania Press, 1971.

Schlesinger, Arthur M., Jr. *A Thousand Days*. New York: Fawcett, 1967.

Speier, Hans. *Divided Berlin: The Anatomy of Soviet Political Blackmail*. New York: Praeger, 1961.

Trewhitt, Henry L. *McNamara*. New York: Harper & Row, 1971.

Whalen, Richard J. *Catch the Falling Flag: A Republican's Challenge to His Party*. Boston: Houghton Mifflin, 1972.

Wills, Garry. *Nixon Agonistes: The Crisis of the Self-Made Man*. Boston: Houghton Mifflin, 1969.

Zasloff, Joseph J., and Goodman, Allen E. *Indochina in Conflict*. Lexington, Mass.: D.C. Heath, 1972.

Index

(Note: The entries included here are listed only in reference to Henry Kissinger. A separate entry for Kissinger has not been used.)